EXPLORING GIFTED EDUCATION

Exploring Gifted Education focusses on the most fundamental and pressing topics in gifted education from across Australian and New Zealand contexts and gives particular attention to evidence-based practices and research findings. The wide variety of topics presented include: identification of gifted learners, creativity, twice-exceptional learners, affective considerations, teaching the gifted, curriculum considerations, programs and services, STEM, early childhood learners, rural and remote contexts, and parents of gifted learners. Each chapter provides guiding questions and key ideas to help orient the reader, and discussion questions synthesise the chapter's concepts at the conclusion.

The first book of its kind to synthesise research-based findings in gifted education from across New Zealand and Australia, it is an essential reference tool for researchers and a key text for courses in gifted education. Practitioners and parents will also find the assembled research illuminating and informative in understanding and addressing the needs of gifted learners.

Jennifer L. Jolly is an Associate Professor at the University of Alabama, and her previous positions include Senior Lecturer at the University of New South Wales. She serves as Association Editor for the National Association for Gifted Children and is a past editor of *Parenting for High Potential*. Her research interests include the history of gifted education, parents of gifted children, and homeschooling gifted children.

Jane M. Jarvis is a Senior Lecturer at Flinders University in South Australia, where her research, teaching, and consultancy work with schools focusses on addressing learner diversity through differentiated curriculum and inclusive educational practices, including for gifted students. Jane is an Associate Editor of the *Australasian Journal of Gifted Education*.

EXPLORING GIFTED EDUCATION

Australian and New Zealand Perspectives

Edited by Jennifer L. Jolly and Jane M. Jarvis

LONDON AND NEW YORK

First published 2018
by Routledge
2 Park Square, Milton Park, Abingdon, Oxon OX14 4RN

and by Routledge
711 Third Avenue, New York, NY 10017

Routledge is an imprint of the Taylor & Francis Group, an informa business

© 2018 selection and editorial matter, Jennifer L. Jolly and Jane M. Jarvis; individual chapters, the contributors

The right of the editor to be identified as the author of the editorial material, and of the authors for their individual chapters, has been asserted in accordance with sections 77 and 78 of the Copyright, Designs and Patents Act 1988.

All rights reserved. No part of this book may be reprinted or reproduced or utilised in any form or by any electronic, mechanical, or other means, now known or hereafter invented, including photocopying and recording, or in any information storage or retrieval system, without permission in writing from the publishers.

Trademark notice: Product or corporate names may be trademarks or registered trademarks, and are used only for identification and explanation without intent to infringe.

British Library Cataloguing-in-Publication Data
A catalogue record for this book is available from the British Library

Library of Congress Cataloging-in-Publication Data
Names: Jolly, Jennifer L., 1972– editor. | Jarvis, Jane M., editor.
Title: Exploring gifted education : Australian and New Zealand perspectives / [edited by] Jennifer L. Jolly and Jane M. Jarvis.
Description: Abingdon, Oxon ; New York, NY : Routledge is an imprint of the Taylor & Francis Group, an Informa Business, [2018] | Includes bibliographical references.
Identifiers: LCCN 2017041979 | ISBN 9780815378853 (hbk) | ISBN 9780815378860 (pbk) | ISBN 9781351227704 (ebk)
Subjects: LCSH: Gifted children—Education—Australia. | Gifted children—Education—New Zealand.
Classification: LCC LC3999.4 .E96 2018 | DDC 371.95099—dc23
LC record available at https://lccn.loc.gov/2017041979

ISBN: 978-0-8153-7885-3 (hbk)
ISBN: 978-0-8153-7886-0 (pbk)
ISBN: 978-1-351-22770-4 (ebk)

Typeset in Bembo
by Apex CoVantage, LLC

CONTENTS

Contributors   *vii*

Introduction   1
Jane M. Jarvis and Jennifer L. Jolly

1   Framing gifted education in Australia and New Zealand   5
Roger Moltzen, Jennifer L. Jolly, and Jane M. Jarvis

2   Identification of gifted and twice-exceptional students   12
Jae Yup Jung and Peta Hay

3   Creativity and giftedness   32
Peter Merrotsy

4   Gifted students with disability: twice-exceptional learners   50
Trevor Clark and Catherine Wormald

5   Supporting the affective needs of gifted learners   66
Janna Wardman

6   Cultivating teachers to work with gifted students   82
Leonie Kronborg

7   Designing and adapting curriculum for academically
gifted students   95
Jane M. Jarvis

vi Contents

8 School programs and strategies for gifted learners 112
Lesley Henderson and Tracy Riley

9 Giftedness in science, technology, engineering,
and mathematics 132
James J. Watters

10 Early childhood environments and education 152
Kerry Hodge and Anne Grant

11 Gifted students in rural and remote settings 171
Margaret Plunkett

12 Parents and gifted and talented children 193
Jennifer L. Jolly

13 Gifted education in Australia and New Zealand:
reflections and future directions 206
Jane M. Jarvis, Jennifer L. Jolly, and Roger Moltzen

Index *213*

CONTRIBUTORS

Trevor Clark, PhD, is a special educator with comprehensive experience and knowledge of educational programs for students on the autism spectrum. He is Director of Research and Senior Education Consultant at Autism Spectrum Australia (Aspect), an Adjunct Associate Professor at Griffith Institute for Educational Research, and a member and past President of the Executive Committee of the Australasian Society for Autism Research (ASfAR).

Anne Grant, PhD, has taught young gifted children, as well as conducted research and published about appropriate curriculum for young gifted children, including online resources. She has taught at university level for many years and is currently involved in pre-service teacher education, research, and writing on the educational needs of young gifted children.

Peta Hay, PhD, is a lecturer in gifted education at the University of New South Wales. She is also a presenter of UNSW's Mini Certificate of Gifted Education, providing professional learning to teachers across Australia.

Lesley Henderson is a Lecturer in the College of Education, Psychology and Social Work at Flinders University, South Australia, where she coordinates postgraduate gifted education courses. She is President of the Australian Association for the Education of the Gifted and Talented, and her research interests include professional learning and leadership in gifted education.

Kerry Hodge, PhD, has researched giftedness in early childhood and lectured at Macquarie University in New South Wales, where she is an Adjunct Fellow. Kerry is currently Manager of Research and Development at a Sydney nonprofit

viii Contributors

organisation delivering research-based education to young children with special learning needs and supporting their parents and teachers.

Jane M. Jarvis, PhD, is a Senior Lecturer at Flinders University in South Australia, where her research, teaching, and consultancy work with schools focusses on addressing learner diversity through differentiated curriculum and inclusive educational practices, including for gifted students. Jane is an Associate Editor of the *Australasian Journal of Gifted Education*.

Jennifer L. Jolly, PhD, is an Associate Professor at the University of Alabama, and her previous positions include Senior Lecturer at the University of New South Wales. She serves as Association Editor for the National Association for Gifted Children and was editor of *Parenting for High Potential*. Her research interests include the history of gifted education, parents of gifted children, and homeschooling gifted children.

Jae Yup Jung, PhD, is a Senior Lecturer, a GERRIC Senior Research Fellow, and a former Australian Research Council DECRA Fellow in the School of Education at The University of New South Wales. He is the editor of the *Australasian Journal of Gifted Education*.

Leonie Kronborg, PhD, is Coordinator of Postgraduate Studies in Gifted Education at the Faculty of Education, Monash University, Australia. She is Vice President and the Australian elected representative on the Executive of the World Council for Gifted and Talented Children and Editor-in-Chief of *Gifted and Talented International*.

Peter Merrotsy, PhD, is a Professor in the Graduate School of Education at the University of Western Australia. His current research focusses on gifted children and youth from backgrounds of so-called disadvantage and on creativity and problem solving.

Roger Moltzen, PhD, is Professor and Dean of the Faculty of Education at the University of Waikato in New Zealand. A former teacher and principal, his career focus as an academic has been in the areas of inclusive education and talent development, and he has published extensively in gifted education. He is Patron of the New Zealand Association of Gifted Children.

Margaret Plunkett, PhD, is an Associate Professor and the Associate Dean (Learning and Teaching) for the Faculty of Education and Arts at Federation University, Australia. She is an Associate Editor of the *Australasian Journal of Gifted Education* and has served as a delegate on the World Council for Gifted and Talented Children since 2006.

Tracy Riley, PhD, is Associate Professor in the Institute of Education and the Dean of Research at Massey University, New Zealand. Creating educational environments that nurture gifted and talented children and young people to develop their individual passions and potential as adaptive, responsive, and engaged citizens is at the heart of her research.

Janna Wardman, PhD, is a Lecturer at the University of Auckland. She currently teaches in post-graduate Initial Teacher Education courses and Master's courses in gifted education, in addition to co-supervising Master's and doctoral candidates. A strong theoretical background, informed by research, supports her practical experience of 30 years in education.

James J. Watters, PhD, is an Adjunct Professor in Education at Queensland University of Technology in Brisbane. He has had over 30 years' experience in gifted education as a classroom science teacher, university lecturer, and researcher. Jim's broad interests focus on the processes of learning and motivation in high-ability people, particularly in domains of STEM.

Catherine Wormald, PhD, is a Lecturer in Education at the University of Wollongong, New South Wales, and a past president of the NSW Association for Gifted and Talented Children and the Australian Association for the Education of the Gifted and Talented. Her areas of interest include gifted students with learning disabilities.

INTRODUCTION

Jane M. Jarvis and Jennifer L. Jolly

Each classroom teacher in Australia and New Zealand has been, or is likely to be, faced with students whose intellectual abilities exceed age-based expectations. Some students enter early childhood education settings as fluent readers, despite having been exposed to no formal reading instruction. Some come to class with mathematical skills far in advance of those required to master grade-level curriculum content, with an enormous fund of factual knowledge and a seemingly insatiable desire to find out more, or with a capacity to understand and play with complex ideas in a way that is entirely unexpected for their age. Young people with above-average and even extraordinarily advanced abilities can be found in every cultural, geographic, and socio-economic strata of Australian and New Zealand society.

Framing the existence of children with very advanced abilities or high intellectual potential as problematic may seem incongruous, particularly in education systems that champion inclusivity, goals of equity and excellence, and the development of high-level critical and creative thinking. Yet, a substantial international evidence base confirms that high intellectual potential is no guarantee of positive educational outcomes or future success. In fact, in the absence of explicit efforts to create educational environments that nurture high potential, many talented individuals flounder. Some become disengaged with an education system that seems more concerned with the mastery of grade-level or minimum standards than it does with nurturing the potential of all students. Others choose to mask their academic abilities in order to be socially accepted, become frustrated when they are continually asked to act as 'mini teachers' to classmates with content they have already mastered instead of advancing their own learning, or experience boredom when they are prevented from working at a pace that matches their rate of learning. Rather than feeling valued as members of diverse, inclusive educational communities, many students who enter school as enthusiastic, capable children learn to expect low-level curriculum or anticipate high grades or accolades for performance that is well below the level of their capabilities, or they encounter negative attitudes towards their abilities from peers and even from some teachers. Both editors of this text have witnessed negative school experiences and poor social and affective outcomes for young people whose educational environments failed to nurture their abilities. Conversely, there is certainly much evidence, both anecdotal and research-based, that highly capable young people are likely to thrive in the right educational circumstances.

While more progress has been made in New Zealand in recent years than in Australia towards a unified national approach, there remains a lack of consistently enforced policy, funding, and practice in both contexts related to the education of highly able students. This is despite long-standing recognition of the intellectual characteristics and special educational needs of this diverse group of students, and even following multiple formal inquiries, reports, and recommendations. Failing to systematically consider best practice in the education of highly able students represents a waste of talent, both for the individual and for broader communities. Dedicated attention to their education is essential not because students with high intellectual potential are more 'special' or more deserving of an appropriate education than any other group of students, but because they are *as* special and *as* deserving as every other student who enters our schools. Yet, in the current educational climate, despite national curriculum and policy documents in both countries that embody the expectation of learning experiences that will cater to the full range of learners, the fate of these students remains largely in the hands of individual teachers, schools, and local education systems.

A significant challenge for the field of gifted education in Australia and New Zealand has been the lack of a coordinated local research base. Gifted education in this part of the world is a relatively young field; just over three decades have elapsed since the establishment of a formal field of study in this context. In 2001, published recommendations of an Australian senate inquiry into the education of gifted and talented children included that the Commonwealth should fund a "national research and resource centre on gifted education" (Senate Employment, Workplace Relations, Small Business and Education Reference Committee, 2001), and submissions to the inquiry suggested a range of research focus areas for this centre, including (a) teaching approaches and programs that can effectively address the educational needs of gifted students, including in the regular classroom; (b) studies of the longitudinal effects of educational interventions for gifted students; (c) approaches to talent development in other domains of endeavor such as sport; and (d) the development of locally appropriate instruments for identifying gifted students (Senate Employment, Workplace Relations, Small Business and Education Reference Committee, 2001). No such national research centre has materialised since that inquiry, and although the research base from Australia and New Zealand has steadily grown, this has occurred without deliberate coordination or reference to a coherent research agenda. Practitioners continue to draw upon research findings and practices from North America, the United Kingdom, and the Asia Pacific region to supplement the local research base.

Even in the absence of a coordinated research centre or agenda, there have certainly been developments in the evidence base concerning the nature and common needs of gifted and talented students, and effective educational approaches for this population, both in Australia and New Zealand and internationally. However, this critical mass of gifted education literature has not previously been collected in a single text to inform both researchers and practitioners working in Australia and New Zealand. Documenting this local knowledge is crucial for the field in order to maintain an identity distinct from that of its Northern Hemisphere cousins, and also to highlight what researchers from Australia and New Zealand can offer the international gifted education community. While acknowledging individual suggestions in relation to a national research agenda, the 2001 senate inquiry report noted, "As to what research priorities should be, this would be a matter for the experts involved" (Senate Employment, Workplace Relations, Small Business and Education Reference Committee, 2001, p. 101). A key additional aim of this text is to define a set of research priorities for the next phase of development in our field.

Exploring Gifted Education: Australian and New Zealand Perspectives presents the most relevant topics in contemporary gifted education. Each chapter presents research from Australia and New Zealand related to a specific aspect of gifted education, reviews international research with a focus on its relevance to local contexts, and identifies key priorities for future research. In each chapter, Indigenous perspectives and implications are addressed, given their central importance to discussions of educational practice in both countries.

The opening chapter frames the discussion of gifted education in the Australian and New Zealand contexts, providing a historical overview and examining its place in an educational landscape of increasingly nationalised curriculum, assessment, and teacher education; greater accountability; a focus on innovation and 21st-century skills; and global trends towards more inclusive educational practices.

Chapters 2–5 contribute to an understanding of the nature and specific needs of children with high potential or advanced performance in academic domains. This includes a discussion of how giftedness is defined and how gifted students can and should be identified in schools (Chapter 2); considerations of creativity in conceptions of giftedness and educational provisions for gifted learners (Chapter 3); gifted students who also live with disability and can be termed 'twice exceptional' (Chapter 4); and common affective characteristics and potential needs of gifted students (Chapter 5).

Chapters 6–8 focus on school-based responses to gifted students, which includes an examination of the role of teachers and teaching in the education of gifted learners (Chapter 6), the elements of curriculum suitable for gifted students and its relationship to curriculum for all learners (Chapter 7), and effective programs and specialised services for gifted learners (Chapter 8).

Beyond discussions of general, school-based approaches to educating gifted students, Chapters 9–12 focus on particular issues relevant to contemporary gifted education in Australia and New Zealand. These include the education of gifted

4 Jane M. Jarvis and Jennifer L. Jolly

students in STEM (Science, Technology, Engineering, and Mathematics) domains (Chapter 9), gifted children in early childhood education settings (Chapter 10), gifted students in rural and remote settings (Chapter 11), and considerations in parenting gifted children (Chapter 12).

The final chapter provides a summary of key ideas across the chapters and synthesises these in proposing a coherent agenda for future research in the field. We reflect on the possibilities for future scholarship and practice in gifted education, with a focus on innovative, context-specific opportunities to improve educational outcomes for students with high potential.

We have chosen to use the term 'gifted' in the title and throughout this text to describe students with high intellectual potential or exhibiting advanced academic performance, because this provides a link to an established field and existing research base. However, we acknowledge that the term can be problematic and is not applied consistently across contexts or even by individuals in the same context. Some authors in this volume use 'gifted', some prefer 'gifted and talented', and some use these terms interchangeably and also refer to students with high ability, advanced abilities, and/or high potential. This usage reflects the diversity of views in the field of gifted education, and each author clarifies their use of terms in the context of the specific chapter. Chapter 1 includes a more thorough discussion of definitions and conceptions of giftedness, but all authors agree that whatever the nuances of usage, we are discussing a very diverse category of individuals characterised by a range of strengths, needs, interests, cultural and family backgrounds, and prior experiences. 'Gifted education' is necessarily a broad term that encapsulates a diversity of educational approaches.

Reference

Senate Employment Workplace Relations Small Business and Education Reference Committee. (2001). *The education of gifted and talented children*. Canberra, ACT: Parliament of the Commonwealth of Australia.

1

FRAMING GIFTED EDUCATION IN AUSTRALIA AND NEW ZEALAND

Roger Moltzen, Jennifer L. Jolly, and Jane M. Jarvis

Current approaches to the education of academically gifted children and young people in Australia and New Zealand must be understood in an historical context. The field of gifted education in both countries has been appreciably influenced by research and practice in the U.S., the UK, and parts of continental Europe and Asia. Yet, the identity of gifted education in this part of the world is unique, with a developmental trajectory shaped by local socio-cultural and political forces. An understanding of this development provides an essential lens through which to critically examine current practices and the state of the research base, and also to consider culturally compatible future directions for the field. In this chapter, we discuss the nature of gifted education in Australia and New Zealand, with a focus on the historical context of scholarship, practices, and understandings of giftedness.

Understanding the past

Gifted education in Australia and New Zealand is relatively young when compared to its American and British cousins. The earliest recorded provisions for gifted students were Opportunity "C" classes in New South Wales, which were established in 1932. Initially offered in just four schools, these classes were available to students in Years 5 and 6 (Robinson, 1992). The 1930s also witnessed New Zealand's father of gifted education, George Parkyn, begin to make observations in regards to gifted children and offer a collection of his thoughts in the seminal text *Children of High Intelligence: A New Zealand Study*, where he noted: "in the ordinary mixed-ability classes of the primary school the bright child often spends a large part of his school time waiting for the next question, the next turn, the next subject, the next task and so on" (1948, p. 145).

Fast forward several decades, and the 1970s witnessed the establishment of regional and state advocacy organizations for gifted children, which would be precursors to the New Zealand Association for Gifted Children and Australian Association for the Education of the Gifted and Talented (AAEGT). Furthermore, it is recognized by Australian scholars that a formal field of study in gifted education was established in 1983 after the World Conference for Gifted and Talented Children was held in Manila that same year. The conference exposed the need for greater national organisation due to the misinformation being provided at the conference about research and practice in regards to gifted education in the Australian context. Prior to this, the field could be characterised as unintentional in purpose and lacking in organisation (Kronborg, 2002).

It may be argued that the relative youth of the field is reflected in common methodological approaches to research, the breadth and depth of the research that has been generated, and the quality and capacity of the research cadre to date. Over the nearly 35 years since the establishment of gifted education as a field, the research trajectory has been uneven. For example, the work completed by Miraca Gross on radical acceleration has had implications not only in Australia but also internationally; however, few other researchers have replicated this level of impact. The 1992 founding of the *Australasian Journal for Gifted Education* (AJGE) by the AAEGT was intended as a mechanism to further advance research in the field and has achieved mixed results (Bailey, 1992). Initially, the journal's audience was to include both researchers and practitioners, but the last two decades have seen a shift towards predominantly theoretical and empirical research articles (Luburic, 2016). The majority of Australian research is published in this outlet, and the journal's impact on the research base and practice throughout Australia could be substantial. As might be expected from a fledgling field of study, the initial five years of the journal included varying levels of methodological rigour and a large diversity of topics; the next five years (1999–2006) saw the journal begin to reflect the research being undertaken in the field, which included research on teacher attitudes towards gifted students and gifted education, research on academic acceleration, and discussion of curricular matters. The level of rigour also began to improve over this period. From 2007 to 2013, a decline was observed, with the bulk of articles described as having lower methodological rigour (Jolly & Chessman, 2016).

The uneven quantity and quality of contributions to the field are symptomatic of broader issues, framed by a lack of federal policy (particularly in Australia) to drive gifted education provisions and funding across all levels and sectors of schooling, including targeted funding for research. Individual Australian states and territories have produced and revised their own policies, with varied fidelity of implementation. Political and financial support for gifted education has fluctuated with successive federal and state governments. In the current climate, the immediate and long-term implications of the national literacy and numeracy assessment regime (NAPLAN) and the national Australian Curriculum established in 2008 and 2014, respectively, have yet to be investigated or fully understood for gifted and talented students.

Gifted education in Australia and New Zealand also can only really be understood within each country's broader educational history. Education in both countries was initially modelled on the English school system and reflected the deeply enshrined notion that children and young people of a particular age form a relatively homogenous group, particularly in terms of their development and learning. This view has informed nearly all major decisions about the structure of educational provisions, from sector divisions to the physical design of schools to the advancement of a national curriculum. The widespread acceptance of the ideas of the age-stage developmental theorists, including Piaget (1929), Erikson (1963), and Kohlberg (1981), reinforced this thinking. These theorists viewed behaviour as discontinuous, such that children and young people move through a series of discrete age-related stages, each marked by relatively predictable and distinct behaviours. This view of development has been subject to increasing challenge, and today's teachers are generally much more conscious of and responsive to the unique nature of each student's cognitive, social, and moral development. However, while acknowledging this philosophical shift, the system still largely reflects and reinforces an age-stage view of development, even if more by default than design.

Much has been written about the influence in both contexts of egalitarianism and its impact on educational provisions (or lack thereof) for gifted students (Gross, 1999; Plunkett & Kronborg, 2007). As Larsson observed:

> In Australia and New Zealand the strong notion of egalitarianism pervades the education system and society and so generally inhibits the variety of educational methods tailored to suit the needs of the talents of the individual. To suggest differentiation of programming to some teachers conjures up the spectre of elitism.
>
> *(Larsson, 1986, p. 215)*

Age-based theories and arguments of egalitarianism have been factors limiting real progress in providing consistently appropriate educational opportunities for gifted or advanced learners.

Conceptualising and defining giftedness

In a society that places a high value on equality, it is not difficult to understand why the very term "gifted" can invite an antagonistic response. Indeed, it was noted in the 2001 Australian senate inquiry into the education of gifted and talented children that the term "gifted" is problematic in this cultural context, based on its unintentional value-ladenness, whereby gifted individuals are implicitly contrasted with the alternative 'non-gifted', and parents may feel embarrassed to refer to their child using that label in order to discuss appropriate educational intervention (Senate Employment, Workplace Relations, Small Business and Education Reference Committee, 2001). It is acknowledged that counterproductive myths, misconceptions, and negative attitudes about giftedness cannot simply be explained in terms of problems with terminology, but it is nevertheless an issue to be considered. New Zealand has preferred the term Children or Students with Special Abilities (C/SWSA).

8 Moltzen et al.

While New Zealand and Australia overlap in their early histories and societal attitudes in relation to gifted education, they have diverged when conceptualising and defining giftedness. Giftedness as high measured intelligence, or IQ, had a relatively short tenure in New Zealand, at least amongst teachers and educators. Instead, the country's egalitarian roots and its suspicion of intelligence testing made it a fertile ground for more liberal, inclusive, and multi-categorical approaches to giftedness – including the definition in the U.S.'s Marland Report (1972). The underpinnings of this definition can be recognised throughout those used in New Zealand. At the turn of the 21st century, New Zealand introduced educational reforms centred on the principles of devolution and decentralisation, which charged schools with developing their own definitions of giftedness. These definitions must be based on the following criteria:

- Reflect a multi-categorical approach that includes an array of special abilities
- Reflect a bicultural approach that incorporates Māori concepts
- Recognise multi-cultural values, beliefs, attitudes, and customs
- Recognise both performance and potential
- Acknowledge that gifted and talented students demonstrate exceptionality in relation to their peers of the same age, culture, or circumstances
- Provide for differentiated educational opportunities for gifted and talented students, including social and emotional support
- Reflect the context and values of the school community
- Acknowledge that giftedness is evidenced in all societal groups, regardless of culture, ethnicity, socioeconomic status, gender, or disability
- Recognise that a student may be gifted in one or more areas
- Recognise that a student's gifts and talents will emerge at times and in circumstances that are unique to that student
- Be grounded in sound research and theories (Ministry of Education, 2012, p. 22)

Primacy has also been given to Māori conceptions of giftedness, with the work of Jill Bevan-Brown informing this impetus (2011). However, the wisdom of leaving the task of defining giftedness to each individual school, rather than establishing a consistent national definition, remains in question. A 2008 survey from the New Zealand Education Review Office (ERO) revealed mixed implementation and operationalisation of the definition of giftedness at the school level. Less than half of schools surveyed had developed a definition that reflected the values of the school community and incorporated Māori or multi-cultural conceptions of giftedness, and that was grounded in research and current theory, while some had no definition at all. Current research is underway to revisit these practices in New Zealand schools.

Overwhelmingly, Australia has adopted a single conceptual model of giftedness, Gagné's Differentiated Model of Giftedness and Talent (DMGT), at least in policy documents (the DMGT is discussed in Chapter 2). Gagné (2007) defined *giftedness* as "the possession and use of outstanding natural abilities, called aptitudes, in at least one ability domain, to a degree that places an individual at least among the top 10% of age peers" (p. 94) and *talent* as

> the outstanding mastery of systematically developed abilities, called competencies (knowledge and skills), in at least one field of human activity to a degree that places an individual at least among the top 10% of age peers who are or have been active in that field.
>
> *(p. 94)*

Consistent with these definitions, many schools rely on IQ and achievement scores to provide guidance for entry into gifted education programs, often using the top 10% as a guideline for selection (Gagné, 2007). However, beyond the designation of 10% as a cut-off mark, there is little evidence that the consensus around one model of giftedness has driven a cohesive and coordinated approach to gifted education throughout Australia (Jarvis & Henderson, 2014). Given that neither country has reached an optimal situation with gifted children and their education, this signals that whatever model or conception of giftedness is adopted must also be supported by strong policy development, funding, and implementation.

Concluding thoughts

The decade from 2000–2010 reflected very different trajectories for gifted education in each country. A sustained national interest in the educational needs of gifted students spurred the New Zealand Ministry of Education to consider policy reforms, resulting in a raft of advice aimed at strengthening gifted education. This culminated in the *Report of the Working Party of Gifted Education* (Office of the Minister of Education, 2001). There is also evidence of a shift in societal attitudes, with greater acceptance that dedicated provisions for gifted students constitute a right rather than a privilege. The progress in Australia has not been as robust. The two Australian Senate Inquiries regarding the education of gifted children (1998, 2001) set forth recommendations for policy and practice which have not resulted in substantive, sustained changes throughout the nation. Meanwhile, societal attitudes towards gifted children have vacillated between ambivalent at best and antagonistic at worst. Gifted students from Aboriginal and Torres Strait Islander backgrounds continue to seriously lag behind in school achievement compared with their non-Indigenous peers, and they are significantly underrepresented in gifted programs (Chaffey, 2009).

The waxing and waning of support for gifted education in Australia and New Zealand is a pattern characteristic of gifted education elsewhere. American researcher Abe Tannenbaum once observed: "The cyclical nature of interest in the gifted is probably unique in American education. No other special group of children has been so alternately embraced and repelled with so much rigor by educators and laypersons alike" (1983, p. 16). Unfortunately, this sentiment transcends contexts and remains as relevant today as it did over 35 years ago.

The subsequent chapters in this book delineate the advances that researchers and practitioners have made in understanding and providing for gifted children, with a focus on Australia and New Zealand. In the context of fluctuating interest and inconsistent policy and funding frameworks, there remain considerable gaps in the research literature and in practice, in some areas more than others. These gaps are also acknowledged in each chapter, with a view towards orienting future efforts in the field. It is hoped that this collected review of research by Australian and New Zealand scholars will help guide a future research agenda and catalyse a renewed, collaborative drive for excellence in educational research and practice for diverse, highly able learners.

References

Bailey, S. B. (1992). From the editor. *Australasian Journal of Gifted Education, 1*, 4.

Bevan-Brown, J. (2011). Indigenous conceptions of giftedness. In W. Vialle (Ed.), *Giftedness from an indigenous perspective* (pp. 10–23). Wollongong, NSW: Australian Association for the Education of the Gifted and Talented.

Chaffey, G. (2009). Gifted but underachieving: Australian indigenous children. In T. Balchin, B. Hymer, & D. J. Matthews (Eds.), *The Routledge international companion to gifted education* (pp. 106–114). London: Routledge.

Erikson, E. H. (1963). *Childhood and society* (2nd ed.). New York, NY: W. W. Norton & Co.

Gagné, F. (2007). Ten commandments for academic talent development. *Gifted Child Quarterly, 51*, 93–118.

Gross, M. U. M. (1999). Inequity in equity: The paradox of gifted education in Australia. *Australian Journal of Education, 43*, 87–103.

Jarvis, J. M., & Henderson, L. (2014). Defining a coordinated approach to gifted education. *Australasian Journal of Gifted Education, 23*(1), 5–14.

Jolly, J. L., & Chessman, A. M. (2016, September). *The landscape of Australian research: 1983–2013.* Session presented at the annual meeting of the Australian Association for the Educaiton of the Gifted and Talented, Sydney, NSW.

Kohlberg, L. (1981). *The philosophy of moral development: Moral stages and the idea of justice (Essays on moral development, volume 1).* New York, NY: Harper & Row.

Kronborg, L. (2002). Foreword. In W. Vialle & J. G. Geake (Eds.), *The gifted enigma: A collection of articles* (pp. vi–xxi). Cheltenham, NSW: Hawker Brownlow Education.

Larsson, Y. (1986). Gifted education policy in Australia. *Gifted Education International, 4*, 49–55.

Luburic, I. K. (2016). *Gifted education in the Australian context: The development of a discipline through the lens of empirical literature* (Unpublished honours thesis). University of New South Wales, Sydney, Australia.

Marland, S. P., Jr. (1972). *Education of the gifted and talented: Report to the congress of the United States by the U.S. Commissioner of Education and background papers submitted to the U.S. Office of Education.* 2 vols (Government Documents, Y4.L 11/2: G36).Washington, DC: U.S. Government Printing Office.

Ministry of Education (NZ). (2012). *Gifted and talented students: Meeting their needs in New Zealand schools.* Wellington, NZ: Learning Media. Retrieved from http://gifted.tki.org.nz/For-schools-and-teachers

Office of the Minister of Education. (2001). *Working party on gifted education: Report to the Minister of Education.* Wellington, NZ: Author.

Parkyn, G. W. (1948). *Children of high intelligence: A New Zealand study*. Wellington, NZ: New Zealand Council for Educational Research.

Piaget, J. T. (1929). *The child's conception of the world*. London: Routledge & Kegan Paul.

Plunkett, M., & Kronborg, L. (2007). Gifted education in Australia: A story of striving for balance. *Gifted Education International, 23*, 72–83.

Robinson, M. (1992). A vision splendid: Gifted education in Australia. *Roeper Review, 14*, 206–208. doi:10.1080/02783199209553431

Senate Employment Workplace Relations Small Business and Education Reference Committee. (2001). *The education of gifted and talented children*. Canberra, ACT: Parliament of the Commonwealth of Australia.

Senate Select Committee. (1998). *The report of the senate select committee on the education of gifted and talented children (The parliament of the commonwealth of Australia)*. Canberra: Australian Government Publishing Service.

Tannenbaum, A. J. (1983). *Gifted children: Psychological and educational perspectives*. New York, NY: Palgrave Macmillan.

2

IDENTIFICATION OF GIFTED AND TWICE-EXCEPTIONAL STUDENTS

Jae Yup Jung and Peta Hay

Guiding Questions

- Why should gifted students be identified?
- What instruments should be selected to identify different sub-populations of gifted students?
- What is an effective process for the identification of gifted students?
- How can twice-exceptional students be identified?

Key Ideas

- The identification of gifted students should reflect the adopted definition of giftedness.
- The purpose of identification is to provide appropriate educational interventions for gifted students.
- The process of identification should make use of data gathered from multiple sources.
- The identification of twice-exceptional students and underserved gifted students requires distinct procedures.

Introduction

The identification of gifted students is critical to providing them with appropriate curriculum to meet their educational needs. Along with creativity, achievement/ underachievement, and talent development, identification appears to be one of the most discussed and researched topics within the field of gifted education (Dai, Swanson, & Cheng, 2011). In particular, attention appears to have focussed on the specific

Gifted and twice-exceptional students **13**

instruments and processes that may be used to identify gifted students, including gifted students with learning difficulties and disabilities (i.e., twice-exceptional students), gifted students from culturally, linguistically, and socioeconomically diverse backgrounds, and young gifted children. Many different instruments and processes are currently used to identify gifted students in Australia and New Zealand (Bourne & Sturgess, 2006; Chaffey, Bailey, & Vine, 2003; Easton, Gaffney, & Wardman, 2016; Jarvis & Henderson, 2015; Niederer, Irwin, Irwin, & Reilly, 2003).

Conceptualisations/definitions of giftedness

The identification of gifted students needs to reflect the conceptualisations and definitions of giftedness that are adopted in the specific national, cultural, school, and other related contexts in which the identification takes place (Worrell & Erwin, 2011). Indeed, Acar, Sen, and Cayirdag (2016) suggest that "identification practices are *operational responses* to the crucial questions about the nature . . . of giftedness" (emphasis added; p. 81). Unfortunately, the lack of consensus among scholars and practitioners on conceptualisations and definitions of giftedness translates into a lack of uniformity in identification practices around the world (Bracken & Brown, 2006; Foreman & Gubbins, 2015; Friedman-Nimz, 2009; Hartas, Lindsey, & Muijs, 2008). Relatedly, variation in the adopted conceptualisations and definitions, and the specific thresholds for giftedness that are chosen, may also result in wide variation in the numbers, characteristics, and types of students who are identified as gifted (Bélanger & Gagné, 2006).

In Australia and parts of New Zealand, Gagné's Differentiated Model of Giftedness and Talent (DMGT) (Gagné, 1985, 1999, 2003, 2009), which distinguishes between the concepts of giftedness and talent, is widely adopted (Catholic Education Office, Sydney, 2007; Easton et al., 2016; Independent Schools Victoria, 2014; Lassig, 2009; Jung & Worrell, 2017). As such, identification practices in these contexts should be directed by, and reflect, the definitions proposed in the DMGT. In this model, Gagné defines *giftedness* as:

> the possession and use of outstanding natural abilities, called aptitudes, in at least one ability domain [i.e., intellectual, creative, social, perceptive, muscular, or motor control] to a degree that places an individual at least among the top 10% of age peers.
>
> *(Gagné, 2009, p. 63)*

In comparison, *talent* is defined as:

> the mastery of systematically developed abilities, called competencies [knowledge and skills], in at least one field of human activity [including the various academic, occupational, and sports fields] to a degree that places an individual at least among the top 10% of age peers who have been active in that field.
>
> *(Gagné, 2009, p. 63)*

Purpose of identification

The main purpose of identification is to ensure that gifted students are provided with appropriate educational interventions (e.g., academic acceleration, ability grouping, withdrawal programs, differentiated curriculum within a mixed-ability setting, mentorships, enrichment activities) that meet their specific needs (Acar et al., 2016). Essentially, the identification of gifted students represents a necessary initial step that informs *whether* any gifted education interventions should be offered and, if so, *which* gifted education interventions may be appropriate. Ideally, any identification process will generate accurate information, which is collected in an efficient and effective manner, on the students who are assessed (Hartas et al., 2008). Moreover, it is imperative that the identification process be *linked* to, and take into consideration, the specific educational interventions that could be made available to the identified students (Acar et al., 2016; Feldhusen, Asher, & Hoover, 1984; Pfeiffer, 2015; VanTassel-Baska, 2006), as economic factors and logistical issues may mean that it will not always be possible to offer the full range of gifted education programs and provisions.

Methods of identification

The various methods used to identify gifted students may be divided into two broad categories (Acar et al., 2016). The *performance* methods generally involve the administration of an instrument (e.g., an IQ test) from which a quantitative score, that is indicative of the respondent's performance on tasks, is obtained. In contrast, the *non-performance* methods refer to methods of identification that typically involve the formation of qualitative judgements by teachers, psychologists, counsellors, parents, and other relevant parties in the giftedness of students (e.g., teacher nominations). Multiple types of performance and non-performance methods are currently available to identify gifted students.

IQ tests

IQ tests are norm-referenced instruments that assess an individual's capacity to solve problems, utilise logic, and recognise patterns and relationships. These instruments appear to be among the most commonly used in the identification of gifted students, possibly due to the strong validity of scores and the usefulness of such scores in the prediction of future academic success (Nesbitt, 2009). In Australia more than in New Zealand (where IQ tests are generally less utilised), the individually administered Wechsler Intelligence Scale for Children (i.e., WISC) and the Stanford-Binet Intelligence Scales are employed in the assessment of general intellectual ability (e.g., Edwards, 2009; Newman, 2008). Both of these instruments produce multiple composite and subscale indices that reflect different aspects of intellectual ability (i.e., verbal comprehension, perceptual reasoning, working memory, processing speed, and composite scores for the WISC; fluid reasoning,

Gifted and twice-exceptional students **15**

knowledge, quantitative reasoning, visual-spatial processing, working memory, and composite scores for the Stanford Binet Intelligence Scales). Unfortunately, where substantial variation exists among these indices, there is contrasting advice about how an individual's scores should be interpreted and the extent to which the composite IQ score represents a valid measure of intellectual ability (Majkut & Rogers, 2005; Rowe, Dandridge, Pawlush, Thompson, & Ferrier, 2014; Rowe, Kingsley, & Thompson, 2010; Watkins, Greenawalt, & Marcell, 2002).

In place of individual IQ tests, which must be administered individually by registered psychologists, are less rigorous alternatives including abbreviated (or short-form) IQ tests and group-administered IQ tests (Pierson, Kilmer, Rothlisberg, & McIntosh, 2012; Pyryt, 2004). Abbreviated IQ tests (e.g., Kaufmann Brief Intelligence Test [K-BIT]), are generally designed to assess the full range of abilities assessed in individual IQ tests, yet they comprise fewer items and/or scales, may be completed in a shorter period of time, and do not always require administration by a registered psychologist (Pierson et al., 2012). In comparison, group-administered IQ tests (e.g., Cognitive Abilities Test [CogAT] and the Australian Council for Educational Research [ACER] General Abilities Tests [AGAT]) are useful as they may be administered simultaneously to large groups of students (Pyryt, 2004). A possible disadvantage in the use of either abbreviated or group-administered IQ tests, in place of individual IQ tests, is the comparative lack of opportunity to collect information on student attitudes, motivation, attention levels, and problem-solving strategies, which may represent useful additional information in the interpretation of test scores (Pierson et al., 2012; Prifitera, Saklofske, & Weiss, 2005). Indeed, mixed evidence exists on the equivalence of the abbreviated or group-administered IQ tests with individual IQ tests. For example, while Grados and Russo-Garcia (1999) found a strong correlation ($r = .86$) between composite K-BIT and full-scale WISC-III scores, there was simultaneously a significant difference in these scores. Similarly, while the correlation between latent factors for the WISC-III Verbal Scale and the CoGAT6 Verbal Battery was strong ($r = .87$), the correlation between the latent factors for the WISC-III Performance Scale and the CogAT6 Nonverbal Battery was more moderate ($r = .64$) in Lohman (2003).

Tests of visual-spatial abilities

Visual-spatial abilities, defined by Lohman (1996) as "the ability to generate, retain, retrieve, and transform well structured visual images" (p. 98), is a multi-faceted component of intelligence that has traditionally not been as extensively tested as verbal or mathematical abilities (Andersen, 2014; Hambrick et al., 2012; Hegarty, Kechner, Khooshabeh, & Montello, 2009). One instrument that may be useful in the assessment of these abilities is the Universal Nonverbal Intelligence Test (UNIT; Bracken & McCallum, 1998), which contains three visual-spatial ability subscales (i.e., cube design, spatial memory, and mazes). Two other options are the Differential Ability Scales (DAS) or the Cognitive Assessment System (CAS), which may be superior in the discrimination of students of high visual-spatial ability in comparison to individual IQ tests (Andersen, 2014). A recently developed instrument is the computerised version of the Spatial Test Battery, which comprises four visual-spatial ability subscales (i.e., surface development, block rotation, visual memory, and perspectives) that have been demonstrated to have adequate levels of test difficulty (i.e., alpha coefficients ranging from .92 to .93 for the total scores on each difficulty level), internal reliability (i.e., alpha coefficients for all subtests that range from .74 to .91), and predictive validity (i.e., a correlation of .29 between Spatial Test Battery scores and a criterion measure of study success; Stumpf, Mills, Brody, & Baxley, 2013).

Non-verbal ability tests

Non-verbal ability tests refer to tests that assess the abilities of students to make inferences, deductions, and extrapolations from figural stimuli (i.e., figural intelligence; Andersen, 2014), without the requirement for any prior verbal, social, or quantitative knowledge (Naglieri & Ford, 2015). These tests are often used with the aim of achieving greater equity in the identification of gifted students from culturally, linguistically, and socioeconomically diverse backgrounds, who may not be identified using traditional IQ measures (Giessman, Gambrell, & Stebbins, 2013; Jung & Worrell, 2017; Naglieri & Ford, 2015; Wellisch & Brown, 2012). Two of the most commonly used non-verbal ability tests are the Ravens Progressive Matrices and the Naglieri Nonverbal Test of Ability (Lohman, Korb, & Lakin, 2008; Naglieri, 1997, 2008; Raven, Court, & Raven, 1996).

A number of cautions may exist with the use of these instruments. In particular, some non-verbal ability tests may not assess *all* the constructs assessed in other tests of ability (Anastasi & Urbina, 1997; Lohman, 2005; Lohman & Gambrell, 2012; Worrell, 2013), while other non-verbal ability tests may have verbal directions and illustrations with culture-specific content (Borland, 2014; Newman, 2008). Additionally, a number of studies suggest that some inequitable identification remains with the use of these instruments (e.g., Carman & Taylor, 2010; Giessman et al., 2013; Lohman et al., 2008). Finally, as students identified as gifted using non-verbal ability tests are likely to be most suited to programs or provisions that focus on non-verbal content (and students identified as gifted using verbal ability tests are likely to be most suited to programs or provisions that focus on verbal content), consideration will need to be given to the nature of the programs or provisions into which the identified students are eventually placed.

Above-level tests

Above-level testing (alternatively called above-grade, off-level, or out-of-level testing) refers to the administration of academic tests that were originally designed for students in higher grades or older age groups (Warne, 2012, 2014). The practice has been used in the field of gifted education for multiple years, particularly in the context of talent searches in Australia (Jung, Barnett, Gross, & McCormick, 2011) and the United States (Assouline & Lupkowski-Shoplik, 2012; Rambo-Hernandez & Warne, 2015). The usefulness of this identification method may lie in the better match that is often achieved between the abilities of gifted students and test content, in comparison to tests designed for particular chronological age groups (Rambo-Hernandez & Warne, 2015). These tests generally function similarly for students of different age groups, except in situations where students have not previously been exposed to the test content (Warne et al., 2016).

Warne (2014) has empirically demonstrated the psychometric rigour (i.e., the reliability of the scores obtained from and the validity of the use) of two common above-level tests (i.e., the Iowa Tests of Basic Skills and the Iowa Tests of Educational Development) in the identification of gifted students, using internal consistency analyses and hierarchical liner modelling. Specifically, he was able to show that these tests may (a) have high test ceilings, (b) have the ability to discriminate among gifted students of different ability levels, (c) have acceptable levels of score reliability, (d) allow for the tracking of individual student progress, and (e) allow for ready comparisons between the performance of gifted students and their older peers.

Nominations

Nominations are qualitative and/or subjective identification processes that may be completed by parties who are familiar with gifted students, including teachers, parents, peers, and the students themselves. A number of scholars have suggested that nomination instruments may be particularly useful due to the unique perspectives that are brought to the identification process (Banbury & Wellington, 1989; Borland, 2014; Jung & Worrell, 2017). For example, parents may be in the best position to contribute information on the cognitive and related milestones that have been reached (Chan, 2009; Ruf, 2009), while peers may be the optimal referents for characteristics such as leadership (Jung & Worrell, 2017). Furthermore, members of Indigenous or ethnic communities may provide valuable community-specific information (Cooper, 2005). For example, Bevan-Brown (2009) noted the usefulness of obtaining nominations from the Māori community to allow for the recognition of "Māori-specific cultural abilities and qualities" (p. 10) that may be related to giftedness. Of the various types of nomination methods, teacher nominations appear to be the most commonly used in Australia, New Zealand, and throughout the world (Easton et al., 2016; Jarvis & Henderson, 2015; McBee, 2006).

Despite some evidence suggesting the effectiveness of nomination instruments, and particularly teacher nomination instruments (Gagné, 1994; McBee, 2006), questions remain over their potential lack of psychometric rigour (Moon & Brighton, 2008; Pfeiffer & Blei, 2008). Indeed, some point to the reliance by nominators on their personal conceptualisations of giftedness (Acar et al., 2016; Pierce et al., 2007; Speirs Neumeister, Adams, Pierce, Cassady, & Dixon, 2007), whereas others note that nominations may reflect factors that are not necessarily connected to giftedness, such as self-efficacy, motivation, and demographic characteristics (Barber & Torney-Purta, 2008; Foreman & Gubbins, 2015; Siegle, Moore, Mann, & Wilson, 2010). Acar et al. (2016) and McBee (2006) also highlight the lower rates of nomination for gifted students of diverse cultural and disadvantaged socioeconomic backgrounds (Acar et al., 2016; McBee, 2006). To address some of these potential weaknesses of nomination methods, McCoach and Siegle (2007) propose that appropriate training needs to be given to nominators prior to their participation in any nomination exercise, while Bracken and Brown (2008) recommend the use of behaviour checklists or rating scales rather than open-ended nomination instruments.

Curriculum-based assessments

Curriculum-based assessments refer to any assessment activities that utilise observation and recording of student performance within a curriculum to inform educational decisions (Hintze, Christ, & Methe, 2006). The usefulness of such an approach to the identification of gifted students appears to be dependent on whether the assessed students reveal their abilities during the learning process (Reichart, 2003). A number of curriculum-based assessment models have been proposed to identify gifted students in Australasia and around the world (Hintze et al., 2006; Jarvis, 2009; Patton, 1992).

In the Provision-Evaluation-Provision (PEP) approach (Tilsley, 1995), the identification process begins with the design and implementation of a curriculum that is appropriate for the prospective areas of giftedness of students in the target group. Thereafter, the nature and quality of student responses to the curriculum are assessed by teachers, to inform decisions about whether any participating students may be gifted (along with decisions about the need for any subsequent modifications to the curriculum). Similar principles underlie the problem-based learning (PBL) approach to identification, which requires teachers to observe and assess students during multiple PBL activities. In Gallagher and Gallagher (2013), the use of the PBL approach resulted in the identification of a group of students who may not be identified using traditional measures, but who display characteristics and produce academic outputs that are very similar to those of the traditionally identified students. A third form of curriculum-based assessment are the various types of performance-based assessments, which introduce challenging and open-ended tasks that emphasise the processes used to arrive at answers, rather than only the answers themselves (Moon, Brighton, Callahan, & Robinson, 2005; VanTassel-Baska, Feng, & Evans, 2007).

Generally, the curriculum-based identification approaches appear to be useful in the identification of gifted students of diverse, disadvantaged backgrounds who may not always be identified using traditional identification instruments, and therefore are typically underrepresented in gifted programs (Gallagher & Gallagher, 2013; VanTassel-Baska et al., 2007). Unfortunately, minimal evidence on the psychometric properties of the various forms of the curriculum-based identification assessments could be identified.

Dynamic assessment

Dynamic assessment is a relatively new, "interactive" approach to the identification of gifted students that, like the non-verbal ability tests and the curriculum-based assessment approaches, is useful in the identification of gifted students who may not have been traditionally identified (Calero, Belen, & Robles, 2011; Chaffey et al., 2003). The approach assumes that gifted students who perform poorly on identification instruments, for cultural or environmental reasons, may demonstrate their "true" performance on these instruments after the provision of appropriate educational interventions (Calero et al., 2011; Noel & Edmunds, 2007). While multiple forms of dynamic assessment exist and are available, one that is commonly utilised follows a pre-test – intervention – post-test format, whereby students are initially tested (e.g., an IQ test) before they are offered an educational intervention informed by the results of the pre-test, and tested again following the educational intervention (Calero et al., 2011; Chaffey et al., 2003). The focus of the analyses is not only on the scores obtained during the two administrations of the test but also on the difference in these scores, to allow for an assessment of "learning capacity" (i.e., with the greatest learning capacity being demonstrated for students with the most substantial gains in scores). The approach appears to be useful in that it may, to some degree, neutralise the inequities in educational opportunity for some segments of the gifted student population.

It is noteworthy that dynamic assessment has been demonstrated to be useful in the identification of gifted students from Indigenous backgrounds in Australia. Chaffey et al. (2003) was successful in the identification of gifted Indigenous students through the development of an approach to dynamic assessment (i.e., Coolabah dynamic assessment) that targeted socioemotional and metacognitive barriers to performance, which have been identified as being potentially problematic for students of minority backgrounds (Tzuriel & Feuerstein, 1992). To address socioemotional issues, Chaffey et al. (2003) required that (a) each session commence with ice-breaker activities designed to ensure that students were comfortable with the assessor and the assessment process; (b) the assessment was presented in a manner that distanced it from usual classwork; and (c) a respected Indigenous community member was present at all times. In comparison, to address the lack of use of metacognitive strategies, the educational interventions were focussed on the learning of effective metacognitive strategies. The approach to the identification of gifted students appears to have achieved substantial support from the Indigenous community in Australia.

Process of identification

The availability of numerous methods to identify gifted students may present multiple challenges for researchers and practitioners who need to make decisions about the specific methods to use, the timing of the use of these methods, and how the results obtained from these methods should be optimally combined. Indeed, multiple scholars (Acar et al., 2016; Chester, 2003; McBee, Peters, & Waterman, 2014) have noted the lack of guidance on the matter. In practice, substantial inconsistency appears to exist among schools in the process of identification. For example, Jarvis and Henderson (2015) noted the use of different combinations of identification methods, differences in the prioritisation given to the results obtained from certain methods, and differences in whether the results obtained from the selected methods are analysed simultaneously or consecutively, among schools in South Australia. In comparison, Easton et al. (2016) noted a general lack of awareness or utilisation of identification policies among teachers in New Zealand, resulting in the adoption of variable and non-systematic identification processes. Similarly, Hartas et al. (2008) identified a "lack of a common metric, inconsistency in handling diverse pieces of evidence, and variable selectors' expertise to judge the documentation provided by the applicants" (p. 13) in the identification of gifted students in the United Kingdom.

Multiple scholars suggest that any process of identification should be informed by data gathered from multiple sources (Acar et al., 2016; Geiser, Mandelman, Tan, & Grigorenko, 2016; Hartas et al., 2008; McBee et al., 2014; Pfeiffer, 2015), as such an approach may have the benefit of being inclusive of students from diverse backgrounds (Acar et al., 2016; Ford & Grantham, 2003; Richert, 1987; Tannenbaum, 2003), while simultaneously providing scope for triangulation to minimise bias (Hartas et al., 2008). Acar et al. (2016) suggest that the identification methods selected for use should incorporate both performance (e.g., IQ tests) and non-performance (e.g., teacher nominations) methods, as these methods do not identify identical groups of students. Nevertheless, to maximise the accuracy of identification, the scores obtained from the selected methods should have reasonable levels of reliability and reasonable levels of correlation with one another (McBee et al., 2014). Generally, the performance methods appear to produce reliable scores that have at least fair levels of correlation with one another, while teacher nominations appear to be the most reliable among the non-performance methods and have the highest levels of correlation with the performance methods (Acar et al., 2016; Geiser et al., 2016).

In terms of the timing of the use of the various identification instruments, Acar et al. (2016) suggest that the selected identification methods should be used *concurrently* rather than consecutively, as the introduction of any preliminary screening phases to the identification process may mean that some gifted students remain unidentified. McBee et al. (2014) propose that the data collected may then be optimally "combined" using one of three approaches: (a) the conjunctive rule (benchmark scores for all identification methods need to be met), (b) the disjunctive rule (benchmark scores for one of the identification methods need to be met), and (c) the compensatory rule (the mean of the scores obtained from the different identification methods need to meet a benchmark score; the benchmark scores set need to be consistent with the conceptualisations and definitions of giftedness that are followed). While the conjunctive rule may be most appropriate for small programs or provisions with major consequences of misidentification (e.g., acceleration), and the disjunctive rule may be most appropriate for large programs with minimal consequences of misidentification (e.g., enrichment), McBee et al. (2014) considered the compensatory rule to be an optimal compromise that balances the rigour of the conjunctive rule with the inclusiveness of the disjunctive rule.

Alternative guidance on the optimal approach to combine scores obtained from performance and non-performance identification methods has been provided by Lohman and Lakin (2007). They proposed that students who meet benchmarks for both identification methods (e.g., an IQ test as the performance method and a teacher nomination as the non-performance method) should be the first to be admitted into gifted programs or provisions. For those who perform below the benchmarks for one or both of these methods, they recommend: (a) enrichment activities (for students who meet the benchmark for the non-performance method but are slightly below the benchmark for the performance method), (b) further monitoring of progress (for students who only meet the benchmark in the performance method), and (c) admission into gifted programs or provisions (for students from disadvantaged backgrounds who rank highly among students of similar backgrounds but do not meet benchmarks for either method).

Pfeiffer (2015) has suggested that an ideal identification process would be ongoing, as the collection of data from multiple sources over an extended period of time may provide the most accurate picture of potentially gifted students' abilities.

Identification of twice-exceptional students

A sub-group of the gifted student population is twice-exceptional students, who are simultaneously gifted *and* possess a disabling condition (Foley Nicpon, Allmon, Sieck, & Stinson, 2011). Despite the existence of multiple disabling conditions, most of the research on twice exceptionality has, until the recent past (i.e., 1990 to 2009), focussed on one of three areas: (a) giftedness and a specific learning disability (SLD), (b) giftedness and attention deficit hyperactivity disorder (ADHD), and (c) giftedness and autism spectrum disorder (ASD; Foley Nicpon et al., 2011). Although research in the area continues, there appear to be some differences in specific approaches for identifying different types of twice-exceptional students.

Gifted and SLD

Multiple methods have been proposed to identify students who are simultaneously gifted and have an SLD (Brody & Mills, 1997; Lovett & Lewandowski, 2006; Lovett & Sparks, 2011; McCoach, Kehle, Bray, & Siegle, 2001; Nielsen, 2002). These include (a) scatter analysis (which deems twice exceptionality when a student who completes an individual IQ test is found to have a substantial difference between the highest and lowest subscale scores), (b) profile analysis (which deems twice exceptionality when certain patterns of poor performance are found in subset clusters of tests), and (c) an ability-achievement discrepancy (with twice exceptionality being deemed when there is substantial difference in measures of ability and achievement;

e.g., two standard deviations). However, all of these identification methods may have potential problems. Specifically, Lovett and Lewandowski (2006) highlight the tendency for most gifted students to have large differences in IQ subscale scores, the lower reliability of individual subtest and subscale scores in comparison to the total score of almost *any* cognitive identification instrument, the lack of empirically derived profiles of twice-exceptional students, and the possible lack of consistency of differences in scores obtained from different instruments over time.

In place of these methods, Lovett and Sparks (2011) propose that the two exceptionalities be assessed separately, with full-scale scores from standardised IQ tests (i.e., a benchmark of at least 120) used to assess giftedness, and norm-referenced academic achievement test scores (i.e., a standard score below 85) used to assess the SLD. The approach appears to represent a variation on the popular ability-achievement discrepancy approach, but with an interpersonal, norm-referenced measure of actual performance to recognise an "actual" academic impairment. As an alternative, some propose the use of the response to intervention (RTI) approach, which arose as the ability-achievement discrepancy approach failed to provide any information on appropriate educational interventions, and relies on the provision of high-quality differentiation that responds to the interests and strengths of a cohort of students, and the subsequent assessment of their performance (Crepeau-Hobson & Bianco, 2011; Lovett & Sparks, 2011; McCallum et al., 2013; Yassel, Adams, Clarke, & Jones, 2014). Crepeau-Hobson and Bianco (2011) suggest that if the RTI approach is integrated with the systematic administration of standardised tests of cognitive ability, it may be effective and useful in the identification of twice-exceptional students.

Gifted and ADHD

For twice-exceptional students who are simultaneously gifted and have ADHD, the process of identification may be complicated by the overlap in some of the characteristics of giftedness and ADHD (e.g., high activity levels, difficulty paying attention, and impulsivity), and by possible "masking" effects that arise from the interaction of the two exceptionalities (Mullett & Rinn, 2015; Rinn & Reynolds, 2012). For example, giftedness may compensate to some degree the expressed ADHD impairments for some students (Zentall, Moon, Hall, & Grskovic, 2001), whereas for others, there may be a decrease in executive functioning (e.g., working memory, processing speed, and auditory verbal memory) to levels that are below those typically observed in gifted students (Brown, Reichel, & Quinlan, 2011).

Mullett and Rinn (2015) suggest that there is no one "litmus test" to identify these students. Behaviour checklists, which are often used to identify students with ADHD, may be inappropriate, as such instruments tend to focus on the expression of behaviours rather than the causes of such behaviours, which may be more relevant for the purposes of identification (Budding & Chidekel, 2012). Similarly, continuous performance tests appear to lack adequate levels of sensitivity and validity to identify twice-exceptional students (Brown et al., 2011; Chae, Kim, & Noh, 2003; Park et al., 2011). In their place, scholars propose that a comprehensive clinical and psychological evaluation, which avoids confounding ADHD symptoms with ADHD-like gifted behaviours, be undertaken of both exceptionalities, by experts in the two disciplines with knowledge of twice exceptionality (Brown et al., 2011; Cordeiro et al., 2011; Reis, Baum, & Burke, 2014).

Gifted and ASD

As for twice-exceptional students who are gifted and have ADHD, scholars suggest that a comprehensive evaluation of the two exceptionalities may be ideal for students who are simultaneously gifted and have ASD. In particular, Assouline, Foley Nicpon, and colleagues note the collective usefulness of the information gathered from individual instruments that assess intelligence, academic achievement, behavioural functioning, social skills, and ASD (Assouline, Foley Nicpon, & Doobay, 2009; Foley Nicpon et al., 2011). The specific instruments used to identify these twice-exceptional students suggested by Assouline et al. (2009) include (a) the Wechsler Intelligence Scale for Children (WISC-IV) to assess intellectual ability, (b) the Woodcock-Johnson (WJ-III) Achievement Battery to assess academic achievement, (c) the Developmental Neuropsychological Assessment (NEPSY-II) to assess neuropsychological functioning (i.e., attention, executive functioning, language, memory, learning, sensorimotor, social perception, and visuospatial processing), (d) the Behavioral Assessment System for Children (BASC-2) to assess psychosocial functioning, (e) the Social Skills Rating System (SSRS) to assess social skills, (f) the Vineland Adaptive Behavior Scales (Vineland-II) to assess adaptive functioning, (g) the Autism Diagnostic Observation Schedule (ADOS) as one measure to assess ASD, and (h) the Autism Diagnostic Review – Revised (ADI-R) as a second measure to assess ASD.

The information gathered from the combination of instruments is likely to allow an accurate assessment of the distinguishing characteristics of twice-exceptional students (e.g., high verbal comprehension and perceptual reasoning abilities, average processing speed, and many social/communication skills that are at levels comparable to students diagnosed with ASD; Assouline et al., 2009). Nevertheless, the time- and resource-intensive nature of the identification process, and the need for collaboration among psychologists, psychiatrists, educators, and other relevant professionals with expertise in two disciplines, may mean that it will not be readily available for all students who have this type of double exceptionality.

Conclusion and recommendations

Despite the existence of gifted education policy documents in Australia and New Zealand, the identification of gifted students continues to be a practice that is not mandated in either country. When any attempts are made to identify gifted students, it is often done in a haphazard manner, without adequate consideration of the multiple issues that determine the composition of the students who are identified as gifted. Fortunately, rigorous empirical research in the international field of gifted education, to which scholars in Australia and New Zealand have contributed, now provide some clear, albeit incomplete, guidelines on the optimal approach to take.

In essence, the current literature states that any strategy to identify gifted students will need to:

(a) be compatible with the definition of giftedness that is adopted (e.g., Gagné's DMGT);
(b) be consistent with the gifted education programs and provisions that will be provided to the identified students (e.g., withdrawal programs in STEM subjects);
(c) ensure that a mix of performance and non-performance identification methods is utilised (with a preference given to a range of psychometrically rigorous identification methods that do not produce results that are highly inconsistent with one another);
(d) concurrently collect data using the selected identification methods;
(e) apply a rule that is consistent with the intended gifted education programs and provisions when analysing data (e.g., the disjunctive rule for enrichment activities in the humanities);
(f) be an ongoing process; and
(g) acknowledge the existence of twice-exceptional students, and adopt separate identification strategies to identify these students.

Further research in the area is nevertheless desirable and necessary to allow for greater effectiveness and clarity in the identification of gifted students. One recommended direction for future research is in the development of a greater number of psychometrically rigorous non-performance identification methods, to address commonly expressed concerns relating to the reliability of the scores obtained from, and the validity of the use of, existing non-performance methods (Acar et al., 2016; Pfeiffer & Blei, 2008). Additionally, research which specifies the optimal *number* and *combination* of identification methods for each adopted definition of giftedness will provide much-needed direction on the specific performance and non-performance identification methods that should be included in any multiple criteria identification process. Similarly, research that provides guidance on the specific combination rules to apply for the full range of available gifted education programs and provisions, may allow for a more sophisticated and nuanced extension to the current guidelines on optimal combination rules proposed by McBee et al. (2014). Finally, the development of more cost- and resource-effective options to identify twice-exceptional students, which may not require comprehensive evaluations of the two exceptionalities by experts in two fields, may eventually allow for greater numbers of twice-exceptional students to be identified for the provision of appropriate educational interventions.

For their part, gifted education practitioners will need to become familiar with what constitutes psychometric rigour in identification instruments (see also Cohen, Swerdlik, & Phillips, 2013) and keep abreast of the advances in research that are taking place in the identification of gifted students (e.g., Acar et al., 2016; McBee et al., 2014), which may necessitate modifications to the currently recommended identification practices. For multiple reasons, it may not be possible to completely follow *all* of the current or future recommended identification practices. In such cases, some practical compromises (e.g., the offering of only a limited range of economically viable gifted education programs and provisions), the pooling of resources (e.g., identification instruments), and the sharing of personnel (e.g., registered psychologists and professionals with expertise in the identification of disabling conditions) may be necessary.

Discussion Questions

- Should only one definition of giftedness be used to guide the identification of gifted students in a school/school system/country?
- Should decisions about the gifted education programs/provisions to be offered precede or follow the identification of gifted students?
- Are there any alternatives to the commonly available methods used to identify gifted students in schools/school systems/countries?
- What are some possible barriers to the identification of gifted students?

References

Acar, S., Sen, S., & Cayirdag, N. (2016). Consistency of performance and non-performance methods in gifted identification: A multilevel meta-analytic review. *Gifted Child Quarterly, 60*, 81–101.

Anastasi, A., & Urbina, S. (1997). *Psychological testing* (7th ed.). Upper Saddle River, NJ: Prentice Hall.

Andersen, L. (2014). Visual-spatial ability: Important in STEM, ignored in gifted education. *Roeper Review, 36*, 114–121.

Assouline, S. G., & Lupkowski-Shoplik, A. (2012). The talent search model of gifted identification. *Journal of Psychoeducational Assessment, 30*, 45–59.

Assouline, S. G., Nicpon, M. F., & Doobay, A. (2009). Profoundly gifted girls and autism spectrum disorder: A psychometric case study comparison. *Gifted Child Quarterly, 53*, 89–105.

Banbury, M. M., & Wellington, B. (1989). Designing and using peer nomination forms. *Gifted Child Quarterly, 33*, 161–164.

Barber, C., & Torney-Purta, J. (2008). The relation of high-achieving adolescents' social perceptions and motivation to teachers' nominations for advanced programs. *Journal of Advanced Academics, 19*, 412–443.

Bélanger, J., & Gagné, F. (2006). Estimating the size of the gifted/talented population from multiple identification criteria. *Journal for the Education of the Gifted, 30*, 131–163.

Bevan-Brown, J. M. (2009). Identifying and providing for gifted and talented Mäori students. *APEX: The New Zealand Journal of Gifted Education, 15*, 6–20.

Borland, J. H. (2014). Identification of gifted students. In J. A. Plucker & C. M. Callahan (Eds.), *Critical issues and practices in gifted education: What the research says* (2nd ed., pp. 323–342). Waco, TX: Prufrock Press.

Bourne, J., & Sturgess, A. (2006). If anyone can, Kiwis can: Every teacher, a teacher of gifted learners. *Australasian Journal of Gifted Education, 15*, 44–50.

Bracken, B. A., & Brown, E. F. (2006). Behavioral identification and assessment of gifted and talented students. *Journal of Psychoeducational Assessment, 24*, 112–122.

Bracken, B. A., & Brown, E. F. (2008). Early identification of high-ability students: Clinical assessments of behaviour. *Journal for the Education of the Gifted, 31*, 403–426.

Bracken, B. A., & McCallum, R. S. (1998). *Examiner's manual for the Universal Nonverbal intelligence test.* Itasca, IL: Riverside.

Brody, L. E., & Mills, C. J. (1997). Gifted children with learning disabilities: A review of the issues. *Journal of Learning Disabilities, 30*, 282–296.

Brown, T. E., Reichel, P. C., & Quinlan, D. M. (2011). Executive function impairments in high IQ children and adolescents with ADHD. *Open Journal of Psychiatry, 1*, 56–65.

Budding, D., & Chidekel, D. (2012). ADHD and giftedness: A neurocognitive consideration of twice exceptionality. *Applied Neuropsychology: Child, 1*, 145–151.

Calero, M. D., Belen, G. M., & Auxiliadora Robles, M. (2011). Learning potential in high IQ children: The contribution of dynamic assessment to the identification of gifted children. *Learning and Individual Differences, 21*, 176–181.

Carman, C. A., & Taylor, D. K. (2010). Socioeconomic status effects on using the Naglieri Nonverbal Ability Test (NNAT) to identify the gifted/talented. *Gifted Child Quarterly, 54*, 75–84.

Catholic Education Office, Sydney. (2007). *Gifted education K-12 position paper.* Retrieved from www.ceosyd.catholic.edu.au/About/Documents/pp-gift-ed.pdf

Chae, P. K., Kim, J. H., & Noh, K. S. (2003). Diagnosis of ADHD among gifted children in relation to KEDI-WISC and TOVA performance. *Gifted Child Quarterly, 47*, 192–201.

Chaffey, G. W., Bailey, S. B., & Vine, K. W. (2003). Identifying high academic potential in Australian Aboriginal children using dynamic testing. *Australasian Journal of Gifted Education, 12*, 42–55.

Chan, D. W. (2009). Dimensionality and typology of perfectionism: The use of the frost multidimensional perfectionism scale with Chinese gifted students in Hong Kong. *Gifted Child Quarterly, 53*, 174–187.

Chester, M. D. (2003). Multiple measures and high-stakes decisions: A framework for combining measures. *Educational Measurement: Issues and Practice, 22*, 32–41.

Cohen, R. J., Swerdlik, M. E., & Phillips, S. M. (2013). *Psychological testing and assessment: An introduction to tests and measurement* (8th ed.). New York, NY: McGraw-Hill.

Cooper, S. (2005). Gifted indigenous programs: Unmasking potential in minority cultures. *Gifted Education International, 19*, 114–125.

Cordeiro, M. L., Farias, A. C., Cunha, A., Benko, C. R., Farias, L. G., Costa, M. T., . . . McCracken, J. T. (2011). Co-occurrence of ADHD and high IQ: A case series empirical study. *Journal of Attention Disorders, 15*, 485–490.

Crepeau-Hobson, F., & Bianco, M. (2011). Identification of gifted students with learning disabilities in a Response-to-Intervention era. *Psychology in the Schools, 48*, 102–109.

Dai, D. Y., Swanson, J. A., & Cheng, H. (2011). State of research on giftedness and gifted education: A survey of empirical studies published during 1998–2010. *Gifted Child Quarterly, 55*, 126–138.

Easton, V., Gaffney, J. S., & Wardman, J. (2016). "I need to do better, but I don't know what to do": Primary teachers' experiences of talented young writers. *Australasian Journal of Gifted Education, 25*, 34–51.

Edwards, K. (2009). Misdiagnosis, the recent trend in thinking about gifted children with ADHD. *APEX: The New Zealand Journal of Gifted Education, 15*, 29–44.

Feldhusen, J. F., Asher, J. W., & Hoover, S. M. (1984). Problems in the identification of giftedness, talent, or ability. *Gifted Child Quarterly, 28*, 149–151.

Foley Nicpon, M., Allmon, A., Sieck, B., & Stinson, R. D. (2011). Empirical investigation of twice-exceptionality: Where have we been and where are we going? *Gifted Child Quarterly, 55*, 3–17.

Ford, D. Y., & Grantham, T. C. (2003). Providing access for culturally diverse gifted students: From deficit to dynamic thinking. *Theory into Practice, 42*, 217–225.

Foreman, J. L., & Gubbins, E. J. (2015). Teachers see what ability scores cannot: Predicting student performance with challenging mathematics. *Journal of Advanced Academics, 26*, 5–23.

Friedman-Nimz, R. (2009). Myth 6: Cosmetic use of multiple selection criteria. *Gifted Child Quarterly, 52*, 248–250.

Gagné, F. (1985). Giftedness and talent: Reexamining a reexamination of the definitions. *Gifted Child Quarterly, 29*, 103–112.

Gagné, F. (1994). Are teachers really poor talent detectors? Comments on Pegnato and Birch's (1959) study of the effectiveness and efficiency of various identification techniques. *Gifted Child Quarterly, 38*, 124–126.

Gagné, F. (1999). My convictions about the nature of abilities, gifts, and talents. *Journal for the Education of the Gifted, 22*, 109–136.

Gagné, F. (2003). Transforming gifts into talents: The DMGT as a developmental theory. In N. Colangelo & G. A. Davis (Eds.), *Handbook of gifted education* (3rd ed., pp. 60–74). Boston, MA: Allyn & Bacon.

Gagné, F. (2009). Building gifts into talents: Detailed overview of the DMGT 2.0. In B. MacFarlane & T. Stambaugh (Eds.), *Leading change in gifted education: The festschrift of Dr. Joyce Van Tassel-Baska* (pp. 61–80). Waco, TX: Prufrock Press.

Gallagher, S. A., & Gallagher, J. J. (2013). Using problem-based learning to explore unseen academic potential. *Interdisciplinary Journal of Problem-Based Learning, 7*, 111–131.

Geiser, C., Mandelman, S. D., Tan, M., & Grigorenko, E. L. (2016). Multitrait – multimethod assessment of giftedness: An application of the correlated traits – correlated (methods – 1) model. *Structural Equation Modeling: A Multidisciplinary Journal, 23*, 76–90.

Giessman, J. A., Gambrell, J. L., & Stebbins, M. S. (2013). Minority performance on the Naglieri nonverbal ability test versus the cognitive abilities test, form 6: One gifted program's experience. *Gifted Child Quarterly, 57*, 101–109.

Grados, J. J., & Russo-Garcia, K. A. (1999). Comparison of the Kaufman brief intelligence test and the Wechsler intelligence scale for children (3rd ed.) in economically disadvantaged African American youth. *Journal of Clinical Psychology, 55*, 1063–1071.

Hambrick, D. Z., Libarkin, J. C., Petcovic, H. L., Baker, K. M., Elkins, J., Callahan, C. N., . . . LaDue, N. D. (2012). A test of the circumvention of-limits hypothesis in scientific problem solving: The case of geological bedrock mapping. *Journal of Experimental Psychology: General, 141*, 397–403.

Hartas, D., Lindsey, G., & Muijs, D. (2008). Identifying and selecting able students for the NAGTY summer school: Emerging issues and future considerations. *High Ability Studies, 19*, 5–18.

Hegarty, M., Keehner, M., Khooshabeh, P., & Montello, D. R. (2009). How spatial abilities enhance, and are enhanced by, dental education. *Learning and Individual Differences, 19*, 61–70.

Hintze, J. M., Christ, T. J., & Methe, S. A. (2006). Curriculum-based assessment. *Psychology in the Schools, 43*, 45–56.

Independent Schools Victoria. (2014). *Students with individual needs.* Retrieved from www.is.vic.edu.au/schools/students/individual-needs.htm

Jarvis, J. M. (2009). Planning to unmask potential through responsive curriculum: The 'famous five' exercise. *Roeper Review, 31,* 234–241.

Jarvis, J. M., & Henderson, L. (2015). Current practices in the education of gifted and advanced learners in South Australian schools, *Australasian Journal of Gifted Education, 24,* 70–86.

Jung, J. Y., Barnett, K., Gross, M. U. M., & McCormick, J. (2011). Levels of intellectual giftedness, culture, and the forced-choice dilemma. *Roeper Review, 33,* 182–197.

Jung, J. Y., & Worrell, F. C. (2017). School psychological practice with gifted students. In M. Thielking & M. D. Terjesen (Eds.), *Handbook of Australian school psychology: Integrating international research, practice, and policy* (pp. 575–593). New York, NY: Springer.

Lassig, C. J. (2009). Teachers' attitudes towards the gifted: The importance of professional development and school culture. *Australasian Journal of Gifted Education, 18,* 32–42.

Lohman, D. F. (1996). Spatial ability and g. In I. Dennis & P. Tapsfield (Eds.), *Human abilities: Their nature and measurement* (pp. 97–116). Mahwah, NJ: Erlbaum.

Lohman, D. F. (2003). *The Wechsler intelligence scale for children III and the cognitive abilities test (Form 6): Are the general factors the same?* Retrieved March 18, 2008, from http://faculty.education.uiowa.edu/dlohman

Lohman, D. F. (2005). The role of nonverbal ability tests in identifying academically gifted students: An aptitude perspective. *Gifted Child Quarterly, 49,* 111–138.

Lohman, D. F., & Gambrell, J. L. (2012). Using nonverbal tests to help identify academically talented children. *Journal of Psychoeducational Assessment, 30,* 25–44.

Lohman, D. F., Korb, K., & Lakin, J. (2008). Identifying academically gifted English language learners using nonverbal tests: A comparison of the Raven, NNAT, and CogAT. *Gifted Child Quarterly, 52,* 275–296.

Lohman, D. F., & Lakin, J. (2007). Nonverbal test scores as one component of an identification system: Integrating ability, achievement, and teacher ratings. In J. VanTassel-Baska (Ed.), *Alternative assessments for identifying gifted and talented students* (pp. 41–66). Waco, TX: Prufrock Press.

Lovett, B. J., & Lewandowski, L. J. (2006). Gifted students with learning disabilities: Who are they? *Journal of Learning Disabilities, 39,* 515–527.

Lovett, B., & Sparks, R. L. (2011). The identification and performance of gifted students with learning disability diagnoses: A quantitative synthesis. *Journal of Learning Disabilities, 46,* 304–316.

Majkut, L., & Rogers, K. B. (2005). Who gets left behind in the WISC-IV? The impact of full-scale vs. index scores upon the identification of gifted and talented learners. *Australasian Journal of Gifted Education, 14,* 5–11.

McBee, M. T. (2006). A descriptive analysis of referral sources for gifted identification screening by race and socioeconomic status. *Journal of Secondary Gifted Education, 17,* 103–111.

McBee, M. T., Peters, S. J., & Waterman, C. (2014). Combining scores in multiple-criteria assessment systems: The impact of the combination rule. *Gifted Child Quarterly, 58,* 69–89.

McCallum, R. S., Bell, S. M., Coles, J. T., Miller, K. C., Hopkins, M. B., & Hilton-Prillhart, A. (2013). A model for screening twice-exceptional students (gifted with learning disabilities) within a response to intervention paradigm. *Gifted Child Quarterly, 57,* 209–222.

McCoach, D. B., Kehle, T. J., Bray, M. A., & Siegle, D. (2001). Best practices in the identification of gifted students with learning disabilities. *Psychology in the Schools, 38,* 403–411.

McCoach, D. B., & Siegle, D. (2007). What predicts teachers' attitudes toward the gifted? *Gifted Child Quarterly, 51,* 246–254.

Moon, T. R., & Brighton, C. M. (2008). Primary teachers' conceptions of giftedness. *Journal for the Education of the Gifted, 31,* 447–480.

Moon, T. R., Brighton, C. M., Callahan, C. M., & Robinson, A. (2005). Development of authentic assessments for the middle school classroom. *The Journal of Secondary Gifted Education, 16*, 119–133.

Mullet, D. R., & Rinn, A. N. (2015). Giftedness and ADHD: Identification, misdiagnosis, and dual diagnosis. *Roeper Review, 37*, 195–207.

Naglieri, J. A. (1997). *Naglieri nonverbal ability test*. San Antonio, TX: The Psychological Corporation.

Naglieri, J. A. (2008). Traditional IQ: 100 years of misconception and its relationship to minority representation in gifted programs. In J. VanTassel-Baska (Ed.), *Alternative assessments for identifying gifted and talented students* (pp. 67–88). Waco, TX: Prufrock Press.

Naglieri, J. A., & Ford, D. Y. (2015). Misconceptions about the Naglieri nonverbal ability test: A commentary of concerns and disagreements, *Roeper Review, 37*, 234–240.

Nesbitt, R. E. (2009). *Intelligence and how to get it: Why schools and cultures count*. New York, NY: W. W. Norton & Company.

Newman, T. M. (2008). Assessment of giftedness in school-age children using measures of intelligence or cognitive abilities. In S. I. Pfeiffer (Ed.), *Handbook of giftedness in children: Psychoeducational theory, research, and best practices* (pp. 161–176). New York, NY: Springer.

Niederer, K., Irwin, R. J., Irwin, K. C., & Reilly, I. L. (2003). Identification of mathematically gifted children in New Zealand. *High Ability Studies, 14*, 71–84.

Nielsen, M. E. (2002). Gifted students with learning disabilities: Recommendations for identification and programming. *Exceptionality, 10*, 93–111.

Noel, K., & Edmunds, A. L. (2007). Constructing a synthetic-analytic framework for precocious writing. *Roeper Review, 29*, 125–132.

Park, M. H., Kweon, Y. S., Lee, S. J., Park, E. J., Lee, C., & Lee, C. U. (2011). Differences in performance of ADHD children on a visual and auditory continuous performance test according to IQ. *Psychiatry Investigation, 8*, 227–233.

Patton, J. M. (1992). Assessment and identification of African-American learners with gifts and talents. *Exceptional Children, 59*, 150–159.

Pfeiffer, S. I. (2015). *Essentials of gifted assessment*. Hoboken, NJ: John Wiley & Sons.

Pfeiffer, S. I., & Blei, S. (2008). Gifted identification beyond the IQ test: Rating scales and other assessment procedures. In S. I. Pfeiffer (Ed.), *Handbook of giftedness in children* (pp. 177–198). New York, NY: Springer.

Pierce, R. L., Adams, C. M., Speirs Neumeister, K. L., Cassady, J. C., Dixon, F. A., & Cross, T. L. (2007). Development of an identification procedure for a large urban school corporation: Identifying culturally diverse and academically gifted elementary students. *Roeper Review, 29*, 113–118.

Pierson, E. E., Kilmer, L. M., Rothlisberg, B. A., & McIntosh, D. E. (2012). Use of brief intelligence tests in identification of giftedness. *Journal of Psychoeducational Assessment, 30*, 10–24.

Prifitera, A., Saklofske, D. H., & Weiss, L. G. (2005). *WISC-IV clinical use and interpretation: Scientist practitioner perspectives*. New York, NY: Elsevier.

Pyryt, M. C. (2004). Pegnato revisited: Using discriminant analysis to identify gifted children. *Psychology Science, 46*, 342–347.

Rambo-Hernandez, K. E., & Warne, R. T. (2015). Measuring the outliers: An introduction to out-of-level testing with high-achieving students. *Teaching Exceptional Children, 47*, 199–207.

Raven, J. C., Court, J. H., & Raven, J. (1996). *Manual for Raven's progressive matrices and vocabulary scales: Section 3. Standard progressive matrices*. Oxford: Oxford Psychologists Press.

Reis, S. M., Baum, S. M., & Burke, E. (2014). An operational definition of twice-exceptional learners: Implications and applications. *Gifted Child Quarterly, 58*, 217–230.

Richert, E. S. (1987). Rampant problems and promising practices in the identification of disadvantaged gifted students. *Gifted Child Quarterly, 31*, 149–154.

Richert, E. S. (2003). Excellence with justice in identification and programming. In N. Colangelo & G. A. Davis (Eds.), *Handbook of gifted education* (pp. 146–158). Boston: Allyn & Bacon.

Rinn, A. N., & Reynolds, M. J. (2012). Overexcitabilities and ADHD in the gifted: An examination. *Roeper Review, 34*, 38–45.

Rowe, E. W., Dandridge, J., Pawlush, A., Thompson, D. F., & Ferrier, D. E. (2014). Exploratory and confirmatory factor analyses of the WISC-IV with gifted students. *School Psychology Quarterly, 29*, 536–552.

Rowe, E. W., Kingsley, J. M., & Thompson, D. F. (2010). Predictive ability of the General Ability Index (GAI) versus the full scale IQ among gifted referrals. *School Psychology Quarterly, 25*, 119–128.

Ruf, D. L. (2009). *Five levels of gifted: School issues and educational options*. Scottsdale, AZ: Great Potential Press.

Siegle, D., Moore, M., Mann, R., & Wilson, H. E. (2010). Factors that influence in-service and pre-service teachers' nominations of students for gifted and talented programs. *Journal for the Education of the Gifted, 33*, 337–360.

Speirs Neumeister, K. L., Adams, C. M., Pierce, R. L., Cassady, J. C., & Dixon, F. A. (2007). Fourth-grade teachers' perceptions of giftedness: Implications for identifying and serving diverse gifted students. *Journal for the Education of the Gifted, 30*, 479–499.

Stumpf, H., Mills, C. J., Brody, L. E., & Baxley, P. G. (2013). Expanding talent search procedures by including measures of spatial ability: CTY's Spatial Test Battery. *Roeper Review, 35*, 254–264.

Tannenbaum, A. J. (2003). Nature and nurture of giftedness. In N. Colangelo & G. A. Davis (Eds.), *Handbook of gifted education* (3rd ed., pp. 45–59). New York, NY: Allyn & Bacon.

Tilsley, P. (1995). The use of tests and test data in identification or recognition of high ability. *Flying High, 2*, 43–50.

Tzuriel, D., & Feuerstein, R. (1992). Dynamic group assessment for prescriptive teaching: Differential effects of treatments. In H. C. Haywood & D. Tzuriel (Eds.), *Interactive assessment* (pp. 187–206). New York, NY: Springer–Verlag.

VanTassel-Baska, J. (2006). A content analysis of evaluation findings across 20 gifted programs: A clarion call for enhanced gifted program development. *Gifted Child Quarterly, 50*, 199–215.

VanTassel-Baska, J., Feng, A. X., & Evans, B. L. (2007). Patterns of identification and performance among gifted students identified through performance tasks: A three-year analysis. *Gifted Child Quarterly, 51*, 218–231.

Warne, R. T. (2012). History and development of above-level testing of the gifted. *Roeper Review, 34*, 183–193.

Warne, R. T. (2014). Using above-level testing to track growth in academic achievement in gifted students. *Gifted Child Quarterly, 58*, 3–23.

Warne, R. T., Doty, K. J., Malbica, A. M., Angeles, V. R., Innes, S., Hall, J., & Masterson-Nixon, K. (2016). Above-level test item functioning across examinee age groups. *Journal of Psychoeducational Assessment, 34*, 54–72.

Watkins, M. W., Greenawalt, C. G., & Marcell, C. M. (2002). Factor structure of the Wechsler intelligence scale for children – Third edition among gifted students. *Educational and Psychological Measurement, 62*, 164–172.

Wellisch, M., & Brown, J. (2012). An integrated identification and intervention model for intellectually gifted children. *Journal of Advanced Academics, 23*, 145–167.

Worrell, F. C. (2013). Identifying gifted learners: Nonverbal assessment. In C. M. Callahan & H. Hertberg-Davis (Eds.), *Fundamentals of gifted education: Considering multiple perspectives* (pp. 135–147). New York, NY: Routledge.

Worrell, F. C., & Erwin, J. O. (2011). Best practices in identifying students for Gifted and Talented Education (GATE) programs. *Journal of Applied School Psychology, 27*, 319–340.

Yassel, N., Adams, C., Clarke, L. S., & Jones, R. (2014). Applying an RTI model for students with learning disabilities who are gifted. *Teaching Exceptional Children, 46*, 42–52.

Zentall, S. S., Moon, S. M., Hall, A. M., & Grskovic, J. A. (2001). Learning and motivational characteristics of boys with AD/HD and/or giftedness. *Exceptional Children, 67*, 499–519.

3

CREATIVITY AND GIFTEDNESS

Peter Merrotsy

Guiding Questions

- What is creativity?
- What is the relationship between creativity and giftedness?
- What does creativity in school children look like?
- What does creativity in schools and classrooms look like?
- What should creativity in schools and classrooms look like?

Key Ideas

- The concept of mini-c creativity (Beghetto & Kaufman, 2007) recognises the creativity inherent in the learning process; it highlights the development of personal forms of creativity; it ensures that creative potential is nurtured.
- There is debate about whether or not creativity is an essential component of giftedness. At the very least, there are many fields for which the expression of creativity is extremely important and others for which it provides a considerable advantage.
- Many models claiming to "teach creativity" emphasise divergent thinking and are set within the structure of Bloom's taxonomy and framed by the Multiple Intelligences, which at best should be seen to be general pedagogy rather than teaching for creativity or teaching for gifted students.
- A suitable model of teaching for creativity will embrace the personal creative potential of children and youth, will focus on the creativity inherent in the learning process, and will provide a framework for the development of creative expression.

Introduction

Creativity is quite a complex construct, a point concisely made by Mark Runco: "Creativity is a reflection of cognition, metacognition, attitude, motivation, affect, disposition, and temperament" (2007, p. 320). Nevertheless, an outside observer would be forgiven for identifying creativity in education with the visual arts. This tendency is reinforced by the language that is commonly used to describe or discuss creativity and by a preponderance of the literature – for example, in a recent handbook, edited by two Australian academics (Thomas & Chan, 2013) and covering a broad sweep of research on creativity, half of the chapters concentrate on the visual and performing arts.

A closer look at educational *praxis* does not shift the observer's gaze far. For what seemed an interminably long time, perhaps for two generations or so of school children, creativity in Australian and New Zealand education mainly comprised activities based on Guilford's (1950) championing of divergent thinking (the process of generating many original ideas), such as by coming up with 100 uses of a brick (Braggett, personal communication, 2004, August 15), and Bloom's (1956) taxonomy, in which synthesis was seen as a creative higher-order cognitive ability (Bailey, personal communication, 2004, March 1). During the 1990s, an apparent shift in educational philosophy towards constructivism resulted in creativity in the classroom merging with (or being confused with) critical thinking, and teachers were "trained" in the art of critical thinking and how to teach it. This marriage of sorts is now articulated as the general capability "critical and creative thinking" in the Australian Curriculum (Australian Curriculum Assessment and Reporting Authority, n.d.) and as effective teaching and learning for gifted and talented students in New Zealand schools (Smith, 2012).

At the same time, there has been a smattering of general education and research literature on creativity in primary and secondary school contexts in Australia and New Zealand. Using my university's database search facilities (which include EDU-CAUSE, ERA, ProQuest, A+Education, ERIC, PsycINFO), I have located only a handful of books published and about 30 master's and doctoral-level research theses completed (although most of these, apparently, have not been reported to a wider audience through journal articles). The books that are accessible tend to be edited offerings (e.g., Lett, 1976; Poole, 1980; Thomas & Chan, 2013). One (small) book by Forster (1998) asked teachers to think about creativity and to challenge learners, "especially in encouraging them to think creatively" (p. 3).

The subjects and nature of the doctoral research studies provide an interesting sequence of snapshots of creativity in antipodean education over the past few decades. Gilchrist (1970) considered the relationship between a selection of cognitive and affective variables and creativity and academic achievement. Wright (1998, 2001) explored the relationship between creativity (*sensu* contemporary performance) and constructivist approaches to learning, for which the sample size N = 1 comprised the author. Hannaford (2001) evaluated approaches to teaching creative thinking and teaching divergent thinking, and concluded, unsurprisingly, that time and the

34 Peter Merrotsy

qualities of the classroom are important. Yashin-Shaw (2001) proposed a cognitive model for creative thinking by analysing creative problem solving by a single participant (i.e., sample size N = 1). Lovesy (2003) found that kinaesthetic teaching and learning practices open up pedagogic spaces in playbuilding that enhance imagination and creativity. Aldous (2005a, 2005b) combined protocol analysis of expert (adult) problem solvers (sample size N = 5) with quantitative analysis of responses to a self-report questionnaire (sample size N = 405 adolescents) to find that "the non-cognitive feeling aspect of novel problem solving, rather than the cognitive rule based aspect, is what is crucial to success" (Aldous, 2005b, p. 421). Corcoran (2006) reported strategies to enhance creativity in the visual art classroom that include creating an environment that encourages motivation and social interaction. And, finally, it would seem that Botticchio (2006) did not break any glass ceilings with her case studies involving adult female participants (sample size *n* = 6):

> The cases challenged the contextual view of creativity by using the contextual framework . . . to determine whether the contextual theory could accommodate . . . experiences of creativity. Analysis of the case studies showed that the women's experience of creativity was captured and explained by the contextual framework [*sic*].
>
> *(p. 1)*

It would be fair to say that, as a whole, the nature of the Australian and New Zealand research on creativity in education has been less than cutting-edge and has had little impact on educational practice.

Creativity and giftedness

Just as '100-uses-of-a-brick' and Bloom's taxonomy were for a long time integral components of 'teaching creativity', they were in some cases the only educational responses to meet the learning needs of 'gifted and talented' students, both in and out of the classroom (Bailey, 1996; Braggett, 1986; Merrotsy, 2003). One reason for this lies in the ambiguity and confusion surrounding conceptions of key terms such as 'creativity' and 'giftedness', and the longing of many teachers to find, and presumably to develop, the creativity and the giftedness in each of their students. The 'gifted education' literature, however, does see a close relationship between 'creativity' and 'giftedness', albeit the nature of this relationship is the subject of heated debate (for a well-researched discussion on the relationship between creativity and giftedness, see Geake, 2009). In Australia and New Zealand, three conceptions of giftedness have been important and influential in this regard.

First, the Marland Report (Marland, 1972) adopted a liberal understanding of giftedness, clearly informed by DeHaan and Havighurst (1957), which resulted in the following U.S. federal definition of giftedness:

> Children and youth with outstanding talent perform or show the potential to perform at remarkably high levels of accomplishment when compared

with others of their age, experience or environment. These children and youth exhibit high performance capability in intellectual, creative and/or artistic areas, possess an unusual leadership capacity or excel in specific academic fields. They require services or activities not ordinarily provided by the school. Outstanding talents are present in children and youth from all cultural groups across all economic strata, and in all areas of human endeavour.

(U.S. Department of Education, 1993, p. 26)

Note the reference to experience and environment, which is significant because of its inclusiveness of children and youth from backgrounds of disadvantage.

Second, in his Three-Ring Conception of Giftedness model, Renzulli proposed that giftedness is a necessary interaction and interlocking of three basic clusters of traits: above average, but not necessarily superior, general ability; high levels of task commitment; and high levels of creativity (Renzulli, 1978). Note here the shift in perspective, radical at the time, to recognising and developing high-level creative-productive behaviour or performance, even if creativity was seen through the lens of "creative" adults in selected fields of endeavour.

Third, in his Differentiated Model of Giftedness and Talent (DMGT), Gagné (1985) distinguishes between natural abilities or aptitudes and developed abilities or skills: "Giftedness corresponds to competence that is distinctly above average in one or more domains of human aptitude. Talent corresponds to performance that is distinctly above average in one or more fields of human activity" (Gagné, 1985, p. 108). Gifts are subdivided into domains, one of which is the creative domain. The point here is that creativity, for Gagné, is not an essential factor of either giftedness or of talent, although of course there are many fields of talent for which the expression of creativity is extremely important and others for which it provides a considerable advantage.

One educational response to these conceptions of giftedness and creativity has been to highlight creativity when identifying "gifted and talented" Aboriginal students in Australia (Merrotsy, 2017a), and Māori and Pasifika students in New Zealand (Smith, 2012). Apart from the vexed problem of how high creative potential might be identified, there is also the deep issue that, for such students, policy and policy guidelines emphasise the visual-and-performing-arts sense of the term creativity, at the expense of high intellectual potential. This implicit racism (or at the very least, stereotyping) means that many aspects of high potential are overlooked, and ways to remove barriers that hinder or block the development of high potential into high performance are not explored (Merrotsy, 2017b).

What is creativity?

There are literally hundreds of definitions of creativity, which appear from time to time over the educational horizon, and, even though they differ in various ways, there are certainly common patterns and elements in the way that they move across the educational landscape. For example, most definitions include a statement to the effect that creativity involves bringing something into being that is original (in

36 Peter Merrotsy

the sense of new, unusual, novel, or unexpected) and also valuable (in the sense of useful, good, adaptive, or appropriate). The earliest expression of this definition was proposed by Stein (1953):

> The creative work is a novel work that is accepted as tenable or useful or satisfying by a group in some point in time. . . . By 'novel' I mean that the creative product did not exist previously in precisely the same form.
>
> *(p. 311)*

For Stein, the extent to which the creative work is novel depends on the extent to which it differs from the status quo, that is, from what has gone before. This could depend on the nature of the problem that is addressed, the context or field in which the problem arises, the characteristics of the creative person, and indeed the characteristics of those with whom the creative person is communicating.

Recent expressions of this definition may be found, for example, by Sternberg (1999), who stated that "creativity is the ability to produce work that is both novel (i.e., original, unexpected) and appropriate (i.e., useful, adaptive concerning task constraints)" (p. 3), and by Lubart (1999), who added, significantly, "from a Western point of view" (p. 339). Such definitions are helpful but need greater explication in practical terms, especially as they relate to school children: the 'something', the 'original', the 'novel', the 'appropriate', the 'useful' and the 'valuable' to which they variously refer are quite ambiguous and may be understood, or construed, in many ways. For an extended discussion of the origins of the standard definition of creativity, see Runco and Jaeger (2012).

What is creativity for school children?

What Stein (1953) in fact was drawing attention to is the difference between objective and subjective forms of creativity. He observed that:

> often, in studying creativity, we tend to restrict ourselves to a study of the genius because the *distance* between what he [sic] has done and what has existed is quite marked. [This tendency] causes us to overlook a necessary distinction between the creative product and the creative experience. . . . In speaking of creativity, therefore, it is necessary to distinguish between internal and external frames of reference.
>
> *(Stein, 1953, pp. 311–312)*

Here, the creative experience is inclusive of subjective or personal forms of creativity and creative expression. The point is that neglecting or ignoring these subjective creative experiences in favour of objectively evaluated creative products leads to a depauperate conception of creativity that excludes consideration of creative potential. And, as it happened, the response to Stein's (1953) concern evolved into the dichotomous notion of Big-C creativity (that is, high level or exceptional creativity) versus little-c creativity (that is, day-to-day creativity). During the 1980s and 1990s, most researchers and writers on creativity recognised only Big C kinds of creativity (Sternberg & Lubart, 1996; for a more complete treatment of the history of the concepts of Big-C and little-c creativity, see Merrotsy [2013]). Indeed, studies tended to be about eminent creators and their eminent creativity, at the expense of creativity by school children.

This exclusion of more subjective forms of creative experience and the lack of consideration of creative potential eventually led, in the 'noughties', to the introduction of a new category of creativity, mini-c creativity: "the novel and personally meaningful interpretation of experiences, actions, and events" (Beghetto & Kaufman, 2007, p. 73). The expanded Four C Model of creativity proposed by Kaufman and Beghetto (2009) comprises four ways in which creativity should be conceptualised, in terms of Big-C, little-c, mini-c, and Pro-c creativity, as shown in Table 3.1.

Clearly, the Four C Model says something important about children and creativity: it recognises personal and subjective forms of creativity including intrapersonal insights and interpretations; and it acknowledges creative ability and expression at various levels of specificity. By including the category of mini-c in their model of creativity, Kaufman and Beghetto (2009) emphasised these important points in two ways:

[it helps to] protect against the neglect and loss of students' creative potential by highlighting the importance of recognizing the creativity inherent in students' unique and personally meaningful insights and interpretations . . . [and to] bring a level of specificity necessary to ensure that the creative potential of children is nurtured (rather than overlooked).

(p. 4)

TABLE 3.1 The Four C Model of creativity (Kaufman & Beghetto, 2009)

Creativity	Characteristics
Big-C	Clear-cut eminent creative accomplishments or contributions, reserved for the great – sometimes called Larger C
little-c	Everyday innovation and creative actions, which can be found in nearly all people – sometimes called smaller c
mini-c	Draws attention to the development of personal knowledge and insights within a particular sociocultural context, and their subsequent creative expression; transformative learning; the creativity inherent in the learning process; also gives recognition to "intrapersonal insights and interpretations, which often live only within the person who created them" (p. 4)
Pro-c	"The developmental and effortful progression beyond little-c" (p. 5); professional-level expertise in a creative field, which usually takes at least ten years to develop

38 Peter Merrotsy

What does creativity in school children look like?

One commonly used checklist for understanding and finding creativity amongst school children is known as the Creativity Characteristics Scale (Renzulli & Hartman, 1971). Note that this is a subscale of the Scales for Rating the Behavioural Characteristics of Superior Students (SRBCSS) (Renzulli & Hartman, 1971; Renzulli et al., 2010), and that later versions are essentially the same as the original (for a critical analysis of these scales, see Merrotsy, 2017). Remember, too, that for Renzulli creativity is a necessary component of giftedness. The characteristics of creativity that may be demonstrated by a student include imaginative thinking; a sense of humour; the ability to come up with unusual or clever responses; a willingness to take risks; the ability to generate a large number of ideas; intellectual playfulness and a willingness to fantasise; and a non-conforming attitude (Renzulli, Smith, White, Callahan, & Hartman, 1976).

I must admit that I have several worries with the Creativity Characteristics Scale (and other aspects of Renzulli's work, for that matter), relating to fundamental issues such as inconsistency in definitions of creativity, the tenuous nature of the support from the literature, and the nature of the evidence in support of instrument validity. For example, at the very least we know that Renzulli (1977) proposed a product-oriented view of creativity, referring to creative-productive giftedness, which is modelled on the behaviour and productivity of creative adults, and the development of which aims to increase the likelihood that more students will become creative in the sense of Big-C creativity or specifically people who will change our culture. Again, the criterion for inclusion of items was that each had been suggested by at least three "research studies" by "well known contributors to the literature" (Renzulli, Hartman, & Callahan, 1971, p. 212). However, "studies" such as a note in a 1940 school bulletin and a vague reference to an edited book do not bolster one's confidence in the external validity of the scale. And again, given Renzulli's (1986) later protestations about differences between schoolhouse giftedness and creative-productive giftedness, it is ironic that the Creativity Characteristics Scale does appear to be good at describing and identifying creative children who are already identified to be gifted, a point made several times by Renzulli et al. (1971).

If the over-emphasis on positive attributes apparent in the Creativity Characteristics Scale is less than satisfying, a dated but probably still the best alternative may be found in Torrance's (1969) Checklist of Creative Positives, which was specifically developed for use with disadvantaged children and youth. It lists a set of indicators that Torrance termed "creative positives," and which his observations suggested occur with a rather high degree of frequency in culturally minority children from disadvantaged backgrounds. This checklist also comes with the advice that particular attributes may sometimes be expressed in non-conformist or unconventional ways. Torrance, Goff, and Satterfield (1998) explained that:

> Not all members of economically disadvantaged groups are gifted in all of these positives; however, these creative positives occur to a high degree

among such groups in general. These creative positives can be observed among poor children by anyone who is willing to become a sensitive, open-minded human being in situations where trust and freedom are established.

(pp. 18–19)

The Checklist of Creative Positives includes the ability to express feelings and emotions; the ability to improvise with commonplace materials and objects; the enjoyment of and ability in visual arts, creative movement, drama, music, and rhythm; the use of expressive speech; fluency and flexibility in figural media; responsiveness to the concrete; humour; richness of imagery in informal language; and originality of ideas in problem solving (Torrance, 1969).

It is evident that a strong affective theme runs through these items. According to Torrance (1998), a compelling reason for encouraging young children from cultural minorities and from backgrounds of poverty to express their emotional capacities is that this will enable an insightful observer to identify high learning potential that may otherwise remain hidden.

How is creativity identified?

If assessing students' creative thinking, creative performance, or creative potential, there needs to be a clear understanding of what is meant by creativity and the main purpose of identification. When these are clear, there is then the difficult problem of how to assess creative production. And then there is the far more difficult problem of how to assess creative potential. With respect to identifying the creativity in creative products, Cropley (2000) compiled and categorised quite a lengthy list of qualities and indicators of creativity relating to products, processes, and personal factors, which included originality, uniqueness, novelty, quality, value, flexibility, complexity, realism, elaboration, synthesis, divergent feelings, intellectual and cultural orientations, and creative attitudes, behaviour, and activities.

Cropley (2000) also analysed a range of tests that are supposed to be indicators of creative potential. These creativity tests attempt to measure so-called creative behaviours and attitudes; cognitive processes such as divergent thinking and making associations; simultaneous cognition; constructions and combinations; independence and differentness; and motivation. To measure such things, the tests vary dramatically in the strategies they use: self-assessment and peer assessment; family and community appraisals; observations of behaviour, attitudes, activities, and products; and word associations, questioning, guessing, supposing, and riddles. The general (and perhaps mischievous) conclusion appears to be that creativity tests actually give little indication of talent, and that the best indicator of creative potential may well be the dedicated pursuit of an interest. In any case, because creativity has been so broadly defined, there is no way of inferring from creativity tests what kind of talent or potential a student may or may not have.

Measures of creativity tend to be inspired by Guilford's (1950) conception of creativity as divergent thinking and by his ideas on test construction, including

40 Peter Merrotsy

the alternative uses (for example, of a brick) task. One such measure of creativity, *How Creative Are You?*, was developed by the Australian David Cohen (1930–2014). Cohen's ideas on providing opportunities for creativity in science teaching appeared in Cohen (1968), and his analysis of creativity measurement theory and related research was presented in Cohen (1972). Cohen (1972) also outlined his creativity instrument and provided a sample of two test items: (1) use given letters to produce pairs of words that make sense together; and (2) use a given shape (that looks like a three-quarters unfolded paper clip) to produce interesting drawings or designs. My university library database search engines have not been able to locate a copy of *How Creative Are You?* nor any subsequent related research articles, and so it would seem that Cohen's measure of creativity has not survived the ravages of time.

One measure of creativity that appears to have withstood the test of time is the Torrance® Test of Creative Thinking (TTCT) (Torrance, 2008). The TTCT was designed to help with the identification of gifted students, especially creatively gifted students in multi-cultural contexts. This test involves verbal (using both verbal and non-verbal stimuli) and non-verbal elements that are assessed with respect to fluency, elaboration, originality, resistance to premature closure, and abstractness of titles. These mental characteristics are scored according to 13 criterion-referenced measures: emotional expressiveness; storytelling articulateness; movement or action; expressiveness of titles; synthesis of incomplete figures; synthesis of lines or circles; unusual visualisation; internal visualisation; extending or breaking boundaries; humour; richness of imagery; colourfulness of imagery; and fantasy (Torrance, 2008). The figural component of the TTCT uses three picture-based exercises, inviting the respondent to draw and give a title to their drawings (pictures) or to write reasons, consequences, and different uses for objects (words), and providing opportunities to ask questions, to guess causes, to guess consequences, to improve products, and to "just suppose". An early and objective discussion of the TTCT concluded, "A reasonably high IQ is probably a necessary condition for adequate performance [in the TTCT], and because of this test scores may provide useful information only with high-IQ children" (Crockenberg, 1972, p. 39).

Another measure of creativity, Urban and Jellen's (1985) Test for Creative Thinking – Drawing Production (TCT-DP), is a non-verbal test of creativity that has found application in several Australian contexts. The TCT-DP uses figural fragments as stimuli, and completed products are evaluated according to a range of elements that include continuation of the figural fragments; additions to the figural fragments; new elements; connections made between figural fragments; connections made to produce a theme or *Gestalt*; boundary breaking, both fragment dependent and fragment independent; use of perspective; use of humour; and unconventionality (Urban & Jellen, 1985). Urban and Jellen (1996) have noted that there are no statistically significant differences between the TCT-DP and the TTCT. They also claim international support for their instrument, but it must be stated that the nature of this support is quite equivocal. In one Australian study, Pears (1994) was led to suggest that teachers tend to be incapable of teaching critical and creative thinking and that some students are better than their teachers at critical and creative thinking. In another study, McCann (2005) argued that creativity is an essential characteristic of giftedness, despite the fact that she found poor correlations between scores on tests of intelligence and tests of creativity, which included the TCT-DP. On the other hand, Brockwell (2008) found that the TCT-DP could be combined with three drawing tasks that specifically involved still life, feelings, and a creative creature, and a discussion with the student about his or her art work, to develop a neat model of identification of young children with high creative ability in the visual arts.

What does creativity in education systems look like?

For a general picture of what creativity in schools and classrooms looks like, we may look to national education documents. The New Zealand Ministry of Education has provided guidelines for schools to support the education of gifted and talented students (Smith, 2012). Here, prominence is given to Renzulli's concept of giftedness (see previous discussion), for which a high level of creativity is a necessary component. Creativity is an "area of giftedness and talent," and refers to students with "general creative abilities as evidenced in their abilities to problem-find and problem-solve, and their innovative thinking and productivity" (p. 23). "Creative thinking characteristics" is one of five categories of behaviour and qualities that may be observed in gifted and talented students (p. 33). The creative gifted child is described as "highly creative but frustrated, bored, questioning, and sometimes rebellious [sic]" (p. 37). Given the important place afforded to creativity in the guidelines, I find it surprising that there is very little mention of creativity in its discussion of differentiated programs for gifted and talented students.

In Australia, such national statements have come only from the Australian Curriculum Assessment and Reporting Authority (ACARA). In its circumlocution of a definition seeking to embrace the creativity in all children, or at least in all successful learners, the National Curriculum Board (2009) explained:

> Creativity enables the development of new ideas and their application in specific contexts. It includes generating an idea which is new to the individual, seeing existing situations in a new way, identifying alternative explanations, seeing links, and finding new ways to apply ideas to generate a positive outcome. Creativity is closely linked to innovation and enterprise [sic], and requires characteristics such as intellectual flexibility, open-mindedness, adaptability and a readiness to try new ways of doing things.
>
> *(p. 12)*

ACARA's (n.d.) more personal view of creativity has since evolved into a view of creative thinking and creative endeavour. ACARA's description of creativity is as follows:

> Creative thinking involves students in learning to generate and apply new ideas in specific contexts, seeing existing situations in a new way, identifying alternative explanations, and seeing or making new links that generate a

42   Peter Merrotsy

positive outcome. This includes combining parts to form something original, sifting and refining ideas to discover possibilities, constructing theories and objects, and acting on intuition. The products of creative endeavour can involve complex representations and images, investigations and performances, digital and computer-generated output, or occur as virtual reality.

(p. 1)

Subsequently, creative thinking, complemented by critical thinking, has become enshrined in the "General capabilities" of the Australian Curriculum and is addressed in each learning or subject area and identified in content descriptions and elaborations.

What does creativity in schools and classrooms look like?

There are several well-known pedagogical models and programs for creativity and problem solving that have found their way to the antipodes, such as The Enrichment Triad (Renzulli, 1977); Discovering Intellectual Strengths and Capabilities while Observing Varied Ethnic Responses (DISCOVER; Schiever & Maker, 1991); Thinking Actively in a Social Context (TASC; Wallace, 2001); Creative Problem Solving (CPS; Treffinger, Isaksen, & Stead-Dorval, 2006); Future Problem Solving (www.fpsp.org.au/; for a formal evaluation in the Australian context, see Volk, 2003); and Tournament of the Minds (TOM) in its various manifestations. Home-grown varieties of programs have tended to be uncritical eclectic mixes of Bloom's Taxonomy (usually Bloom, 1956), although occasionally the revision by Anderson et al. (2001), is used as a framework with Gardner's (1993) Multiple Intelligences, various programs associated with de Bono (1985), and a range of programs claiming to have research support from cognitive neuroscience. These models and frameworks, the nature of their research support, and the extent to which they may or may not meet the needs of creative and gifted and talented students have been critically appraised in Merrotsy (2017). Because of space limits for this chapter, an overview of just one model is provided, *Wheel Work* (Mackay & Hoy, 2002), which has been developed and applied in Australian contexts. This model was chosen because it is in many ways a good example of the typical curriculum response to 'teaching creativity' and to the education of students who are gifted. I have also found it to be a very powerful tool when working with primary-aged gifted children who are significantly underachieving at school.

There appears to be no formal research showing that *Wheel Work* is more effective than other models in developing critical and creative thinking, or supporting its implementation in particular contexts or with particular groups of students. However, some anecdotal evidence suggests that it can be quite effective in addressing the learning needs of students who are underachieving at school. There is also some evidence, arising from research not specifically studying aspects of the model, that *Wheel Work* has been particularly successful in addressing underachievement by overlooked gifted students from very low socioeconomic backgrounds and from cultural minority backgrounds, and has been instrumental in helping these students to achieve at school. Examples of these applications can be found in Merrotsy (2013, in both a rural and regional Indigenous context, and a very low socioeconomic regional context) and in the Achievement Integrated Model (Bousnakis et al., 2011, in a very low socioeconomic metropolitan context).

The *Wheel Work* model (Mackay & Hoy, 2002) was developed in response to classroom teaching of gifted and talented children and was aimed at encouraging students to engage in critical and creative thinking. It provides a structured pedagogical process that integrates standard curriculum learning outcomes with key competencies, information literacy skills, and Bloom's taxonomy, and that responds to the diversity of students. Students learn to take control and have ownership over their own learning, and they have opportunities to apply their knowledge, understandings, and skills, learnt across all curriculum Key Learning Areas, to new tasks and situations. Through this integration they are able to demonstrate deeper understanding as they manipulate information and ideas to solve problems and create new meanings and understandings.

Wheel Work is set within the conceptual framework of lifelong learning. A lifelong learner has an understanding of the nature of knowledge and of metacognition, uses the skills of a discipline to solve problems, is prepared to question, is able to transfer skills across domains, and is able to express creativity. *Wheel Work* is also a process structured around Bloom's Taxonomy (unfortunately, it uses the 1956 version of the taxonomy). In this process, the teacher works (actively) as a "director" while students progress from skill lessons to planning, working, evaluating, and celebrating. Along the way, students will grow in three important areas of learning. First, they will develop greater competence in the 'information literacy process', which comprises six stages or steps (define, locate, select, organise, present, and evaluate). Second, they will develop greater proficiency in the 'key competencies': collect, analyse, and organise information; communicate ideas and information; plan and organise activities; work in teams; use mathematical ideas and techniques; solve problems; use technology; and check, monitor, and assess own progress. Third, they will display growing self-belief, especially by engaging in risk taking, and by recognising and responding to freedom of choice.

The *Wheel Work* process is easy for both teachers and students to learn and to apply. Within a particular curriculum or program framework, students select a topic and use the wheel to choose and organise their learning activities and their products appropriate to their level of ability and development (see Figure 3.1).

Overall, *Wheel Work* aims to be a holistic, school-based program that offers an apparently robust conceptual framework for each student to choose, plan, develop, and evaluate a unit of work, through independent learning or contract work, which addresses a problem that is real to each student and that is at a level suitable to each student's level of ability, development, and readiness. For students who underachieve, including overlooked gifted students, because the degree of difficulty of the task being attempted closely matches the cognitive abilities and skills of each student, this appears to be a successful pedagogical model (Merrotsy, 2013).

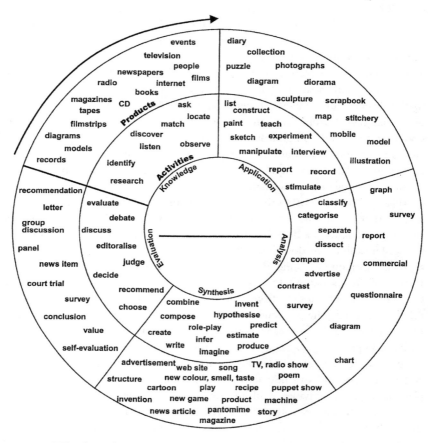

FIGURE 3.1 Wheel Work

Source: Mackay and Hoy (2002, p. 68), with permission from Coolabah Publishing

What should creativity in schools and classrooms look like?

A model for teaching related to creativity for school students must be set within an appropriate pedagogical framework. Such a framework must take into account how children and adolescents learn and must equip them with the means and media to develop their creative potential and to express their creativity. Such a framework must acknowledge the knowledge and skills of the professional teacher and his or her leadership role in curriculum development and implementation, in assessment and evaluation of student learning, and in providing a safe and comfortable yet challenging learning environment.

What exactly, then, is the role of the teacher in teaching for creativity? In response to this question, Merrotsy (2017) has developed a model for teachers to develop and implement a pedagogy for creative problem solving, which is called *Middle C* and which draws on aspects of culture, cognition, constructivism, and creativity. *Middle C* comprises 14 elements that are necessary (but probably not sufficient) for pedagogy for creativity and for the expression of creativity.

Some of these elements refer to professional standards for excellence in teaching. A theoretical framework for teaching should be personally liberating for both the teacher and the students, and should promote and sustain active teaching and active learning. The teacher will have mastery of subject area content knowledge and pedagogical content knowledge. The teacher understands how students best learn and understands how high-ability students best learn. The teacher uses current best-practice models for curriculum planning and development, for planning assessment of student learning, and for evaluating the quality of student learning.

Other elements refer to the nature of the creative learning and teaching environment. Inclusiveness, participation, feelings of social solidarity, face-to-face relationships, impartiality, shared cognition, challenge, quest for meaning, modelling, deliberation, questioning, discussion, reasonableness, thinking for oneself and reflection – all of these provide the best teaching and learning environment for the development of creative potential. A psychologically healthy and strong internal learning environment is best supported by goal-oriented processes, especially those related to metacognition, volition, and self-regulation.

One element of *Middle C* refers specifically to culture. Culture is fundamental to creativity: creativity is an expression of culture; culture is an expression of creativity. The culturally proficient teacher will honour differences, appreciate the benefits of diversity, relate knowledgeably and respectfully with people from other cultures, enjoy a holistic understanding of creative potential, and remove barriers to authentic cultural creative expression.

Two other elements of *Middle C* refer specifically to cognitive ability and creativity, and demand a more dynamic understanding of intellectual ability, creative ability, and high intellectual and creative potential. In particular, a suitable model of teaching for creativity will embrace personal creativity and the creativity of children and youth, will focus on the creativity inherent in the learning process, and will provide a framework for the development of creative expression. Explicit in both Gagné's (2015) DMGT and his understanding of high natural ability, and Kaufman and Beghetto's (2009) Four C Model of creativity and their conception of mini-c creativity, is the notion of potential. Implicit in both of these models, at least for the professional teacher, is a statement about professional practice. The teacher's role is not so much to identify high performance in students. Rather, the teacher has the responsibility to identify students with high potential and to do something real about developing the high potential into high performance.

46 Peter Merrotsy

Topics for further research in this area could include how Runco's (2007) notion of creative potential is to be understood in the cultural contexts of Australia and New Zealand; how creative potential should be understood, recognised, and identified in children and youth; and when "teaching creativity" (in its various pedagogical guises), what is effective, to what extent, and why? What is actually learned by the students?

Discussion Questions

- Choose a model or program that aims to "teach creativity". Critically appraise its strengths and weaknesses with respect to developing creative potential and to meeting the learning needs of gifted children and youth.
- Describe what creativity should look like in your classroom and in your school.
- What is a teacher's role in nurturing creative potential? What are some specific behaviours in which a teacher can engage?

References

Aldous, C. R. (2005a). *Creativity in problem solving: Uncovering cognitive and non-cognitive systems of reasoning in the solving of novel mathematics problems* (Unpublished doctoral thesis). Flinders University, Adelaide, SA.

Aldous, C. R. (2005b). Attending to feeling: Productive benefit to novel mathematics problem-solving. *International Education Journal, 7*, 410–422.

Anderson, W. L., Krathwohl, D. R., Airasian, P. W., Cruikshank, K. A., Mayer, R. E., Pintrich, P. R., Raths, J., & Wittrock, M. C. (Eds.) (2001). *A taxonomy for learning, teaching, and assessing: A revision of Bloom's taxonomy of educational objectives* (Abridged edition). New York, NY: Longman.

Australian Curriculum Assessment and Reporting Authority [ACARA]. (n.d.). *Critical and creative thinking*. Retrieved from www.australiancurriculum.edu.au/GeneralCapabilities/Pdf/Critical-and-creative-thinking

Bailey, S. (1996). *Personal bests*. Armidale, NSW: Tall Poppy Educational.

Beghetto, R. A., & Kaufman, J. C. (2007). Toward a broader conception of creativity: A case for 'mini-c' creativity. *Psychology of Aesthetics, Creativity, and the Arts, 1*(2), 73–79.

Bloom, B. S. (Ed.) [with Englehart, M. D., Furst, E. J., Hill, W. H., & Krathwohl, D. R.] (1956). *The taxonomy of educational objectives. The classification of educational goals. Handbook I: Cognitive domain*. New York, NY: David McKay.

Botticchio, M. (2006). *Creativity under the glass ceiling: A study using a contextual theory of creativity as a framework* (Unpublished doctoral thesis). University of Wollongong, Wollongong, NSW.

Bousnakis, M., Burns, T., Donnan, L., Hopper, S., Mugavero, G., & Rogers, K. B. (2011). Achievement integrated model: Interventions for gifted Indigenous underachievers. In W. Vialle (Ed.), *Giftedness from an indigenous perspective* (pp. 43–77). Wollongong, NSW: AAEGT.

Braggett, E. (1986). The education of gifted and talented children in Australia: A national overview. In K. Imison, L. Endean, & D. Smith (Eds.), *Gifted and talented children: A national concern* (pp. 13–27). Toowoomba, QLD: Darling Downs Institute Press.

Brockwell, H. (2008). *Identification of aptitude in the creative visual arts within an Australian primary schooling context* (Unpublished BEd Honours thesis). University of New England, Armidale, NSW.

Cohen, D. (1968). Opportunities for creativity. *Australian Science Teachers' Journal, 14*, 6–19.

Cohen, D. (1972). The development of a creativity test. *Research in Science Education, 2*(1), 82–95.

Corcoran, K. (2006). *Enhancing creativity: Strategies implemented in the senior secondary visual art classroom* (Unpublished doctoral thesis). Griffith University, Brisbane, QLD.

Crockenberg, S. B. (1972). Creativity tests: A boon or boondoggle for education? *Review of Educational Research, 42*, 27–45.

Cropley, A. J. (2000). Defining and measuring creativity: Are creativity tests worth using? *Roeper Review, 23*, 72–79.

deBono, E. (1985). *Six thinking hats*. Boston, MA: Little Brown.

DeHaan, R. F., & Havighurst, R. J. (1957). *Educating gifted children*. Chicago, IL: University of Chicago Press.

Forster, J. (1998). *Think about . . . creativity*. Cheltenham, VIC: Hawker Brownlow.

Gagné, F. (1985). Giftedness and talent: Reexamining a reexamination of the definitions. *Gifted Child Quarterly, 29*, 103–112.

Gagné, F. (2015). Academic talent development programs: A best practices model. *Asia Pacific Education Review, 16*(2), 281–295.

Gardner, H. (1993). *Creating minds*. New York, NY: Basic Books.

Geake, J. G. (2009). Neuropsychological characteristics of academic and creative giftedness. In L. V. Shavinina (Ed.), *International handbook on giftedness* (pp. 261–273). New York, NY: Springer.

Gilchrist, M. B. (1970). *The relation of some personality and ability variables to creativity and academic achievement* (Unpublished doctoral thesis). University of Melbourne, Melbourne, VIC.

Guilford, J. P. (1950). Creativity. *American Psychologist, 5*, 444–454.

Hannaford, J. (2001). *An evaluation of approaches to teaching creative and divergent thinking* (Unpublished doctoral thesis). Macquarie University, Sydney, NSW.

Kaufman, J. C., & Beghetto, R. A. (2009). Beyond big and little: The Four C model of creativity. *Review of General Psychology, 13*(1), 1–12.

Lett, W. R. (Ed.) (1976). *Creativity and education*. Melbourne, VIC: Australia International Press.

Lovesy, S. C. (2003). *Drama education secondary school play building: Enhancing imagination and creativity in group play building through kinaesthetic teaching and learning* (Unpublished doctoral thesis). University of Western Sydney, Sydney, NSW.

Lubart, T. I. (1999). Creativity across cultures. In R. J. Sternberg (Ed.), *Handbook of creativity* (pp. 339–350). Cambridge: Cambridge University Press.

Mackay, B., & Hoy, L. (2002). *Wheel work: An educational approach to life long learning*. West Tamworth, NSW: Coolabah Publishing.

Marland, S. P., Jr. (1972). *Education of the gifted and talented: Report to the congress of the United States by the U. S. Commissioner of Education and background papers submitted to the U. S. Office of Education. 2 vols* (Government Documents, Y4.L 11/2: G36). Washington, DC: U.S. Government Printing Office.

McCann, M. (2005). Quest for the holy grail of psychometric creativity: The links with visual thinking ability and IQ. *Gifted and Talented International, 20*(1), 19–29.

Merrotsy, P. (2003). The education of gifted students in NSW – an appraisal. *Australasian Journal of Gifted Education, 12*(2), 18–27.

Merrotsy, P. (2013). Invisible gifted students. *Talent Development & Excellence, 5*(2), 31–42.

Merrotsy, P. (2017a). *Pedagogy for creative problem solving*. Melbourne, VIC: Routledge.

48 Peter Merrotsy

Merrotsy, P. (2017b). Gagné's differentiated model of giftedness and talent in Australian education. *Australasian Journal of Gifted Education, 26*(2), 29–42.

National Curriculum Board. (2009). *The shape of the Australian curriculum.* Retrieved from www.acara.edu.au/_resources/The_Shape_of_the_Australian_Curriculum_May_2009_file.pdf

Pears, G. (1994). *Critical thinking skills in schools* (Unpublished doctoral thesis). Curtin University of Technology, Perth, WA.

Poole, M. (Ed.) (1980). *Creativity across the curriculum.* North Sydney, NSW: George Allen & Unwin.

Renzulli, J. S. (1977). *The enrichment triad model: A guide for developing defensible programs for the gifted and talented.* Mansfield Center, CT: Creative Learning Press.

Renzulli, J. S. (1978). What makes giftedness? Re-examining a definition. *Phi Delta Kappan, 60,* 180–184, 261.

Renzulli, J. S. (1986). The three-ring conception of giftedness: A developmental model for creative productivity. In R. J. Sternberg & J. Davidson (Eds.), *Conceptions of giftedness* (pp. 53–92). Cambridge: Cambridge University Press.

Renzulli, J. S., & Hartman, R. K. (1971). Scale for rating behavioral characteristics of superior students. *Exceptional Children, 38,* 243–248.

Renzulli, J. S., Hartman, R. K., & Callahan, C. M. (1971). Teacher identification of superior students. *Exceptional Children, 38,* 211–214.

Renzulli, J. S., Smith, L. H., White, A. J., Callahan, C. M., & Hartman, R. K. (1976). *Scales for rating the behavioural characteristics of superior students.* Mansfield Center, CT: Creative Learning Press.

Renzulli, J. S., Smith, L. H., White, A. J., Callahan, C. M., Hartman, R. K., Westberg, K. L., Gavin, M. K., . . . Reed, R. E. S. (2010). *Scales for rating the behavioural characteristics of superior students* (3rd ed.). Waco, TX: Prufrock Press.

Runco, M. A. (2007). *Creativity theory and themes: Research, development, and practice.* Amsterdam, The Netherlands: Academic Press.

Runco, M. A., & Jaeger, G. J. (2012). The standard definition of creativity. *Creativity Research Journal, 24,* 92–96.

Schiever, S. W., & Maker, C. J. (1991). Enrichment and acceleration: An overview and new directions. In G. Davis & N. Colangelo (Eds.), *Handbook of gifted education* (pp. 99–110). Boston, MA: Allyn & Bacon.

Smith, C. (Ed.) (2012). *Gifted and talented students: Meeting their needs in New Zealand schools.* [Ministry of Education.] Wellington, NZ: Learning Media.

Stein, M. I. (1953). Creativity and culture. *Journal of Psychology, 36,* 311–322.

Sternberg, R. J. (1999). The concept of creativity: Prospects and paradigms. In R. J. Sternberg (Ed.), *Handbook of creativity* (pp. 3–15). Cambridge: Cambridge University Press.

Sternberg, R. J., & Lubart, T. I. (1996). Investing in creativity. *American Psychologist, 51,* 677–688.

Thomas, K., & Chan, J. (Eds.) (2013). *Handbook of research on creativity.* Cheltenham, UK: Edward Elgar.

Torrance, E. P. (1969). Creative positives of disadvantaged children and youth. *Gifted Child Quarterly, 13,* 71–81.

Torrance, E. P. (1998). Talent among children who are economically disadvantaged or culturally different. In J. F. Smutny (Ed.), *The young gifted child: Potential and promise. An anthology* (pp. 95–118). Cresskill, NJ: Hampton Press.

Torrance, E. P. (2008). *The Torrance tests of creative thinking: Norms.* [Technical manual.] Bensenville, IL: Scholastic Testing Service.

Torrance, E. P., Goff, K., & Satterfield, N. B. (1998). *Multicultural mentoring of the gifted and talented.* Waco, TX: Prufrock Press.

Treffinger, D. J., Isaksen, S. G., & Stead-Dorval, K. B. (2006). *Creative problem solving: An introduction* (4th ed.). Waco, TX: Prufrock Press.

Urban, K. K., & Jellen, H. G. (1985). *Der TSD-Z: Test zum schöpferischen Denken – zeichnerisch.* [Arbeitsstelle HEFE, Paper 6.] Hannover, Germany: Universität Hannover. Made available by the corresponding author.

Urban, K. K., & Jellen, H. G. (1996). *Test for creative thinking – drawing production (TCT-DP).* Lisse, The Netherlands: Swets & Zeitlinger.

U.S. Department of Education. (1993). *National excellence: A case for developing America's talent.* Washington, DC: U.S. Government Printing Office.

Volk, V. (2003). *Confidence building and problem solving skills* (Unpublished doctoral thesis). University of New South Wales, Sydney, NSW.

Wallace, B. (2001). *Teaching thinking skills across the primary curriculum: A practical approach for all abilities.* London: David Fulton (A NACE/Fulton Publication).

Wright, D. G. (1998). *Creativity and embodied learning: A reflection upon and a synthesis of the learning that arises in creative expression, with particular reference to writing and drama, through the perspective of the participant and self organising systems theory* (Unpublished doctoral thesis). University of Western Sydney, Sydney, NSW.

Wright, D. G. (2001). Creativity and learning: Creative work and the construction of learning. *Reflective Practice, 2*(3), 261–273.

Yashin-Shaw, I. (2001). *A cognitive model for understanding creative thinking* (Unpublished doctoral thesis). Griffith University, Brisbane, QLD.

4

GIFTED STUDENTS WITH DISABILITY

Twice-exceptional learners

Trevor Clark and Catherine Wormald

Guiding Questions

- How is dual exceptionality defined?
- How are students identified as twice exceptional (2e), and who should be involved in the identification process?
- What are some of the common learning needs of twice-exceptional students?
- What are key elements of differentiated educational programs to address the learning needs of twice-exceptional students?

Key Ideas

- The term twice exceptional (2e) is used to describe students who can be considered intellectually gifted, but who also have a diagnosed disability or learning difficulty.
- Due to the broad range of disability types which are characterised by different areas of specific need, and the considerable inter-individual variation in both the 'gifted' and 'disability' categories, it is important to recognise that 2e students are very diverse. It follows that appropriate educational responses to 2e students will also be highly individual.
- The identification and assessment of students as 2e should employ multiple measures, collected and interpreted by multi-disciplinary teams that include professionals with expertise in both giftedness and disability.
- The provision of appropriate, differentiated educational programs tailored to the identified learning needs of 2e students is associated with school success and positive long-term post-school outcomes.

- There is a lack of Australian and New Zealand research related to the identification and education of 2e students, particularly Indigenous students. There is a need for robust research evaluating the outcomes of educational programs designed to address the needs of 2e students.
- As for other groups of learners, it is important to include 2e students in the processes of identification, educational planning, and program evaluation.

Introduction

Within the larger cohort of students considered intellectually gifted is a diverse group of students who have diagnosed disabilities. Previously referred to as 'gifted students with a learning disability' (or GLD), the term 'twice-exceptional' (2e) is now widely used to describe these students. This chapter reviews key issues related to the identification and education of 2e students. These issues are introduced through the case study of an Australian student, which illustrates the sometimes-paradoxical nature of giftedness and learning disability. It highlights the importance of the early identification and assessment of 2e students in both mainstream and special education settings and the provision of appropriate differentiated educational programs. The link between differentiated educational programs and the post-school outcomes of 2e students is made. Where it exists, Australian and New Zealand research is outlined, and gaps in the literature identified to guide future research in this important area of gifted education.

Case study

From an early age, Todd was an exceptional child. However, whilst verbally precocious, able to build cities from Lego blocks, and complete complex puzzles, he could not dress himself even by the age of 5 years. After starting pre-school, it became obvious that Todd had significant physical problems. He could not sit on a chair and would accidentally bump other children whilst sitting on the floor. He avoided any fine motor tasks such as painting and avoided any physical activity at school. Despite these issues and his dyspraxia (a condition that makes it difficult to plan and coordinate movement), Todd was keen to learn. His Full-Scale IQ was assessed at the 97th percentile.

Todd has had to overcome bullying from peers and disbelief by his teachers that he is capable of achieving. At school, he was harassed by other students and physically manhandled, which pushed him to the limits of his tolerance. He became verbally abusive, using his finely honed verbal skills to strike back at his tormentors. Stress and anxiety were constant issues for Todd, and he developed various ways of coping. When he was younger, he would jump on the trampoline or use a swing to relax. As he got older, he would draw maps and mazes and, later still, design whole shopping centres as well as build whole cities using building bricks. Todd often felt overwhelmed, but with the support of a counsellor he began to negotiate due dates and workloads with his teachers. In secondary school, Todd participated in discussions with teachers and other professionals concerning various educational interventions and special programs that were required to address his specific learning needs.

Todd is a student who is 2e in that he displays gifts, or exceptional abilities, alongside his disabilities; Todd has a physical disability, dyspraxia, and also a specific learning disability. The juxtaposition of two contrary conditions in the one student – high-level skills alongside a diagnosed disability – presents the paradox. Todd was not provided with a differentiated educational program to address his unique learning needs until much later in his schooling years.

The failure by teachers to recognise potential or identify the exceptional skills of students who are 2e and to provide them with a differentiated educational program related to their needs has major implications for their school success and long-term post-school outcomes. A survey of 300 high-functioning adults with autism spectrum disorder (ASD), many of whom may be classified as twice-exceptional (Autism Spectrum Australia, 2013), revealed that less than 50% had some form of employment. Post-school outcomes for people diagnosed with ASD universally show poor employment, social, and life outcomes (Baldwin, Costley, & Warren, 2014; Howlin, Goode, Hutton, & Rutter, 2004; Howlin & Moss, 2012). Given the poor post-school outcomes of adults with autism, it is particularly important that students with ASD and who display exceptional or advanced skills or gifts are identified in the early years of their schooling and provided with appropriate differentiated educational programs. Unless teachers and counsellors identify and develop the strengths of all 2e students, these individuals may fail to develop their talents and instead underachieve in relation to their intellectual potential (Reis, McGuire, & Neu, 1997). There is a consensus among scholars in the field of gifted education that 2e students require access to enrichment activities in their areas of interest and strength and a focus on talent development (Baum & Owen, 1988; Clark, 2001; Hallowell, 2005; Neihart, 2008; Nielsen, 2002).

The case of Todd serves to highlight the challenges for teachers and parents in the provision of appropriate differentiated educational programs for 2e students, no matter the exceptionality, disability, or educational setting. The research into post-school outcomes of students who are 2e is limited and is confined to studies of a small cohort of the much larger and diverse 2e population. This type of research is important as it will help to inform the type and nature of school-based differentiated programs that are likely to enhance post-school outcomes.

Definition and identification

The terminology used to refer to students who are 2e has changed over time. Initially in the literature these students were referred to as gifted with a learning disability (GLD) (Baum, 1988; Brody & Mills, 1997), whilst more recent research refers to them as twice exceptional (2e), which is now the internationally accepted term (Foley Nicpon, Allmon, Sieck, & Stinson, 2011).

Students who are 2e may have disabilities in (but not limited to) the following areas: attention-deficit hyperactivity disorder (ADHD), dyslexia (specific reading disability), autism spectrum disorder (ASD), emotional and behavioural disorder (EBD), specific learning disability (SLD), speech and language disorder, visual or auditory processing disorder, and physical and/or sensory disabilities. Due to the range of disabilities that may co-exist with giftedness, it is difficult to define this diverse group of students, and there is no nationally consistent operational definition of this group of students in Australia or New Zealand. A comprehensive definition developed by Reis, Baum, and Burke (2014) defines students with dual exceptionalities as:

> students who demonstrate the potential for high achievement or creative productivity in one or more domains such as math[s], science, technology, the social arts, the visual, spatial or performing arts or other areas of human productivity AND who manifest one or more disabilities as defined by federal or state eligibility criteria. These disabilities include specific learning disabilities; speech and language disorders; emotional/behavioural disorders; physical disabilities; autism spectrum disorders (ASD); or other health impairments such as Attention Deficit/Hyperactivity Disorder (ADHD). These disabilities and high abilities combine to produce a unique population of students who may fail to demonstrate either high academic performance or specific disabilities. Their gifts may mask their disabilities and their disabilities may mask their gifts.
>
> *(p. 222)*

This definition recognises the diverse nature of students who are 2e. This diversity and juxtaposition of gifts and disabilities can make appropriate identification challenging. This difficulty is compounded by the fact that there is also no firmly agreed-upon national definition of giftedness. Currently, there is no agreed identification protocol that takes into account the possibility that a student may be gifted and have a learning disability or disabilities. Identification processes for giftedness and learning disabilities are mutually exclusive (Assouline, Foley Nicpon, & Whiteman, 2010; Wormald, 2009).

Baum, Owen, and Dixon (1993) have suggested that there are three groups of 2e students. One group includes students who have been identified as gifted and are placed in specialist gifted programs; for many of these students, the student's learning disability is not apparent until the work becomes more difficult. Another group includes students identified as having a learning difficulty or disability and placed in a specialist remedial program; the fact that these students might also be gifted is not even considered. The final group includes those students who are not recognised as being either gifted or having learning disabilities. This is because students in this group are managing to achieve average grades, such that neither exceptionality is recognised.

Rogers (2011) recommends a number of important elements to be considered in the identification of 2e students:

- A tiered system of identification, whereby the first tier is a general screening process using such tools as behavioural checklists, and successive tiers involve more sophisticated, targeted instruments.
- An identification team, with specific training in using an identification protocol.
- Use of the WISC-IV (by a registered psychologist) as a tool to assist in identifying discrepancies among index scores that may be indicative of dual exceptionality.
- Consideration of family history of giftedness and/or learning disabilities or difficulties in the overall assessment process (this would be a standard component of a comprehensive assessment by a psychologist).
- Awareness that while identification of 2e students may be easier in classes for gifted students (where specific difficulties may become evident in the context of increasingly demanding content), consideration should be given to seeking out 2e students in mixed-ability classrooms, where both giftedness and disabilities may be masked.
- Awareness that 2e female students may be particularly adept at masking both their learning difficulties and giftedness in an attempt to fit in socially.
- Support for parents to understand the importance of early identification in order to access appropriate educational supports.

Given the complexity of identification for many 2e individuals, researchers recommend that multi-disciplinary teams familiar with both giftedness and disability work to compile a body of relevant evidence (Pereles, Omdal, & Baldwin, 2009; Wormald, 2009). Identification and assessment should include data consisting of test scores, profile analysis, observations of behaviour across situations, and product evaluations. While not responsible for formal diagnosis of specific disabilities, teachers may be in a good position to collect data about a student's classroom performance and behaviour across varied tasks and situations, and to provide specific work samples reflecting both exceptional abilities and specific areas of difficulty. Teachers may also be the first to recognise that a student has a particularly uneven profile of strengths and weaknesses, and to suggest a referral for more formal assessment; the capacity to recognise a pattern of abilities that is potentially consistent with dual exceptionality relies on the teachers' professional knowledge of giftedness and disability.

It is difficult to provide accurate prevalence rates for dual exceptionality among students in Australia and New Zealand, since neither country collects comprehensive national data on students identified as gifted, and definitions of both 'gifted' and 'twice exceptional' vary among schools, districts, and states. Understanding prevalence rates is important to inform advocacy, plan interventions, and track outcomes over time. In her review of research on 2e students in Australia, Ronksley-Pavia (2015) estimated the prevalence of 2e in Australia to be approximately 41,156 students aged 0–14 years. This estimate was based on the prevalence rates of students with disabilities (Australian Bureau of Statistics, 2012) and the presumed prevalence of giftedness among Australian students. If accurate, this estimate suggests that a considerable number of students may require support for both giftedness and disability, which warrants a concerted effort to clarify a definition and set of guidelines for identification and educational intervention for this group of students.

Legislative and policy context

Despite recognition of dual exceptionality by researchers and scholars in gifted education, those outside the field may be confused by or even resistant to the selection of students with disabilities for educational experiences designed for gifted students (Foley Nicpon, Assouline, & Colangelo, 2013). Some practitioners consider the terms *giftedness* and *disability* to be incompatible (Baum, Rizza, & Renzulli, 2006), or observe that 2e students may be overlooked for advanced-level programs (Schultz, 2011). Internationally, educational practices that result in a denial of services to 2e students may be considered discriminatory. In the U.S., for example, Federal Law (Section 504 Title II) requires that qualified students who are 2e be given the same opportunities as students without disabilities to compete for and benefit from accelerated programs and classes.

A Commonwealth Senate review into gifted education was undertaken in Australia in 2000 (Parliament of Australia, 2001). This review highlighted that Australia's schools have struggled to understand the diverse nature of children who are gifted, and even more so, the concept of 2e. Although inclusivity and equity in education underpin the policies of 21st-century education in Australia (Gray & Beresford, 2008; Organisation for Economic Co-operation and Development [OECD], 2008), the fact that no legislation exists within Australia mandating provisions for students who are 2e suggests the issue of discrimination may be 'alive and well' in this country.

The Australian *Disability Standards for Education* (Department of Education and Training, 2005) were introduced and are formulated under the federal *Disability Discrimination Act 1992* (DDA). The primary purpose of the Standards is to clarify, and make more explicit, the obligations of education and training service providers under the DDA and the rights of people with disabilities in relation to education and training. The Standards prescribe that education providers must "ensure that students with disabilities are able to access and participate in education and training on the same basis as those without disability" (DEEWR, 2013, para. 1). Although the Standards were developed to ensure the rights of students with disabilities, no explicit reference is made to the existence of students who are 2e.

All Australian government and non-government schools are required annually to participate in the nationwide Nationally Consistent Collection of Data on School Students with Disability (Education Council, 2015). The aim of this data collection process is to identify the number of school students with disability and the level of reasonable educational adjustment provided for them at school. As for the DDA, no explicit reference is made to students who are 2e in the national data collection framework.

In New Zealand, the Ministry of Education's (2013) National Administrative Guidelines (NAG 1(c) iii) include students who are gifted and talented within the broader category of students with special needs. However, there are no national definitive guidelines for the identification and evaluation of individuals who are gifted and talented. Each school community therefore defines who is included or excluded, according to their own understanding of the concept (Russell & Riley, 2011). Programs continue to be developed for students who are academically at-risk, with extra academic and socioemotional support (New Zealand Ministry of Education, 2010; Russell, 2013). However, identification of at-risk individuals is key to this process, and at present there are no policies or procedures in place for the specific identification and evaluation of students who are 2e in New Zealand schools.

The confusion that currently exists in the field of 2e in relation to an agreed appropriate definition and identification measures (Foley Nicpon et al., 2013) is likely to have resulted in the under-identification of 2e students. The lack of legislation protecting the educational needs of this group of students may also contribute to the under-identification of 2e students in Australian and New Zealand schools.

Educational supports and interventions for 2e students

While somewhat limited, research has been undertaken in relation to developing and providing appropriate educational programs for students who are 2e (Baum, 1988; Bees, 1998; Hishinuma & Nishimura, 2000; Rogers, 2011; Weinfeld, Barnes-Robinson, Jeweler, & Shevitz, 2002). In alignment with their comprehensive definition of twice-exceptional students, Reis et al. (2014) state that these students require an individualized education plan (IEP) or an accommodation plan with specific goals and strategies that enable them to achieve at a level and rate commensurate with their abilities.

Crim, Hawkins, Rubin, and Johnson (2008) compared the academic accommodations provided within the IEPs of SLD/low-ability (n = 225), SLD/average ability (n = 708), and SLD/high ability (n = 112) students. The researchers found that the students with high ability were offered fewer accommodations than other groups in the study. Yet, the accommodations likely to benefit 2e students do not appear to be extraordinarily intensive. Mann (2006) noted that a caring atmosphere that focusses on strengths-oriented accommodations and student-centred learning were considered best practices for gifted students who have a learning disability. Olenchak's (2009) study of 57 gifted students with specific learning disabilities found substantial affective gains (self-concept) for students engaged in Schlichter's Talents Unlimited program, coupled with individual counselling. Certainly, Weinfeld et al.'s (2002) study of gifted students with severe learning disabilities showed the efficacy of placing these students in special "Centre" classrooms that focus on self-direction, self-reflection, problem solving, and inquiry-based curriculum experiences. Likewise, Baum, Cooper, and Neu's (2001) description of Project High Hopes indicated that helping gifted students with SLD focus on problem-solving, analysis, and creativity was educationally beneficial to them. Nielsen (2002) concluded that, not only must these students' strengths be addressed, as they work in learning environments with others like themselves, but they must also be supported to develop compensatory strategies for their weaknesses.

Rogers (2011) found that 2e students had distinct learning differences that needed to be addressed by implementing a number of teaching and support strategies. Because no single technique for addressing a particular issue is likely to result in sustained, long-term effectiveness, it is necessary to review and refresh strategies over time. Rogers (2011) concluded that:

> strategies must be developed and integrated within the differentiated curriculum to cover several components of the whole learner . . . a child profiling team must plan the specific strategies that address the child's strengths and weaknesses . . . it is important not to water down the gifted curriculum provided for the 2e child.
>
> *(pp. 62, 65)*

Research on programs and strategies that have focussed on students' giftedness rather than their disabilities has documented student outcomes including increased self-esteem, improved learning behaviour, and creative productivity. For example, Bees (1998) studied a program that included resource room support for the student's learning disability and enrichment for their advanced abilities, and concluded that providing meaningful opportunities for gifted students with learning disabilities to feel a sense of connectedness to school contributed to the success of the program. Baum and Owen (1988), in their research comparing high-ability students, high-ability students with learning disability, and average-ability students with a learning disability, concluded that feelings of self-efficacy are improved by providing programs that recognize 2e learners' giftedness as well as their learning disability, and this in turn leads to greater achievement when the students' gifts are acknowledged. In another study, Baum, Emerick, Herman, and Dixon (1989) undertook case studies of four programs specifically designed for gifted students with learning disabilities led and concluded that when the students' giftedness was recognised and nurtured, there was an increased willingness by the students to complete tasks and a decrease in behaviours which negatively affected their learning (including disruptive tendencies, inattentiveness, short attention span, task avoidance, and manipulation tactics).

Baum (1988), in a study of an enrichment program for seven gifted students with learning disabilities in grades 4–5, concluded that as a result of the enrichment program, students demonstrated improvement in motivation and behaviour when they were allowed to choose their own area of study and final product. As a result of this work, she constructed guidelines for educators working with gifted students with learning disabilities. These guidelines include provision of a talent-supportive environment, instruction in compensatory strategies, and support to develop awareness of personal strengths and weaknesses. Both she and Hannah and Shore (1995) have confirmed the efficacy of these guidelines since their initial introduction. In another example, Weinfeld et al. (2002) established that four major components are required for successful programs for gifted students with learning disabilities. These components were the result of a specialist program that was developed and implemented in one county in the U.S. Their guidelines were very similar to Baum's earlier list, with the addition of comprehensive case management to coordinate all aspects of the student's individualised education plan.

A recent mixed-methods study by Willard-Holt, Weber, Morrison, and Horgan (2013) updated the field on the most recent innovations in practice for students who are 2e. The findings suggested that 2e "students would like to exert more control over what they study, how they learn, how quickly they learn and how they demonstrate their learning" (p. 258). Additionally, these students wanted more flexibility when engaging in group work, suggesting that the groups be constructed by the teachers and their disabilities taken into account. Compensatory strategies suggested by 2e students included "study skills, organisation, time management, technology to assist in communication" (p. 258). In addition, they recommended academic acceleration (Assouline & Whiteman, 2011), interest-based learning with authentic curriculum (Baum et al., 2001), and strength-oriented enrichment accommodations (Leggett, Shea, & Wilson, 2010; Pereles et al., 2009).

A recent important addition to the literature with regard to programming is a New Zealand qualitative study (Ng, Hill, & Rawlinson, 2016) that explored the experiences of three 2e students during their transfer (transition) to a high school. Successful transition has been shown to depend on such factors as the timely handover of accurate and complete student records. Barriers to successful transition can result in disruption in curriculum continuity, which can be especially detrimental for learners with special needs. The findings of this study suggest that the way in which students who are 2e experienced transition influenced the development of their personal capabilities as learners in the education setting. The provision of an IEP appeared to assist in the process of transition to high school for these students.

Although there is currently limited research on appropriate programming for 2e students in Australia or New Zealand, Wormald (2009) demonstrated that many teachers are interested in learning more about these students and how to meet their educational needs. She noted that teachers were aware these students existed and that there were many reasons they were not being identified or receiving appropriate educational programs that enabled them to reach their potential. The teachers in Wormald's study expressed an interest in pursuing further professional development in order to gain knowledge about students who are twice exceptional. To date, research undertaken in Australia and New Zealand has mainly been limited to small, single-case studies rather than studies with larger sample sizes (Dixon & Tanner, 2013; Lewis, 2015; Townsend & Prendergast, 2015).

Case study of an Australian program for 2e students

An example of a large, multiple-case study involving an evaluation of a differentiated educational program in Australia is the *Savant Skill Curriculum* (Clark, 2001). Although designed specifically for a group of 2e students with autism spectrum disorder (ASD), the principles underpinning this program are consistent with many of the programming recommendations outlined previously in this chapter.

In this study involving 22 children (aged 4 to 16 years) with ASD, a longitudinal, multiple-replication case study design was used. Each participant displayed a variety of savant (or 'splinter') skills. Savant skills are exceptional skills in a specific area, and estimates of their occurrence in individuals with ASD range from 10% to almost 30% (based on a 2009 study by Howlin et al., 2004), compared with less than 1% of individuals without ASD. Savant skills are usually exhibited in the domains of memory, hyperlexia, art, music, mechanical or spatial skill, calendar calculation, mathematical calculation, sensory sensitivity, or athletic ability (Hill, 1978; Howlin, Goode, Hutton, & Rutter, 2009; Treffert, 2009). Although these skills appear remarkable in contrast to the difficulties associated with ASD, they may also be remarkable in contrast to the person without a disability and are classified as prodigious skills (Treffert, 2009).

The *Savant Skill Curriculum* (Clark, 2001) is an example of dual-programming for 2e students based on recommendations by Weinfeld et al. (2002). The curriculum attempted to harness the motivation and interest displayed by the students in their exceptional skill areas to develop adaptive or compensatory behaviours in relation to deficits inherent in ASD (such as social-communication impairments, sensory processing issues, and challenging behaviours). The conceptual framework for the curriculum is based on merging the two fields of gifted and autism education. The *Savant Skill Curriculum* included a range of educational strategies used to support gifted students (acceleration, enrichment, and mentorships), as well as autism-specific intervention strategies (social stories, visual supports for communication, and the use of areas of obsessive interest as positive reinforcement and motivators to learning). A focus on the inclusion of strengths and interests in a challenging curriculum with academic acceleration is a key strategy in the development of programs for 2e students (Assouline & Whiteman, 2011).

The assessment of each student's savant skills was undertaken by a multi-disciplinary team that included school counsellors, teachers, and speech pathologists (Pereles et al., 2009). An individual education plan (IEP) was developed for each of the students and included teaching goals and strengths-oriented enrichment activities based upon the student's savant strengths and interests, a strategy recommended for students who are twice exceptional (Reis et al., 2014). Both the students and their parents were involved in the development of each IEP and, for some, parents acted as mentors for their own children in some domains of exceptional ability (Dole, 2000; Wormald, 2009).

The results of the study indicated a significant improvement in the functional application of the children's savant skills (t [14] = − 2.6, p < .05) over the course

60 Trevor Clark and Catherine Wormald

of the curriculum. Qualitative gains were reported for some students in relation to their adaptive functioning. A comprehensive overview of the study and a step-by-step guide to the differentiated educational program is available in a text by Clark (2016).

The role of families in supporting achievement in twice-exceptional students

Parents are usually the first to understand that their child not only displays the characteristics of giftedness but also demonstrates some areas of difficulty in their development. The disability may be recognised first, but this is not always the case (Reis et al., 2000). In some cases, a child's advanced abilities are initially recognised, and the disability only becomes apparent when the student goes to school and encounters increased cognitive demands. Wormald (2009) conducted a study of five 2e students in Australia and found that parents were the first to recognise their child's dual exceptionalities, rather than school staff; in fact, most parents reported that teachers were reluctant to believe that a child could be gifted as well as having learning disabilities. Family members reported feeling that they had to compensate at home for the lack of appropriate education at school (Wormald, 2009). The majority of participants engaged in out-of-school programs in order to achieve the intellectual challenge they craved and to experience success, which in turn appeared to enhance their feelings of self-esteem and self-efficacy (Reis et al., 1997, 2000; Ruban & Reis, 2005). Dole (2000) found that parents who provided emotional support for their 2e children contributed to developing resilience in their children. Out-of-school programs can provide not only an opportunity for the student to find like-minded peers but also the chance for parents to develop a support network. Through this socialisation, parents may also be able to source information, strategies, and resources to support their efforts to help their children to develop their giftedness and cope with their learning disabilities.

Considerable time and money can be spent by parents of 2e children in order to have their children assessed by various professionals during the initial identification process and at other key times, eventuating in a range of assessments and interventions to support their child being sought across the school years (Wormald, 2009). Identification and appropriate educational planning for students who are twice exceptional requires the cooperation of parents, teachers, and other allied professionals, and this cooperation can help ensure that these students have appropriate educational opportunities. This is a shared responsibility for all involved.

Student voices

In many cases, students who are twice exceptional know that they are different. They may feel confused as they recognise that they are very capable in some areas while significantly struggling in others. Research has demonstrated that 2e students may experience low self-esteem and anxiety (Assouline & Whiteman, 2011; Foley

Nicpon et al., 2013). Many do not want to go to school and may feign illness in order to stay at home. One student in Wormald's (2009) study commented:

> You don't know what it's like when you bring me to this place. It's like a nuclear bomb going off in my stomach, it spread to my head and I can't think and it spreads to my hands and I can't make them move.
>
> *(p. 168)*

In her Australian study of the lived experiences of twice-exceptional students, Ronksley-Pavia (2015) concluded that researchers need to ensure that they do not use oppressive discourses which seek to "speak and act on behalf of those children that [research frequently] . . . constructs as inexperienced, passive, and intellectually immature" (p. 132). Her study sought to elicit the lived experiences of children with dual exceptionalities, not on the presumption of a unitary identity, but rather focussing on their experiences as being first and foremost those of children who are active and experienced 'voices' of intellectual strength and maturity.

Provisions for twice-exceptional Indigenous students

Little attention has been paid to the research or documented practice to twice-exceptional students from Indigenous backgrounds – namely, Aboriginal and Torres Strait Islander students in Australia and Māori and Pasifika students in New Zealand. In her review of Māori gifted education in New Zealand, Mahu-ika (2007) concluded that although gifted and talented education continues to develop as a field of study, a specific focus on Māori within this broader body of work remains in its infancy. Several key gaps in the research were identified, including a need to clarify the variations of a Māori conception of giftedness, as Māori are a diverse people and suggestions for identifying and providing for Māori students who are gifted and talented will not apply to all Māori learners with special abilities (Bevan-Brown, 2004). Other knowledge gaps include an understanding of the role of gender, sexuality, and age in the experience and development of giftedness in Indigenous students, and the development and evaluation of effective programs and structures relevant to the advancement of Māori gifted and talented education.

Future research on twice-exceptional students

Although there is an emerging interest in the identification and recognition of students who are 2e, and the need to develop differentiated educational programs for these students, there is a dearth of research on twice exceptionality in both Australia and New Zealand. A key to future research in this field is the pressing need to develop, or agree upon, a clear operational definition of dual exceptionality that will guide identification and programming for this group of students. Such an agreement would allow for prevalence studies of 2e students in Australia and New

Zealand, which is an important prerequisite for supporting advocacy and informing policy makers.

To date, most of the 2e research in Australia and New Zealand has consisted of small case studies. This is perhaps not surprising given the relatively small numbers of 2e students in any setting and the wide individual variation among 2e students, which makes it difficult to treat them as a single research population. These limitations notwithstanding, there is a need for larger, mixed-methods and longitudinal studies, which include a focus on the development and evaluation of differentiated educational programs for diverse 2e learners. Research should also explore the post-school outcomes of students who are 2e, which would in turn serve to inform the type and nature of school-based programs. More studies should be centred on the inclusion of the 'voice' and lived experience of students who are 2e and also that of their families. Research regarding the transition of students who are 2e from grade to grade, and school to school, is also required to ensure that specialised programs and supports provide continuity to students as they progress to higher grades of schooling.

Given the resounding lack of research in relation to Indigenous students who are 2e, research in this area must be prioritised in both countries. Given the interest expressed by teachers (Wormald, 2009) in pursuing further professional development in relation to students who are 2e, this should also be considered an important area for future research in the field of gifted education.

Conclusion

Despite a growing awareness of and knowledge about students who are twice exceptional, identification systems and appropriate services have yet to be comprehensively developed or implemented for this population of learners internationally. The adoption of an agreed operational definition of dual exceptionality in both Australia and New Zealand is likely to encourage policy makers, professionals, and parents to work together to identify more of these students and to develop appropriate differentiated educational programs to address their common and individual educational and learning needs.

Discussion Questions

- What factors may be contributing to relatively low rates of identification and insufficient programming for twice-exceptional students in Australian and New Zealand?
- While acknowledging the considerable diversity among individuals, what should be considered the essential elements of a differentiated program for twice-exceptional students?
- What are some key areas of focus for future research into twice-exceptional students and their education in Australia and New Zealand?

References

Assouline, S. G., Foley Nicpon, M., & Whiteman, C. (2010). Cognitive and psychosocial characteristics of gifted students with written language disability. *Gifted Child Quarterly*, *54*, 102–115.

Assouline, S. G., & Whiteman, C. S. (2011). Twice-exceptionality: Implications for school psychologist in the post-IDEA 2004 era. *Journal of Applied School Psychology*, *27*, 380–302.

Australian Bureau of Statistics. (2012). *Disability, ageing and careers, Australia: Summary of findings* (Cat. No. 4430.0). Retrieved from www.ausstats.abs.gov.au/ausstats/subscriber.nsf/0/9C2B94626F0FAC62CA2577FA0011C431/$File/44300_2009.pdf

Autism Spectrum Australia. (2013). *We belong: The experiences, aspirations and needs of adults with Asperger's disorder and high functioning autism*. Sydney, NSW: Author.

Baldwin, S., Costley, D., & Warren, A. (2014). Employment activities and experiences of adults with high-functioning autism and Asperger's disorder. *Journal of Autism and Developmental Disorders*, *44*, 2440–2449.

Baum, S. M. (1988). An enrichment program for gifted learning disabled students. *Gifted Child Quarterly*, *32*, 226–230.

Baum, S. M., Cooper, C. R., & Neu, T. W. (2001). Dual differentiation: An approach for meeting the curricular needs of gifted students with learning disabilities. *Psychology in the Schools*, *38*, 477–490.

Baum, S. M., Emerick, L. J., Herman, G. N., & Dixon, J. (1989). Identification, programs and enrichment strategies for gifted learning disabled youth. *Roeper Review*, *12*, 48–53.

Baum, S. M., & Owen, S. V. (1988). High ability/learning disabled students: How are they different? *Gifted Child Quarterly*, *32*, 321–326.

Baum, S. M., Owen, S. V., & Dixon, J. (1993). *To be gifted and learning disabled: From identification to practical intervention strategies*. Melbourne, VIC: Hawker Brownlow Education.

Baum, S. M., Rizza, M., & Renzulli, S. (2006). Twice-exceptional adolescents: Who are they? What do they need? In F. A. Dixon & S. M. Moon (Eds.), *The handbook of secondary gifted education* (pp. 137–164). Waco, TX: Prufrock Press.

Bees, C. (1998). The GOLD program: A program for gifted learning disabled adolescents. *Roeper Review*, *21*, 155–161.

Bevan-Brown, J. (2004). Gifted and talented Māori learners. In D. McAlpine & R. Moltzen (Eds.), *Gifted and talented: New Zealand perspectives* (2nd ed., pp. 171–197). Palmerston North, NZ: Kanuka Grove Press.

Brody, L. E., & Mills, C. J. (1997). Gifted children with learning disabilities: A review of the issues. *Journal of Learning Disabilities*, *30*, 282–296.

Clark, T. R. (2001). *The application of savant and splinter skills in the autistic population through curriculum design: A longitudinal multiple-replication case study design* (Unpublished doctoral thesis, University of New South Wales, Sydney, Australia).

Clark, T. R. (2016). *Exploring giftedness and autism: A study of a differentiated educational program for autistic savants*. London: Routledge.

Crim, C., Hawkins, J., Ruban, L., & Johnson, S. (2008). Curricular modifications for elementary students with learning disabilities in high- average- and low-IQ groups. *Journal of Research in Childhood Education*, *22*, 233–245.

Department of Education, Employment, & Workplace Relations. (2013). *Annual report 2012–2013*. Retrieved from https://docs.education.gov.au/system/files/doc/other/deewr_annual_report_2012-13.pdf

Department of Education and Training. (2005). *Disability standards for education 2005*. Retrieved from https://docs.education.gov.au/system/files/doc/other/disability_standards_for_education_2005_plus_guidance_notes.pdf

Dixon, R. M., & Tanner, K. (2013). The experience of transitioning two adolescents with Asperger syndrome in academically focused high schools. *Australasian Journal of Special Education, 37*, 28–48.

Dole, S. (2000). The implications of the risk and resilience literature for gifted students with learning disabilities. *Roeper Review, 23*, 91–96.

Education Council. (2015). *Nationally consistent collection of data: School students with disability*. Retrieved from https://docs.education.gov.au/system/files/doc/other/2015-nccd-guidelines.pdf

Foley Nicpon, M. F., Allmon, A., Seick, B., & Stinson, R. D. (2011). Empirical investigation of twice-exceptionality: Where have we been and where are we going? *Gifted Child Quarterly, 55*, 3–17.

Foley Nicpon, M. F., Assouline, S. G., & Colangelo, N. (2013). Twice-exceptional learners: Who needs to know what? *Gifted Child Quarterly, 57*, 169–180.

Gray, J., & Beresford, Q. (2008). A 'formidable challenge': Australia's quest for equity in indigenous education. *Australian Journal of Education, 52*, 197–223.

Hallowell, E. (2005). The problem with problems. *Independent School, 65*(1), 30–38.

Hannah, C. L., & Shore, B. M. (1995). Metacognition and high intellectual ability: Insights from the study of learning-disabled gifted students. *Gifted Child Quarterly, 39*(2), 95–109.

Hill, A. L. (1978). Savants: Mentally retarded individuals with special skills. *International Review of Research in Mental Retardation, 9*, 277–298.

Hishinuma, E. S., & Nishimura, S. T. (2000). Parent attitudes on the importance and success of integrated self-contained services for students who are gifted, learning disabled, and gifted/learning disabled. *Roeper Review, 22*, 241–250.

Howlin, P., Goode, S., Hutton, J., & Rutter, M. (2004). Adult outcomes for children with autism. *Journal of Child Psychology and Psychiatry, 45*, 212–229.

Howlin, P., Goode, S., Hutton, J., & Rutter, M. (2009). Savant skills in autism: Psychometric approaches and parental reports. *Philosophical Transactions of the Royal Society B: Biological Sciences, 364*, 1359–1367.

Howlin, P., & Moss, P. (2012). Adults with autism spectrum disorders. *The Canadian Journal of Psychiatry, 57*, 275–283.

Leggett, D. G., Shea, I., & Wilson, J. A. (2010). Advocating for twice-exceptional students: An ethical obligation. *Research in the Schools, 17*(2), 1–10.

Lewis, T. (2015). *An investigation into the classroom interactions of twice exceptional students in comparison to their typically developing peers* (Unpublished Master's thesis). University of Canterbury, Christchurch, New Zealand.

Mahuika, R. (2007). Māori gifted and talented education: a review of the literature. *MAI Review, 1*, 1–13.

Mann, R. L. (2006). Effective teaching strategies for gifted/learning-disabled students with spatial strengths. *Journal of Secondary Gifted Education, 17*, 112–121.

Neihart, M. (2008). Identifying and providing services to twice exceptional children. In S. I. Pfeiffer (Ed.), *Handbook of giftedness in children: Psychoeducational theory, research, and best practices* (pp. 115–137). New York, NY: Springer.

New Zealand Ministry of Education. (2010). *Easing the transition from primary to secondary schooling: Helpful information for schools to consider*. Retrieved from www.educationcounts.govt.nz/publications/schooling/98196/key-points

New Zealand Ministry of Education. (2013). *The National Administrative Guidelines (NAGs)*. Retrieved from https://education.govt.nz/ministry-of-education/legislation/nags/

Ng, S. J., Hill, M. F., & Rawlinson, C. (2016). Hidden in plain sight: The experiences of three twice-exceptional students during their transfer to high school. *Gifted Child Quarterly, 60*, 296–311.

Nielsen, M. E. (2002). Gifted students with learning disabilities: Recommendations for identification and programming. *Exceptionality, 10*(2), 93–111.

Olenchak, F. R. (2009). Effects of talents unlimited counselling on gifted/learning disabled students. *Gifted Education International, 25,* 143–162.

Organisation for Economic Co-operation and Development. (2008). *Education at a glance 2008: OECD indicators.* Retrieved from www.oecd.org/education/skills-beyond-school/41284038.pdf

Parliament of Australia. (2001). *The education of gifted and talented children.* Retrieved from https://docs.education.gov.au/system/files/doc/other/disability_standards_for_education_2005_plus_guidance_notes.pdf

Pereles, D. A., Omdal, S., & Baldwin, L. (2009). Response to intervention and twice-exceptional learners: A promising fit. *Gifted Child Today, 32*(3), 40–51.

Reis, S. M., Baum, S. M., & Burke, E. (2014). An operational definition of twice-exceptional learners: Implications and applications. *Gifted Child Quarterly, 58,* 217–230.

Reis, S. M., McGuire, J. M., & Neu, T. W. (2000). Compensation strategies used by high-ability students with learning disabilities who succeed in college. *Gifted Child Quarterly, 44,* 123–134.

Reis, S. M., Neu, T. W., & McGuire, J. M. (1997). Talents in two places: Case studies of high ability students with learning disabilities who have achieved. *Exceptional Children, 63,* 463–479.

Rogers, K. B. (2011). Thinking smart about twice exceptional learners: Steps to find them and strategies for catering to them appropriately. In C. Wormald & W. Vialle (Eds.), *Dual exceptionality* (pp. 57–70). Wollongong, NSW: University of Wollongong.

Ronksley-Pavia, M. (2015). A model of twice-exceptionality: Explaining and defining the apparent paradoxical combination of disability and giftedness in childhood. *Journal for the Education of the Gifted, 38,* 318–340.

Ruban, L. M., & Reis, S. M. (2005). Identification and assessment of gifted students with learning disabilities. *Theory into Practice, 44,* 115–124.

Russell, V. (2013). *A program for gifted Māori in an English-medium secondary school* (Unpublished Master's thesis). University of Auckland, Auckland, New Zealand.

Russell, V., & Riley, T. (2011). Personalising learning in secondary schools: Gifted education leading the way. *APEX, 16*(1), 1–9.

Schultz, J. J. (2011). *Nowhere to hide: Why kids with ADHD and LD hate school and what we can do about it.* New York, NY: Wiley-Blackwell.

Townsend, G., & Prendergast, D. (2015). Student voice: What can we learn from twice-exceptional students about the teacher's role in enhancing or inhibiting academic self-concept. *Australasian Journal of Gifted Education, 24*(1), 37–51.

Treffert, D. A. (2009). The savant syndrome: An extraordinary condition. A synopsis: Past, present, future. *Philosophical Transactions of the Royal Society B: Biological Sciences, 364,* 1351–1357.

Weinfeld, R., Barnes-Robinson, L., Jeweler, S., & Shevitz, B. (2002). Academic programs for gifted and talented/learning disabled students. *Roeper Review, 24,* 226–233.

Willard-Holt, C., Weber, J., Morrison, K. L., & Horgan, J. (2013). Twice-exceptional learners' perspectives on effective learning strategies. *Gifted Child Quarterly, 57,* 247–262.

Wormald, C. (2009). *An enigma: Barriers to the identification of gifted students with a learning disability* (Doctoral thesis). University of Wollongong, Sydney, Australia. Retrieved from http://ro.uow.edu.au/theses/3076

5

SUPPORTING THE AFFECTIVE NEEDS OF GIFTED LEARNERS

Janna Wardman

Guiding Questions

- What affective needs do gifted learners commonly exhibit and to what extent are these unique to gifted learners?
- What types of supports may gifted children require for their affective development?
- How should the affective needs of gifted learners need be considered across the lifespan?
- Are affective needs culturally specific to Indigenous populations of gifted learners in Australia and New Zealand?

Key Ideas

- Affective outcomes for gifted children can be understood in terms of the interactions between individuals and their social, emotional, cultural, and academic environments.
- While there is not strong evidence for unique affective characteristics of gifted children, it is important for educators to be aware of the potential difficulties gifted students may encounter due to inadequate curriculum or program options, asynchronous development, feelings of difference, and high expectations from self and others.
- Gifted children are diverse and may require different social and emotional supports across their lifespan.
- A good fit between gifted learners and the curriculum and academic programs provided can help to avoid or ameliorate potential affective difficulties.

- To support the positive affective development of gifted students from Indigenous backgrounds, culturally responsive environments and practices are critical.

Introduction

In its broadest sense, the term *affective* is interpreted as related to an individual's feelings or emotions. Throughout the history of gifted education, there has been considerable debate over the extent to which intellectually gifted students exhibit unique social and emotional (affective) characteristics and needs. Are affective vulnerabilities commonly noted in gifted students a function of individual characteristics associated with giftedness, or do they depend on the interactions between individuals and environments that may provide an inappropriate 'fit' for their characteristics and needs? This chapter provides an overview of the research on the affective characteristics and needs of gifted students, including those from Indigenous backgrounds, and considers ways that gifted students can be supported socially and emotionally across the lifespan. While acknowledging the common needs and characteristics of gifted students, they are diverse and will present with individual needs, interests, goals, and experiences, which shape their developmental pathways and determine appropriate educational responses.

To what extent do gifted learners have unique affective needs?

The earliest research on gifted children concentrated on refuting the myths held by many in the general public, including that that highly precocious children suffered from mental illness and were often subject to "early ripe, early rot". Terman's longitudinal study of 1,528 gifted children throughout California found that these children did not have special social and emotional needs and were as emotionally healthy as the general population of school children, if not more so (Terman & Oden, 1947). Working in parallel to Terman, Hollingworth found similar results. The notable exception in her sample was the profoundly gifted students, who required additional academic acceleration and access to appropriate social peers to lessen the sense of loneliness and isolation they otherwise experienced (Hollingworth, 1942). This mismatch between the intellectual characteristics of gifted students and the learning environments in which they are placed is often where affective difficulties originate. In Australia, Gross (2004) identified a similar need among profoundly gifted students, noting that, "In every case, the young people who have been radically accelerated have found both outstanding academic success and the 'sure shelter' of a warm and supportive friendship group" (p. 281). Alice, a student in Gross's study, claimed that it was only when she reached university that

68 Janna Wardman

she found her "intellectual home," highlighting the relationship between the academic and affective domains:

> There is such a sense of belonging . . . such a joyful interaction. It's not just being interested in the same things; it's being passionate about the same things. When one has known deep loneliness and social isolation, the affection and acceptance of friends become especially important. When one differs from one's age-peers so profoundly and in so many respects, intellectually, academically, emotionally and in one's interests and values . . . friendship can be difficult to achieve or sustain.
>
> *(p. 280)*

Six decades after Terman and Hollingsworth's work, Reis and Renzulli (2004) led a task force of psychologists and education experts, which confirmed the conclusions that gifted students are at least as well-adjusted, on average, as students in the general population. In Australia, Vialle, Heaven, and Ciarrochi's (2007) study of 65 gifted high school students, drawn from a longitudinal study of over 950 students, similarly found no significant difference between the measured self-esteem of gifted students and others, and no significant correlation between self-esteem and academic achievement in identified gifted learners. Moreover, teachers reported that gifted students were well-adjusted and less likely to have emotional or behavioural difficulties than their non-identified peers.

Despite the general lack of evidence for unique affective characteristics or needs of gifted students, Peterson (2009) cautions that the tendency to positively stereotype gifted students can deter efforts to acknowledge potential vulnerabilities and support the affective development of individuals. Educators need to be aware of the potential difficulties gifted learners might face as they navigate educational and social environments that are often out of synch with their intellectual characteristics and needs. Indeed, Reis and Renzulli (2004) also noted that gifted students could encounter situations that may place their social and emotional development at risk. For example, schools may not offer programs which enable gifted students to work at an appropriate pace and level of complexity and challenge that keeps them engaged in their learning (Gross, 2004; Wardman, 2009; Wardman, 2015a).

However, acknowledging that the mismatch between individual characteristics and social and academic environments might give rise to affective difficulties is not the same as concluding that all gifted children will experience affective difficulties, or that gifted students as a population have unique affective needs when compared with the general population. Gifted students are diverse, and the assumptions that all gifted students will experience difficulties or, on the other hand, that all gifted students will easily overcome affective challenges and become well-adjusted adults are equally problematic. With these general points in mind, some of the particular areas of focus in the literature on the affective needs and outcomes of gifted students are discussed in the following sections.

Perfectionism

Perfectionism is often discussed in the gifted education literature as a common trait of gifted students. Perfectionism is characterised as a multi-dimensional construct with different types, some of which are considered more adaptive than others. For example, some authors distinguish points along a continuum between 'normal' perfectionism in which individuals strive for outstanding performance and positive growth, and 'neurotic' perfectionism in which individuals tend to fixate excessively on their mistakes, which may result in anxiety and a sense of failure that impedes growth (Schuler, 2000).

The prevalence of perfectionism in gifted students in comparison to the general population has not been strongly established in the research literature (Neumeister, Williams, & Cross, 2007). However, negative manifestations of perfectionism may be of concern for gifted students who are exposed to very high expectations from those around them (and, in turn, high self-expectations) and a disproportionate emphasis on consistently high-level performance. Neumeister et al. (2007) did observe that perfectionistic tendencies, regardless of origin, could be abated with appropriate academic and social supports. By proposing mastery goals and fostering a growth-oriented mindset, students with perfectionistic tendencies can be supported to view their mistakes in a more positive light (Mofield, Parker Peters, & Charkraborti-Ghosh, 2016). That is, if the learner believes intelligence is not a fixed, innate characteristic, but can be further developed, mistakes can be re-framed from a threat to one's self-worth and perceived competency to an opportunity to facilitate growth towards mastery.

Resilience

In the broader developmental psychology research, the concept of resilience – the capacity to 'bounce back' and cope with adverse circumstances – is well-documented as a critical protective factor in positive developmental outcomes for individuals experiencing hardship (Masten & Obradović, 2006). Intelligence (or general cognitive reasoning ability) has been identified as a protective factor associated with the development of effective coping skills and a capacity to overcome challenges (Mueller, 2009). For gifted students living in difficult circumstances, or for those required to overcome significant personal hardships during their education, the capacity for high-level reasoning may be an important strength that can be leveraged to support positive outcomes (Neihart, 2002). Gifted students may encounter bullying at school (Peterson & Ray, 2006), have challenging home environments (Ballam, 2009; Ballam, 2013; Christie, 2011), experience difficulties associated with a disability (Barber & Mueller, 2011), have difficulty reconciling their identification as gifted with a sense of cultural identity (Moore, 2005), struggle to adjust to the academically challenging environment of gifted programs in which they are no longer considered the 'brightest' student (Vogl & Preckel, 2014), or encounter any number of other challenges. A sense of resilience is important for students' capacity to cope in all of these circumstances.

Olszewski-Kubilius (2000, 2008) suggests that coping with difficult personal circumstances may actually help some individuals develop the ability to cope with high levels of stress, take intellectual risks, and cultivate a desire for challenge, all of which are essential in the talent development process. Research by Duckworth, Peterson, Matthews, and Kelly (2007) and Duckworth (2016) identified a number of traits displayed by talented individuals who achieved high levels of success, including cognitive ability, creativity, vigour, emotional intelligence, and resilience. One trait they identified as being displayed by many talented leaders was a type of resilience they described as "grit", which was defined as "perseverance and passion for long term goals" (2016, p. 1087). The elements of passion and perseverance in the concept of grit find parallels in Renzulli's (1978) concept of task commitment, which has long been associated with the process of development towards high-level performance in a domain. Within the talent development approach to gifted education, psychological coaching is advocated as an important element of programming, in recognition of the critical role that factors such as persistence, motivation, and resilience play over the course of long-term development of domain-specific talents (Subotnik, Olszewski-Kubilius, & Worrell, 2011). These are important areas for continued research and should be considered by educators working with gifted learners in all contexts.

Underachievement

The extent to which some gifted students fail to fulfil their perceived academic potential, and even evidence poor academic outcomes, is a topic of discussion in the literature. No agreed definition of gifted underachievement exists; however, the field does recognise particular behaviours which denote the presence of underachievement. Specifically, the discrepancy between ability (or potential) and achievement (or performance), however defined, is considered to denote underachievement (Reis & McCoach, 2000). Reis & McCoach (n.d.) identify three main causes of underachievement in gifted students. These include:

1 An apparent underachievement problem masks more serious physical, cognitive, or emotional issues.
2 The underachievement is symptomatic of a mismatch between the student and his or her school environment.
3 Underachievement results from a personal characteristic such as low self-motivation, low self-regulation, or low efficacy. (para. 6)

Vialle et al. (2007) note that adverse experiences such as being bullied can have a negative impact upon a gifted learner's motivation (and in turn their achievement), or that underachievement could become an avoidance coping strategy. One long-term consequence of underachievement may be that students disengage from or drop out of formal schooling. Anecdotal evidence of this outcome is available, and Renzulli and Park (2000) suggest that up to 20% of high school dropouts may be gifted. In Australia and New Zealand, there are no current data available to the public on the proportion of students who fail to complete high school who would be considered gifted. However, educators should recognize that giftedness is no guarantee of academic success (Richotte, Rubenstein, & Murry, 2015). Like other students, gifted learners need to be supported in targeted ways to overcome challenges to their academic achievement at different stages of their development. While the causes may be varied, academic underachievement is a factor to consider in the affective and intellectual development of gifted learners, especially given the potentially serious consequences if not addressed.

Affective development across the lifespan

Giftedness develops and manifests in disparate ways across the lifespan, and different social and emotional challenges may be prominent at divergent times. Asynchronous development – the mismatch between cognitive, physical, and emotional development that is characteristic of many gifted students – can play a significant role in the developmental trajectory of a student's gifts and talents and impact the way individuals respond to different challenges across their schooling years (Cross & Cross, 2015). One result of asynchronous development is that gifted children have often been observed to prefer socialising with older students who may share complementary interests. Older students may provide a more acceptable context within which to ask questions, receive constructive criticism, set mastery and performance goals, and strive for success. This preference for older peers may appear at a very young age for some gifted children (Cross & Cross, 2015).

Relatedly, a social and emotional challenge for gifted children across the lifespan concerns making friends. While this is a central concern for all children, Riley, Sampson, White, Wardman, and Walker (2015) reported that without similar-ability friends, tensions can emerge for gifted children, including bullying, loneliness, a mismatch of interests, and the difficulty of working in mixed-ability groups in regular classrooms. These findings emerged from a qualitative study of gifted children in New Zealand, in which participants identified distinct friendship groups for discrete settings and described the stress of having to 'multi-task' in order to cater for friends with varying academic abilities and interests. This research confirmed the importance for gifted students of having at least one 'like-minded' friend at school, to whom they can relate:

> Connectedness is a fundamental need among humans. It is the sense of belonging that comes from the bonds within a reciprocal relationship. Through reciprocity, acceptance, value, and importance are bestowed on all involved, company is enjoyed, and the needs for companionship and support are met.
>
> (p. 24)

Friendship and social acceptance may play out differently across the lifespan, but the specific social context of the school plays an important role in understanding these experiences for individual gifted students. A phenomenological study of academically advanced students in three different school settings in Australia demonstrated that these students were more likely to establish positive peer relationships and experience widespread peer acceptance in settings with a formal social and emotional program (Eddles-Hirsch, Vialle, McCormick, & Rogers, 2012). Peer acceptance is critical for gifted students from a young age, and without it even very young students can learn to 'mask' their abilities in order to fit in socially (e.g., Gross, 1993).

By adolescence, this desire for social acceptance may lead gifted students to emphasise their sporting abilities over their academic abilities, or to otherwise downplay their intellectual gifts in the presence of peers (Cross, Coleman, & Terhaar-Yonkers, 2014). Phillips and Lindsay (2006) suggested that although resilient individuals are able to withstand negativity from peers, others, especially adolescent girls, might find it difficult to find the right balance between social acceptance and high levels of academic achievement (Crawford, 2016; Gaerlan-Price, Wardman, Bruce, & Millward, 2016; Vialle, 2007; Watts, 2006; Wood, 2015). Teenage years can be an especially confusing time, and many adolescents report concerns regarding their feelings, emotions, future aspirations, and relationships (Jen, Wu, & Gentry, 2016).

Beyond the role of social acceptance and peer relationships, the curricular and instructional environment provided by schools and teachers is an important influence on social and emotional outcomes for gifted students. Affective challenges may be compounded for gifted students when the administrative needs of a school (e.g., timetabling structures) take precedence over the learning needs of a student who would benefit from an accelerated academic program (Wardman & Hattie, 2012). Gifted students and their parents may experience frustration at having to constantly advocate for their academic needs to be addressed. In her longitudinal study of 70 gifted children in the UK, Freeman (2006) observed:

> Sometimes far too much of the young people's energy had gone into fighting their school regimes and teachers supposedly there to help them. Too many had dissipated their time and energies into wrong channels because of poor educational guidance. At times, the youngsters told me that they had known exactly what they had wanted to do but were thwarted by reasons such as school timetables or teacher opinion.
>
> *(p. 397)*

Although research into the experiences of gifted students in tertiary education is relatively rare (Hèbert & McBee, 2007; Rinn & Plucker, 2004), a small number of studies have highlighted ongoing challenges for students when their intellectual and affective needs are not addressed within university settings. A study in New Zealand investigated the lived experiences of talented undergraduate students in three university settings (Rubie-Davies et al., 2015). Common findings were boredom with the pace of some courses and frustration at the prescriptive nature of assignments set by some university lecturers. Positive findings included relationships with individual university lecturers who had acted as unofficial mentors. Many of the gifted undergraduates, however, had learned not to share their high grades with classmates, as in the past they had experienced negative reactions. These students reported sharing pride in their academic achievements within their own families, the support of whom many had credited for their successful studies. They appreciated an initiative by the university in which they were invited to a social gathering of other high-achieving undergraduates in the same faculty and to meet other students who were 'going for it'. The participants universally disliked the 'gifted' label, preferring 'talented', although some students remarked the term was like something out of a Miss Universe Contest. They also reported feelings of being set up to be 'got at' by using the term gifted (Rubie-Davies et al., 2015). Some students reported verbal put-downs made by university staff and fellow students in the guise of humour; in some cases, significant bullying was reported. One student who participated in the study later emailed a personal reflection. As space is limited in this chapter, only five of the 13 stanzas are given here.

Ode to Those Bright and Bullied

Thus it passed the jealous haters
Feeling dominance was theirs
Continued unchecked to spread nasty
Gossip, which brought me many tears

And, yes, I've learned some lessons
Tho' not the ones you'd expect
Not friendship or notions of beauty
Nor feelings of mutual respect

I've learnt never to stick my head up
Or on fellow students depend
Administrators seem to be players
Who will string you along for their ends

Whatever you do, don't be helpful
Accepting responsibility
That sets you apart from others
Least you be viewed differently

For diversity's a tricky ideal here
Oft spoke of, but seldom embraced
And enlightenment's good in theory
But not acted upon in this place

Do gifted Indigenous populations have culture-specific affective needs?

While there exists great diversity between and among individuals from Indigenous backgrounds as well as between gifted students, it is important to consider affective

74 Janna Wardman

outcomes for Indigenous Australian and New Zealand students as a subset of the gifted population, and to reflect on the ways that Indigenous cultural understandings and experiences may interact with giftedness in an individual's development. In New Zealand for many years, Jill Bevan-Brown was a sole voice in terms of academic research on gifted Māori students, although there have been more recent contributions from other academics. Bevan-Brown (2011) observed that gifted students can be found among people of all cultures and ethnicities, but noted the underrepresentation of Māori students in gifted programs in New Zealand and a misunderstanding of conceptions of giftedness among culturally diverse populations; for example, the Māori perspective is different from more Western conceptions in several areas, including creativity and leadership (Bevan-Brown, 2004, 2005, 2011). Creativity in the Western concept of giftedness centres on original or novel ideas developed by individuals who 'stand out' from the crowd, whereas, in the Māori concept, it is the combined notion of creativity, *kotahitanga* (acting in unity) that is valued (Bevan-Brown, cited in McCann, 2005).

Service to others is also viewed highly as a core quality in Māori culture, as is the brand of leadership identified by Bevan-Brown as *awhinatanga* – the "behind-the-scenes genre, where the leader provides emotional support, guidance and inspiration in a quiet unassuming way" (Bevan-Brown, 2005, p. 151). Mentoring is also seen as an important element in providing an holistic program for gifted Māori students. Mentoring is also mentioned as being a traditional tool: "This strategy was used to nurture gifted individuals in traditional Māori society and is seen as equally relevant and effective today" (Bevan-Brown, 2009, p. 18). Bevan-Brown elaborated:

> For example, a child who is intellectually gifted must also be nurtured in the affective domain, in fact, traditionally Maori do not separate these two spheres of development: a person's 'hinengaro' is the source of both their thoughts and emotions.
>
> *(2009, p. 18)*

At the core is the belief that gifts and talents belong to the group, not the individual, and should result in a benefit to society at large. Only if those conditions are met can the collective culture celebrate the gifts. This has caused individual Māori students to turn down selection into gifted programs, as to accept would be seen as *whakahihi* (big-headed). Bevan-Brown (2004) explained that in Māori culture there are strong sanctions against boasting. As one proverb says, "It's not for the kumara to say how sweet it is" (p. 186–187). Māori students and their *whanau* (extended family) are more likely to regard gifted programming as an option if it can be achieved in a group, rather than individual, setting. Gifted Māori students and those of other ethnic minority groups could/should be identified and catered for in ways that match a student's cultural norms. Bevan-Brown (2005) urged all teachers to understand and value Indigenous cultures in order to provide holistic programs that would identify and provide for all gifted students, in a way that would support rather than undermine their affective development.

In the Australian context, Christie (2011) observed that schooling in general seems to be "failing Aboriginal people in remote communities these days" (p. 41). In his study of the traditional Yolnu society, he observed the same sense of gifts belonging to the group, not solely the individual. This has also been observed in Māori and Cook Island Māori cultures. One elder stated that you can tell the gifted children as they are the ones who help the other kids when the teacher is not watching, "They are not competitive. They already know that they are people with destiny" (p. 41). The Yolnu elders also explained that there is an understanding of spirit and *nayanu*, which he translated as "the seat of the emotions" (p. 40). It is through *nayanu* that the feeling of connectedness to extended family and country is expressed. This is core to developing a sense of belonging. Christie also explains the notions of *gakal*, where through an individual's actions, he or she becomes "one with their ancestors and their land" (p. 37). He likens the process to self-actualisation, which is the highest level in Maslow's (1971) hierarchy of needs. Thus the people of the Yolnu society have similar needs to Western cultures, but they may be observed in different ways.

As with the negative stereotypes of Australian Aboriginal school participation, Webber (2011) urges us to address the perception of negative Māori participation and achievement in gifted programs. She observes that although schools work to achieve equitable learning environments, Māori students "are not encouraged, directly or indirectly, to develop a knowledge and pride in their own culture" (Webber, 2011, p. 101). If racial-ethnic identities are developed, self-concept and achievement will improve. When introducing themselves, it is traditional for Māori to recount their *whakapapa* (genealogy), as ancestors play a large part in Māori culture (Macfarlane, 2006). This traditional knowledge and sense of belonging has been lost to many urban Māori. Webber (2011) suggests that the study of *whakapapa* can create a culturally responsive environment where gifted Māori learn to be proud of their culture and identity.

Gibson and Vialle (2007) examined the importance of language in general, as opposed to specific languages, in Australian Aboriginal culture. There is a similarity with Webber in terms of a key aspect of the culture being lost in the movement of people to city environments. Individual languages, which had been used for 40,000 years, have been lost in the last 100 years. Gibson and Vialle (2007) set the challenge for educators to develop the confidence and sense of identity of Australian Aboriginal children through nurturing and respecting the traditional values and beliefs that remain as many have been lost.

Webber (2008) observes the importance of the learner's sense of belonging. For Indigenous learners, underlying this is the construction of a positive ethnic identity: "Belonging is about opening doors for students, so that they can see themselves in the various communities within which they live and learn" (p. 107.) As with all cultures, love and belonging are Maslovian needs, which are required to be met.

While there may be differences between Western cultures and the Indigenous cultures of Australasia, there are also similarities, and it is important to consider culture in supporting the affective development of all students.

Programming strategies to support the affective needs of gifted learners

As cognitive and affective development are closely related, both can be addressed through specific curricular offerings or educational services that provide for social-emotional needs. Social and emotional struggles already discussed in this chapter include perfectionism, unrealistic goals, asynchronous development, and underachievement. Regardless of the origin or symptom of difficulties experienced by individual gifted students, targeted responses are required to address these issues.

Appropriate learning environments that meet gifted children's learning needs address both the cognitive and affective needs of gifted children. Gifted programs that provide a differentiated curriculum and a continuum of services can be highly effective in this two-pronged approach. These can include supports provided in regular classrooms and in special programs for gifted students, and may comprise approaches such as grouping strategies, learning centres, special classes, after-school programs, and/or acceleration (see Chapter 8).

Acceleration is one of the most extensively researched approaches in the field of gifted education and has shown positive outcomes for cognitive and affective growth in gifted students. In Lee, Olszewski-Kubilius, & Thomson's (2012) study of whole-grade accelerated students, it was found that they had high academic self-concepts, and their overall self-concepts were more positive than for the comparison group. Early entrance to elementary (primary) school also resulted in students having improved socialization and self-esteem when compared to their peers who had not been accelerated (Rogers, 2002).

Bibliotherapy and its closely related ally, cinematherapy, has been shown to have positive results in supporting gifted learners when they are experiencing difficulties. For example, Fumer and Kenney (2011) used bibliotherapy as a strategy to help students feel at ease with their math ability in a mixed-ability classroom. By reading books that reflected similar situations, young people with advanced mathematical abilities helped students in their class to accept their abilities and cease "de-geniusing". Other examples of bibliotheraphy can be found in the literature with similar positive outcomes (e.g., Hebert, 2000; McCulliss & Chamberlin, 2013; Pagnani, 2013).

Peterson and Lorimer's (2011) five-year longitudinal study of gifted students in years five to eight at a private school for gifted children explored the impact of weekly discussion groups structured around building social-emotional development. Two hundred and sixty students participated in weekly topical discussions addressing a range of current school or societal issues led by the teachers. Overall and over time, students perceived the program to be a positive experience. The authors concluded that, "work with social and emotional development, in contrast to academic knowledge acquisition, involves complex student-student and teacher-student interaction, self-reflection in new ways, unique and unpredictable group dynamics, and ambiguity regarding 'product' from time invested" (Peterson, & Lorimer, 2011, p. 176).

Mentoring or coaching can also be an important tool in the development of a gifted individual, with some mentors providing career guidance and affective

Supporting gifted learners **77**

encouragement (Lewis, 2002). Regular contact with a mentor or counsellor, individually or in small group situations, has been found to reduce stress and feelings of isolation (Vialle et al., 2007). Rogers' (2002) meta-analysis found significant positive socialization effect sizes of .50 for mentorships. Mentoring may be especially effective for gifted females in high school, who often grapple with career choices due to multi-potentiality. Mentors can provide opportunities for students to discuss career trajectories and role advancement (Maxwell, 2007). While mentoring is recognized as beneficial, not all gifted leaners have access to a mentor, especially those in rural and low socio-economic areas (Sampson Jr. & Chason, 2008).

Conclusion

Contrary to early assumptions, gifted students are not more likely than others to experience negative affective outcomes. However, healthy affective development depends upon a good 'fit' between the individual and his or her environments, and educators should be aware of potential difficulties that can be experienced by gifted students when this fit is inappropriate. Providing an educational environment that fosters the affective development of gifted students may include early identification of giftedness; supporting gifted students to form relationships with peers with whom they can share interests and experience intellectual stimulation; providing consistently challenging learning environments, such as through enrichment and various forms of acceleration; valuing and supporting the development of cultural identity; and providing appropriate mentors. Future research could investigate the affective consequences for gifted students of different educational interventions.

Of all the concerns raised by parents and students in the literature, the failure of schools to provide learning at an appropriate level and pace is the most frequently cited and most often contributes to affective difficulties for gifted students. With a coordinated approach (Jarvis & Henderson, 2014) between home and school, both the cognitive and affective needs of gifted and talented children can be addressed.

Discussion Questions

- What might be the consequences of negatively or positively stereotyping affective characteristics and outcomes for gifted students?
- What are some potential affective difficulties that gifted students may experience when the educational environment does not provide a good fit for their abilities?
- How might asynchronous development impact a gifted student at different stages of their schooling?
- How can schools value and acknowledge cultural identity among Indigenous students, including through approaches to gifted education?

78 Janna Wardman

References

Ballam, N. (2009). Gifted and growing up in a low-income family: Mindsets, resilience and interventions. *Teachers and Curriculum, 11*, 17–20.

Ballam, N. (2013). *Defying the odds: Gifted and talented young people from low socioeconomic backgrounds* (Doctoral thesis). University of Waikato, Hamilton, New Zealand. Retrieved from http://hdl.handle.net/10289/8424

Barber, C., & Mueller, C. T. (2011). Social and self-perceptions of adolescents identified as gifted, learning disabled, and twice exceptional. *Roeper Review, 33*, 109–120.

Bevan-Brown, J. (2004). Gifted and talented Maori learners. In D. McAlpine & R. Moltzen (Eds.), *Gifted and talented: New Zealand perspectives* (2nd ed., pp. 171–197). Palmerston North, NZ: Kanuka Grove Press.

Bevan-Brown, J. (2005). Providing a culturally responsive environment for gifted Maori learners. *International Education Journal, 6*(2), 150–155.

Bevan-Brown, J. M. (2009). Identifying and providing for gifted and talented Maori students [Electronic Version]. *APEX: The New Zealand Journal of Gifted Education, 15*, 6–20. Retrieved from www.giftedchildren.org.nz/apex

Bevan-Brown, J. M. (2011). Indigenous conceptions of giftedness. In W. Vialle (Ed.), *Giftedness from an indigenous perspective* (pp. 10–23). Wollongong, NSW: Australian Association for the Education of the Gifted and Talented.

Christie, M. (2011). Some aboriginal perspectives on gifted and talented children and their schooling. In W. Vialle (Ed.), *Giftedness from an indigenous perspective* (pp. 36–42). Wollongong, NSW: Australian Association for the Education of the Gifted and Talented.

Crawford, M. (2016) *Acceleration and gifted girls* (Doctoral thesis). Massey University, Palmerston North, NZ.

Cross, T. L., Coleman, L. J., & Terhaar-Yonkers, M. (2014). The social cognition of gifted adolescents in schools: Managing the stigma of giftedness. *Journal for the Education of the Gifted, 37*, 30–39.

Cross, T. L., & Cross, J. R. (2015). Clinical and mental health issues in counseling the gifted individual. *Journal of Counseling and Development, 93*, 163–172.

Duckworth, A. (2016). *Grit: The power of passion and perseverance*. New York, NY: Scribner.

Duckworth, A., Peterson, P., Matthews, M. D., & Kelly, D. R. (2007). Grit, perseverance and passion for long term goals. *Journal of Personality and Social Psychology, 92*, 1087–1101.

Eddles-Hirsch, K., Vialle, W., McCormick, J., & Rogers, K. (2012). Insiders or outsiders: The role of social context in the peer relations of gifted students. *Roeper Review, 34*, 53–62.

Freeman, J. (2006). Giftedness in the long term. *Journal for the Education of the Gifted, 29*, 384–403.

Fumer, J. M., & Kenney, C. (2011). Counting on Frank: Using bibliotherapy in mathematics to prevent de-geniusing. *Pythagoras, 32*, 133–140.

Gaerlan-Price, E., Wardman, J., Bruce, T., & Millward, P. (2016). The juggling act: A phenomenological study of gifted and talented girls' experiences with Facebook. *Roeper Review, 38*, 162–174.

Gibson, K., & Vialle, W. (2007). The Australian Aboriginal view of giftedness. In S. N. Phillipson & M. McCann (Eds.), *Conceptions of giftedness: Sociocultural perspectives* (pp. 169–196). Mahwah, NJ: Lawrence Erlbaum Associates.

Gross, M. U. M. (1993). *Exceptionally gifted children*. London: Routledge.

Gross, M. U. M. (2004). *Exceptionally gifted children*. London: Routledge.

Hèbert, T. P. (2000). Helping high ability students overcome math anxiety through bibliotherapy. *Journal of the Secondary Gifted Education, 8*, 164–178.

Hèbert, T. P., & McBee, M. (2007). The impact of an undergraduate honors program on gifted university students. *Gifted Child Quarterly, 51*, 136–151.

Hollingworth, L. S. (1942). *Children above 180 IQ, Stanford-Binet: Their origin and development.* New York, NY: World Books.

Jarvis, J. M., & Henderson, L. (2014). Defining a coordinated approach to gifted education. *Australasian Journal of Gifted Education, 23*(1), 5–14.

Jen, E., Wu, E., & Gentry, M. (2016). Social and affective concerns high-ability adolescents indicate they would like to discuss with a caring adult implications for educators. *Journal of Advanced Academics, 27*, 39–59.

Lewis, G. (2002). Alternatives to acceleration for the highly gifted child. *Roeper Review, 24*, 130–133.

Macfarlane, A. H. (2006). Becoming educultural: te whakawhitinga on ngā mātauranga. *Kairaranga: Weaving Educational Threads, Weaving Educational Practice, 7*(2), 41–43.

Maslow, A. (1971). *The farther reaches of human nature.* New York, NY: Viking.

Masten, A. S., & Obradović, J. (2006). Competence and resilience in development. *Annals of the New York Academy of Sciences, 1094*, 13–27.

Maxwell, M. (2007). Career counseling is personal counseling: A constructivist approach to nurturing the development of gifted female adolescents. *The Career Development Quarterly, 55*, 206–224.

McCann, M. (2005). International perspectives on giftedness: Experimental and cultural observations of IQ and creativity with implications for curriculum and policy design. *International Education Journal, 6*, 125–135.

McCulliss, D., & Chamberlain, D. (2013). Bibliotherapy for youth and adolescents – School-based application and research. *Journal of Poetry Therapy, 26*(1), 13–40.

Mofield, E., Parker Peters, M., & Chakraborti-Ghosh, S. (2016). Perfectionism, coping, and underachievement in gifted adolescents: Avoidance vs. approach orientations. *Education Sciences, 6*(3), 21.

Moore III, J. L. (2005). Underachievement among gifted students of color: Implications for educators. *Theory into Practice, 44*, 167–177.

Mueller, C. E. (2009). Protective factors as barriers to depression in gifted and nongifted adolescents. *Gifted Child Quarterly, 53*, 3–14.

Neihart, M. (2002). Risk and resilience in gifted children: A conceptual framework. In M. Neihart, S. M. Reis, N. M. Robinson, & S. M. Moon (Eds.), *The social and emotional development of gifted children: What do we know?* (pp. 113–122). Waco, TX: Prufrock Press.

Neumeister, K. L. S., Williams, K. K., & Cross, T. L. (2007). Perfectionism in gifted high school students: Responses to academic challenge. *Roeper Review, 29*, 254–263.

Olszewski-Kubilius, P. (2000). The transition from childhood giftedness to adult creative productiveness: Psychological characteristics and social supports. *Roeper Review, 23*, 65–71.

Olszewski-Kubilius, P. (2008). The role of family in talent development. In S. I. Pfeiffer (Ed.), *Handbook of giftedness in children: Pscho-educational theory, research and best practices* (pp. 53–70). New York, NY: Springer.

Pagnani, A. R. (2013). Gifted male readers: Current understandings and suggestions for future research. *Roeper Review, 35*, 27–35.

Peterson, J. S. (2009). Myth 17: Gifted and talented individuals do not have unique social and emotional needs. *Gifted Child Quarterly, 53*, 280–282.

Peterson, J. S., & Lorimer, M. R. (2011). Student response to a small-group affective curriculum in a school for gifted children. *Gifted Child Quarterly, 55*, 167–180.

Peterson, J. S., & Ray, K. E. (2006). Bullying and the gifted: Victims, perpetrators, prevalence, and effects. *Gifted Child Quarterly, 50*, 148–168.

Phillips, N., & Lindsay, G. (2006). Motivation in gifted students. *High Ability Studies, 17*, 57–73.

Reis, S., & McCoach, B. (n.d.). *Underachievement in gifted and talented students with special needs.* Retrieved from http://gifted.uconn.edu/schoolwide-enrichment-model/gifted_underachievers/

80 Janna Wardman

Reis, S. M., & McCoach, D. B. (2000). The underachievement of gifted students: What do we know and where do we go? *Gifted Child Quarterly, 44,* 152–170.

Reis, S. M., & Renzulli, J. S. (2004). Current research on the social and emotional development of gifted and talented students: Good news and future possibilities. *Psychology in the Schools, 41,* 119–130.

Renzulli, J. S. (1978). What makes giftedness? Re-examining a definition. *Phi Delta Kappan, 60,* 180–184, 261.

Renzulli, J. S., & Park, S. (2000). Gifted dropouts: The who and the why. *Gifted Child Quarterly, 44,* 261–271.

Richotte, J., Rubenstein, L., & Murry, F. (2015). Reversing underachievement of gifted middle school students. *Gifted Child Today, 38,* 103–113.

Riley, T., Sampson, C., White, V., Wardman, J., & Walker, D. (2015). Connecting like-minded learners through flexible grouping. *Set, 1,* 25–33.

Rinn, A. N., & Plucker, J. A. (2004). We recruit them, but then what? The educational and psychological experiences of academically talented undergraduates. *Gifted Child Quarterly, 48,* 54–67.

Rogers, K. B. (2002). *Re-forming gifted education: How parents and teachers can match the program to the child.* Scottsdale, AZ: Great Potential Press.

Rubie-Davies, C. M., Wardman, J., Millward, P., Bicknell, B., Ballam, N., & Riley, T. (2015). *What about our talented students? Phase 3.* Final Report Northern Regional Hub Project Fund, AKO Aotearoa, Wellington, NZ.

Sampson, J. P., Jr. & Chason, A. K. (2008). Helping gifted and talented adolescents and young adults. In S. I. Pfeiffer (Ed.), *Handbook of giftedness in children* (pp. 327–346). New York, NY: Springer.

Schuler, P. A. (2000). Perfectionism and gifted adolescents. *Journal of Secondary Gifted Education, 11,* 183–196.

Subotnik, R. F., Olszewski-Kubilius, P., & Worrell, F. C. (2011). Rethinking giftedness and gifted education: A proposed direction forward based on psychological science. *Psychological Science in the Public Interest, 12*(1), 3–54.

Terman, L. M., & Oden, M. (1947). *The gifted child grows up.* Palo Alto, CA: Stanford University Press.

Vialle, W. (2007). Paris or pink. *Australasian Journal of Gifted Education, 16*(1), 5–11.

Vialle, W., Heaven, P. C., & Ciarrochi, J. (2007). On being gifted, but sad and misunderstood: Social, emotional, and academic outcomes of gifted students in the Wollongong youth study. *Educational Research and Evaluation, 13,* 569–586.

Vogl, K., & Preckel, F. (2014). Full-time ability grouping of gifted students: Impacts on social self-concepts and school related attitudes. *Gifted Child Quarterly, 58,* 51–68.

Wardman, J. (2009). Secondary teachers', student teachers' and education students' attitudes to full-year acceleration for gifted students. *Australasian Journal of Gifted Education, 18*(1), 25–36.

Wardman, J. (2015a). Full-year acceleration at high school: Parents support the social and emotional challenges of their children. *Gifted and Talented International, 29*(2), 49–62.

Wardman, J., & Hattie, J. (2012). Administrators' perceptions of full-year acceleration at high school. *Australasian Journal of Gifted Education, 21*(1), 32–41.

Watts, G. (2006). Teacher attitudes to the acceleration of the gifted: A case study from New Zealand. *Gifted and Talented, 10*(1), 11–19.

Webber, M. (2008). *Walking the space between: Identity and Maori/Pakeha.* Wellington, NZ: NZCER Press.

Webber, M. (2011). Look to the past: Stand tall in the present: The integral nature of positive racial-ethnic identity for the academic success of Māori students. In W. Vialle (Ed.),

Giftedness from an indigenous perspective (pp. 100–110). Wollongong, NSW: Australian Association for the Education of the Gifted and Talented.

Wood, D. M. (2015) *Beauty or brains? The impact of popular culture on the development of adolescent rural gifted girls' identity and subsequent talent development* (Doctoral thesis). University of Wollongong, NSW. Retrieved from http://ro.uow.edu.au/theses/4520

6

CULTIVATING TEACHERS TO WORK WITH GIFTED STUDENTS

Leonie Kronborg

Guiding Questions

- Why do teachers need to know research and gifted education theory? Why is it so important?
- What policies, standards, and professional development experiences influence teaching practice in gifted education?
- What theories and models of giftedness inform professional learning for teachers?
- What educational provisions best provide for students with high abilities, and what is the teacher's role in relation to these provisions?

Key Ideas

- Understanding the prior knowledge and experiences of pre-service and in-service teachers when starting professional development is critical in creating meaningful learning experiences.
- Professional development for teachers in gifted education can have a significant influence on teachers' attitudes towards gifted students, their understanding of the needs of gifted and highly able students, and their ability to identify and provide effective education for these learners.
- Departments of Education and universities have a crucial role in providing guidelines, policies, and criteria to develop better learning environments for gifted and talented students; creating options for professional development; and developing standards to unify procedures, knowledge, and efforts in the field. The extent to which this role is undertaken is often closely related to the political climate and leadership.

- The selection of particular theories and conceptions of giftedness and talent development will inform teachers' efforts to identify gifted students and recognise particular characteristics of gifted children as they emerge in a given environment.
- The selection of educational provisions for gifted and talented students appears to be related to teachers' level of knowledge about giftedness and gifted education.

Personal professional insights: teacher education and professional learning programs

In teaching postgraduate and pre-service teachers in gifted education at a leading Australian university, I have found it critical at the beginning of a course to understand what experiences my students have had in relation to gifted children. In which context is the postgraduate student currently working? Their prior experience of teaching gifted students, understanding of the phenomenon of giftedness, and understanding of the process of talent development, among others, are key areas that will inform their engagement with the gifted education research. Additional questions about individual students' background may further explore personal and professional experiences with gifted children; for example, were they ever considered gifted as a child? Do they have gifted siblings and/or are they the parent of a gifted child? Have they experienced teaching in a school that provided for gifted learners? Have they had the experience of being in a selective learning environment for high-ability or gifted students? Modelling this questioning behaviour can be useful to students in their reflection on giftedness and gifted students.

Pre-service teachers arrive at course work aiming to gain a general perspective of giftedness and gifted education. This includes key aspects such as ways to identify gifted, talented, and twice-exceptional students; the social and emotional needs of gifted students; and strategies to provide a supportive social classroom context for learning. In addition, pre-service teachers typically want to learn effective instructional strategies and educational provisions that can be implemented in their classrooms and schools to support gifted students' talent development. They are often hoping to be employed following their studies, as teachers of a class that will include some gifted students. Postgraduate teachers are often already teaching gifted students in a school in Victoria or another Australian state or territory, or even in New Zealand, and are keen to learn more about the educational needs of gifted students. Often included in this postgraduate population are psychologists and international students wanting to take their knowledge and skills to apply in their home contexts.

All this information provides pathways via which to differentiate my teaching and further model appropriate strategies for meeting the needs of the gifted. This is a form of formative assessment which is helpful in engaging teachers who

84 Leonie Kronborg

are expected to motivate, develop, and extend gifted students' potential and talent development in their own teaching.

The impact of pre-service or professional learning in gifted education

A national survey of gifted programs in the United States, conducted by Callahan, Moon, and Oh (2014), found that there was "limited transfer if any at all, of the work of experts (research and theory development) into the field of practice" (p. 10). This is a disappointing finding; if such a survey were replicated in Australia, it could yield similar findings. Hence, increased professional learning experiences and teacher education in gifted education is extremely important in order to overcome this ignorance of the research literature in gifted education and to cultivate effective Australian and New Zealand teachers of the gifted and talented.

Research literature in gifted education evidences that teachers' participation in pre-service gifted education studies and/or professional learning, which has informed them about the needs of gifted and talented students, translates to the effective teaching of students in selective secondary programs and in mixed-ability high school settings (Kaman & Kronborg, 2012; Knopfelmacher & Kronborg, 2003; Kronborg, 2015; Kronborg & Plunkett, 2008, 2012, 2013, 2015). Teachers in these studies were found to provide a range of instructional strategies that engaged gifted students in challenging learning experiences across diverse subject domains and that motivated the students intrinsically and extrinsically (Kronborg & Plunkett, 2012, 2013; Plunkett & Kronborg, 2007). There is evidence for the efficacy of specific learning interventions and instructional strategies for students with advanced talent in academic domains (Assouline, Colangelo, VanTassel-Baska, & Lupkowski-Shoplik, 2015), which supports the rationale for providing quality professional learning experiences for teachers of the gifted.

Effective teachers are at the heart of successful student learning experiences. Research has indicated that effective professional learning is the "critical component of improving the quality of education" (Jones & Dexter, 2014, p. 368). Studies have shown that teachers have a strong impact on their students' learning, and that gifted students are particularly influenced by their teachers' attitudes and actions (Croft, 2003; Roberts, 2006). What makes an outstanding teacher of the gifted? Teachers of the gifted demonstrate particular characteristics and competencies, and use a range of teaching practices to achieve optimal learning experiences for their gifted students (Chan, 2001; Knopfelmacher & Kronborg, 2003; Kronborg, 2017; Kronborg & Plunkett, 2015; Maker & Schiever, 2010; VanTassel-Baska, McFarlane, & Feng, 2006).

In a study of teachers' professional development at a new Victorian government co-educational selective high school for Year 9 and 10 gifted and highly able students, five key characteristics were identified by the teachers of the gifted as most important for teaching gifted and highly able students. These included their ability to be enthusiastic about students with high ability; to strive for excellence and high achievement so that they could model that behaviour to students; to recognise the individual differences amongst gifted and highly able students; to respect the individuality of gifted students, personal self-images, and personal integrity; and to be able to create warm, safe, democratic environments so that gifted students could speak their minds and not be limited in the classroom by peers who stifled or were intimidated by classroom discussions. These teachers went beyond treating gifted students as stereotypes and acknowledged the need for individual intellectual stimulation and challenging curriculum (Kronborg & Plunkett, 2013).

This study of teachers' perspectives on effective teaching practice supported a focus on seeing things from the student's point of view, guiding students rather than trying to coerce them, being able to work with culturally diverse high-ability students, and respecting those differences. Teachers valued developing students' self-concepts, while encouraging an understanding of their own learning needs. As a consequence, these effective teachers provided learning experiences which were based on students' interests whenever possible. Moreover, as a result of professional learning, these teachers identified the importance of a range of teaching and learning strategies they preferred to use with gifted students, such as providing students with the choice to work alone, modelling metacognitive strategies, encouraging brainstorming ideas and alternative ways of thinking, teaching higher-level thinking, encouraging debate amongst students, and a range of other strategies which were perceived to make students' learning meaningful (Kronborg & Plunkett, 2013).

Teacher attitudes towards the gifted play a critical role in student responses, as gifted students will be affected by their teachers' attitudes and actions (Croft, 2003; Roberts, 2006). Often, teachers with little knowledge of gifted education do not understand the academic needs of highly able students (Geake & Gross, 2008; Lassig, 2009; Plunkett, 2002). Not until teachers engage in professional learning in gifted education is there a change or improvement in attitudes towards the gifted and an awareness or consciousness of gifted students' academic or educational needs (Geake & Gross, 2008; Lassig, 2009; Kronborg & Plunkett, 2012; Pedersen & Kronborg, 2014 ; Plunkett & Kronborg, 2011).

When teachers have not experienced professional learning or pre-service education about the academic needs of gifted or highly able students, negative teacher attitudes or misconceptions can lead to inappropriate education for gifted students (Geake & Gross, 2008; Plunkett, 2002; Plunkett & Kronborg, 2011). Therefore, "teachers need to have positive attitudes towards gifted students in order to be effective educators to them" (Kronborg & Plunkett, 2012, p. 35), and to take responsibility for their own development and learning (Knopfelmacher & Kronborg, 2003). Consequently, most teachers participate in professional learning because they want to become more effective teachers, and professional development provides an opportunity for increased competence and increased professional satisfaction (Guskey, 1986).

Policies, standards, and professional development

When reflecting on gifted education policy in Australia and New Zealand, one could argue it is always a work in progress. As a result of constant political change and ongoing debate, little has been acknowledged as essential gifted education practice in policy. In Australia, there remains a need for a national policy for gifted students that can be developed and modified, and acknowledged as an essential part of education for gifted students and their talent development. In contrast to the Australian context, New Zealand has managed to achieve acknowledged national guidelines for gifted education in schools since 2002 (New Zealand Ministry of Education, 2002).

Change in Australian state and territory governments often disrupts teacher expectations and provisions for gifted and talented students. The research evidence base in gifted education, which should underpin the need for gifted education policy and hence the professional learning required for teachers, is often overlooked with changes in state government or even changes in school leadership. In turn, this lack of consistent, dedicated focus on quality teaching for gifted and talented students, based on research evidence, impacts government funding and opportunities available for teacher education in universities. It also limits the commitment to professional learning in schools, an essential factor in developing competent educators for pre-school, primary, and secondary gifted students in Australian and New Zealand schools. Course costs and distance to professional learning opportunities have been found to limit teachers' opportunities to further their knowledge and skills. Principals have noted that, "even current fringe benefit tax laws also act as a disincentive for schools to fund teachers' postgraduate studies in gifted education" (Education and Training Committee Report, 2012, p. 224).

In Australia, the need for teacher education based on research in the field of gifted education was acknowledged formally in the second national Senate Inquiry into the Education of Gifted Children (Senate References Committee, 2001), and followed in 2005 when the Gifted and Talented Education Professional Development Package was produced as a computer-based course with six modules on the education of gifted and talented students. These modules were produced by the Gifted Education Research Resource and Information Centre (GERRIC, 2005) at the University of New South Wales and funded by the Australian Government Department of Education, Science and Training (DEST). A copy was provided to every school in Australia for teachers to learn about teaching gifted students.

Subsequently, the Victorian Inquiry into Gifted Education (Parliament of Victoria Education and Training Committee, 2012) had Australia–wide submissions with implications for all states and territories. Of the 65 recommendations of the Parliamentary Committee's final report (Parliament of Victoria Education and Training, 2012), 10 recommendations focussed on the need for improved teacher education and training. In particular, the Education and Training Committee recommended "that the Victorian Government provide scholarships for teachers to undertake postgraduate study in gifted education" and "that the Victorian Government support schools to support teachers to undertake postgraduate study in gifted education" (p. xxxiv). Following a subsequent change of state government, this recommendation has not been implemented by the Department of Education.

Other Australian states and territories have also experienced vacillating support for teacher education and professional learning for gifted students from their State Departments of Education. In 2001, the Australian Senate report recommended that all state and territory education authorities should require, as a condition of employment, that all graduated teachers have at least one semester unit on the special needs of gifted students in their degrees (Senate Report, 2001, para. 4.67). In 2017, this recommendation has only been implemented by a handful of Australian universities, with gifted education studies offered as an elective at a minority of other universities.

In contrast to Australia, New Zealand's policy for teacher professional learning in gifted education became noticeably stronger between 2004 and 2014, based on a review of gifted education practices in New Zealand schools (Riley & Bicknell, 2013). A review of 327 New Zealand schools (13% of all schools invited to participate in the study) indicated that the percentage of schools providing professional learning and development for teachers in gifted education increased from 22.1% in 2004 to 27.3% in 2014. Of teachers at participating schools, 14.6% had engaged in university studies, 59.4% of the schools indicated they had developed gifted and talented policies, and 57.7% of schools reported curriculum delivery policies that addressed the needs of gifted and talented students (Riley & Bicknell, 2013). In 2005, all New Zealand schools were required to identify gifted and talented students and to develop strategies to effectively respond to their needs (Bourne & Sturgess, 2006).

Additionally, the New Zealand Ministry of Education (2012) argues that educators need specific development and clear understanding of the concepts of giftedness and talent, as well as knowledge in areas such as identification, programming and teaching methods, and the ability to work with different populations of gifted students in terms of gender, culture, and sociodemographic characteristics. However, participation in nationally offered professional development is a matter of school choice, and schools are responsible for administering their own professional learning and development funds (Easton, Gaffney, & Wardman, 2016). In New Zealand, convincing schools of the benefits of teacher education for gifted students, provided by universities, remains important.

The Australian Professional Standards for Teachers (Australian Institute for Teaching and School Leadership [AITSL], 2017) is a set of evidence-informed Australian standards or expectations that all teachers and teacher education graduates need to develop and acknowledge. The knowledge, skills, and capabilities listed in these standards were developed for all teachers, to ensure that they can respond effectively to the needs of all students. Each of these teaching standards can be reflected upon, adapted, and extended to consider how they apply to the educational needs of gifted and talented students across Australia, but this will only have real impact if teachers understand how to apply gifted education models and strategies to these standards.

Countries such as the U.S. have defined teacher standards specifically for the field of gifted education, as a way to establish the critical knowledge and skills that teachers need to know to be effective in teaching gifted and talented students (VanTassel-Baska & Johnsen, 2007). In the same way, the American Psychological Association (APA, 2015) described 20 principles from psychology to improve pre-K to 12 teaching and learning processes. A panel of experts in the field of gifted education updated and expanded these 20 principles, to include a focus on creative, talented, and gifted students (APA, 2017).

Australian teachers do not just need a set of standards; teachers need to be specifically mindful of the evidence-based educational needs of gifted and talented students (Kronborg & Plunkett, 2012, 2013; Lassig, 2009), because as indicated previously, teachers with negative attitudes towards gifted students and their academic needs may be unable to identify gifted students in their classrooms due to their stereotypical beliefs and misconceptions about high-ability students (Kronborg & Meyland, 2003; Plunkett & Kronborg, 2011; Preckel, Matheis, & Kronborg, 2015). Positive attitudes, instead, are critical for being an effective teacher of gifted and talented students (Kronborg & Plunkett, 2012).

Theories and models of giftedness to support professional learning

Across Australia and New Zealand, educators and teachers have different understandings of what is considered to be giftedness and what is considered to be a talent. Gifted education in Australia and New Zealand is underpinned by a range of theoretical perspectives (Kronborg, 2017). Gagné's (2003) Differentiated Model of Giftedness and Talent (DMGT) is the main theory promoted by the various Departments of Education across the states and territories of Australia (Kronborg & Plunkett, 2012). Nevertheless, the new Australian curriculum encourages educators (Australian Curriculum, Assessment and Reporting Authority [ACARA], 2015) to acknowledge the theories of Gagné (2003), Tannenbaum (2003), and Renzulli (1986). These theories of giftedness and talent development are important for teaching gifted students, whether at pre-school, primary, or secondary levels.

Gagné (2013a) defines giftedness in his DMGT as designating "the possession and use of untrained and spontaneously expressed natural abilities or aptitudes (called gifts) in at least one ability domain, to a degree that places an individual at least among the top ten percent of age peers." (p. 193), whereas the concept of talent is described as "the outstanding mastery of systematically developed competencies (knowledge and skills) in at least one field of human activity to a degree that places an individual at least among the top ten percent of learning peers" (Gagné, 2013b, p. 5). In this theory, it is acknowledged that teachers and parents can influence the environment, which can catalyse students' gifted potential into talent. According to Gagné (2013a), talents progressively emerge from the transformation of the students' outstanding natural abilities or gifts into the well-trained and systematically developed competencies characteristic of a particular field of human activity.

Another theory that has had a strong influence on teachers in Australian schools is Tannenbaum's Sea Star Theory of Giftedness. According to Tannenbaum (2003), giftedness in a child is the potential to become an adult with a developed talent. Tannenbaum asserted that there are two types of gifted individuals: creators who produce either things or ideas; and performers who interpret or re-create things or ideas. Tannenbaum maintained that these two kinds of gifted individuals demonstrate their talent either creatively by adding something new or original, or proficiently by having high levels of developed skill. Like Gagné's model, Tannenbaum's model attempts to explore the process by which ability becomes actual achievement. He identifies five factors that influence this conversion: superior general intellect; distinctive special aptitudes; a supportive array of non-intellective traits such as personality, self-concept, and motivation; a challenging and facilitative environment; and chance.

The New Zealand Ministry of Education (2012) also recommends theories for teachers to consider in their professional learning when educating gifted students. These are similar, but slightly different from the models presented in the Australian Curriculum documents, and include Renzulli's Three-Ring Conception of Giftedness (1986) and his social capital model (2002). Gagné's model (2008, 2009) is strongly recommended, in addition to Gardner's theory of Multiple Intelligences (1993, 1998), to underpin school policies. Additionally, New Zealand has developed sets of criteria that schools can use for developing definitions of giftedness and talent that reflect their own local contextual characteristics (Ministry of Education, 2012). A cultural concept of giftedness that considers gifted and talented Māori students (Bevan-Brown, 2009) is also acknowledged in the New Zealand policies, together with an explanation of potential cultural indicators of giftedness based on Bevan-Brown's research (2009) into how special abilities are interpreted and manifested in different cultures in New Zealand.

Theories and models that underpin the conceptions of giftedness selected for different contexts have important repercussions for the education of gifted and talented students. The conceptualisation of giftedness has implications for the identification process, the types of opportunities provided to nurture talent development, and ultimately the success of gifted education (Schroth & Helfer, 2009).

Educational provisions for students with high abilities

From studies of the beliefs of Australian pre-service teachers (Plunkett & Kronborg, 2011) and postgraduate teachers (Kronborg & Meyland, 2003), initial misconceptions before engaging in teacher education commonly include that accelerated learning and ability grouping for gifted students or students with high abilities are considered inappropriate educational strategies. It was not until pre-service teachers (Plunkett & Kronborg, 2011) and postgraduate teachers in these studies had learned about conceptions of giftedness, identification practices, and curriculum for the gifted (Kronborg & Meyland, 2003) that most teachers began to acknowledge the academic benefits of accelerated learning for many gifted students (Kronborg & Meyland, 2003; Plunkett & Kronborg, 2011). A body of research suggests that teachers often deny the benefits of practices such as academic acceleration when they are

90 Leonie Kronborg

not aware of the research evidence on its effectiveness, and this finding was again supported in a recent meta-analysis of research on ability grouping and accelerated learning for gifted students (Steenbergen-Hu, Makel, & Olszewski-Kubilius, 2016).

Many of the pre-service and postgraduate teachers in the Victorian studies believed before engaging in their studies of gifted education issues that teaching homogeneously grouped gifted and highly able students was not beneficial to gifted students (Kronborg & Meyland, 2003; Plunkett & Kronborg, 2011). This negative perspective in regard to grouping students with high abilities together, that educators often perpetuate, is consistent with the egalitarian values of Australian and New Zealand society (Frantz & McClarty, 2016; Moltzen, 2011; Riley, 2000). Furthermore, this idea is perpetuated by many Australian and New Zealand teachers who maintain that mixed-ability classes are the preferred educational provision for gifted and highly able students, because every teacher "should have the knowledge rather than just having one teacher who has all the knowledge" in regard to teaching gifted students (Education and Training Committee, 2012, p. 220). Yet, the evidence tells us that gifted students in government schools are more likely to achieve highly in selective programs where they are grouped with other students of a similar achievement level (VCE School Ranking, 2016). The U.S. Study of Mathematically Precocious Youth (SMPY) also provides extensive data in support of early identification of young intellectually able students in mathematics who qualify for accelerated educational programming (Lubinski, 2016; Lubinski & Benbow, 2006).

Final thoughts

Teachers' knowledge and understandings of the educational needs of gifted students can be informed greatly by effective professional learning and teacher education in universities that is evidence-based and taught by experts in the field of gifted education. If we want to nurture students who can benefit and improve society, and perhaps contribute to finding solutions to complex problems that currently seem out of reach, then investing in the education of gifted and talented students, many of whom may have the capacity to make valuable contributions to broader society, seems like a logical next step.

This chapter discussed the importance of knowing and engaging with the base knowledge and prior experiences of pre-service and practicing teachers when designing meaningful professional learning experiences related to gifted education. The impact of professional development in gifted education is related to its effects on teacher attitudes, teacher knowledge of the nature and needs of gifted children, and teacher competence in recognising gifted children and providing effective learning experiences. There are important roles to be played by informed academics in universities, supported by key Department of Education and Ministry of Education personnel who can provide and review guidelines, policies, and criteria to develop better learning environments for gifted and talented students. Both academics and policy makers have a role to play in developing quality, sustainable options for teacher education and professional development in gifted education

> ## Discussion Questions
>
> - What would happen if teacher education/professional learning in gifted education were "compulsory" for pre-service and practicing teachers in Australia and New Zealand? What effects might this have on teachers' pedagogy?
> - Is the teacher education and professional development currently implemented in Australia and New Zealand addressing the needs of most teachers of gifted students? How do we know?
> - Are the teaching strategies commonly used to support gifted students in Australian and New Zealand classrooms based on research evidence, or do they sometimes stem from misconceptions about giftedness and gifted students?
> - Would it be beneficial to have a set of professional teaching standards for Australia and New Zealand that are specifically designed for teachers in the field of gifted education?
> - What might be the advantages and disadvantages, in terms of teacher education, of ability-grouped classes for advanced primary school students and selective schools for academically advanced secondary students?

References

American Psychological Association, Center for Psychology in Schools and Education. (2017). *Top 20 principles from psychology for PREK – 12 creative, talented, and gifted students' teaching and learning*. Retrieved from www.apa.org/ed/schools/teaching-learning/top-twenty-principles.aspx

American Psychological Association, Coalition for Psychology in Schools and Education. (2015). *Top 20 principles from psychology for PREK – 12 teaching and learning*. Retrieved from www.apa.org/ed/schools/cpse/top-twenty-principles.pdf

Assouline, S., Colangelo, N., VanTassel-Baska, J., & Lupkowski-Shoplik, A. (2015). *A nation empowered: Evidence trumps the excuses holding back America's brightest students*. University of Iowa: The Connie Belin & Jacqueline N. Blank International Centre for Gifted Education and Talent Development.

Australian Curriculum, Assessment and Reporting Authority [ACARA]. (2015). *Student diversity*. Retrieved from www.australiancurriculum.edu.au/studentdiversity/gifted-and-talented-students

Australian Institute for Teaching and School Leadership [AITSL]. (2017). *Australian professional standards for teachers*. Retrieved from www.aitsl.edu.au/australian-professional-standards-for-teachers/standards/list

Bevan-Brown, J. (2009). Identifying and providing for gifted and talented Māori students. *APEX, 15*(1), 6–20. Retrieved from www.giftedchildren.org.nz/apex/v15no1.php

Bourne, J., & Sturgess, A. (2006). If any one can, Kiwis can: Every teacher, a teacher of gifted learners. *The Australasian Journal of Gifted Education, 15*(1), 44–50.

Callahan, C. M., Moon, T. R., & Oh, S. (2014). *National surveys of gifted programs: Executive summary*. Retrieved from www.nagc.org/sites/default/files/key%20reports/2014%20Survey%20of%20GT%20programs%20Exec%20Summ.pdf

Chan, D. W. (2001). Characteristics and competencies of teachers of gifted learners: The Hong Kong teacher perspective. *Roeper Review, 23*, 197–202.

Croft, L. J. (2003). Teachers of the gifted: Gifted teachers. In N. Colangelo & G. A. Davis (Eds.), *Handbook of gifted education* (3rd ed., pp. 558–571). Boston, MA: Allyn and Bacon.

Easton, V., Gaffney, J. S., & Wardman, J. (2016). "I need to do better, but I don't know what to do": Primary teachers' experiences of talented young writers. *Australasian Journal of Gifted and Talented, 25*(2), 34–51.

Education and Training Committee. (2012). *Inquiry into the education of gifted and talented students*. Melbourne, VIC: Parliament of Victoria. Retrieved from https://www.parlia ment.vic.gov.au/images/stories/committees/etc/Past_Inquiries/EGTS_Inquiry/Final_Report/Gifted_and_Talented_Final_Report.pdf

Frantz, R. S., & McClarty, K. L. (2016). Gifted education's reflection of country-specific cultural, political, and economic features. *Gifted and Talented International, 31*(1), 4658.

Gagné, F. (2003). Transforming gifted into talents: The DMGT as a developmental theory. In N. Colangelo & G. A. Davis (Eds.), *Handbook of gifted education* (3rd ed., pp. 64–74). Boston, MA: Allyn and Bacon.

Gagné, F. (2008). Building gifts into talents: Brief overview of the DMGT 2.0. *Gifted, 152*, 5–9.

Gagné, F. (2009). Building gifts into talents: Detailed overview of the DMGT 2.0. In B. Mac-Farlane & T. Stambaugh (Eds.), *Leading change in gifted education: The festschrift of Dr. Joyce Van Tassel-Baska* (pp. 61–80). Waco, TX: Prufrock Press.

Gagné, F. (2013a). Yes, giftedness (aka "innate" talent) does exist!. In S. B. Kaufman (Ed.), *The complexity of greatness* (pp. 191–222). New York, NY: Oxford University Press.

Gagné, F. (2013b). The DMGT: Changes within, beneath, and beyond. *Talent Development & Excellence, 5*(1), 5–19.

Gardner, H. (1993). *Frames of mind: The theory of multiple intelligences* (2nd ed.). London: Fontana.

Gardner, H. (1998). Are there additional intelligences? The case for naturalist, spiritual and existential intelligences. In J. Kane (Ed.), *Education, information and transformation* (pp. 111–131). Upper Saddle River, NJ: Merrill Prentice Hall.

Geake, J. G., & Gross, M. U. M. (2008). Teachers' negative affect toward academically gifted students: an evolutionary psychological study. *Gifted Child Quarterly, 52*, 217–231.

GERRIC. (2005). *Professional development package for teacher*. Retrieved from https://educa tion.arts.unsw.edu.au/about-us/gerric/resources/pd-package/

Guskey, T. R. (1986). Staff development and the process of teacher change. *Educational Researcher, 15*(5), 5–12.

Jones, W. M., & Dexter, S. (2014). How teachers learn: The roles of formal, informal, and independent learning. *Education Technology and Research Development, 62*, 367–384.

Kaman, Y., & Kronborg, L. (2012). Perceptions of learning at a select entry accelerated high school for high ability students. *Australasian Journal of Gifted Education, 21*(2), 47–61.

Knopfelmacher, S., & Kronborg, L. (2003). *Characteristics, competencies and classroom strategies of effective teachers of gifted and talented students*. Proceedings of the 9th National Conference of the AAEGT.

Kronborg, L. (2015, October). *Understanding of teachers motivated to teach gifted and highly able students in diverse schooling environments: providing for their academic, social and emotional needs students?* Paper session presented at the Gifted Futures Forum for Talent Enhancement at the University of NSW, Sydney, Australia.

Kronborg, L. (2017, January). *Effective teaching of gifted and highly able secondary students for talent development: a case study*. Paper session presented at the PhD research on Honours education translated into practice program for researchers and teachers in Honors programs in higher education, at Hanze University of Applied Sciences, Groningen, The Netherlands.

Kronborg, L. (2017). Gifted education in Australia and New Zealand. In S. J. Pfeiffer (Ed.), *Handbook of giftedness and talent* (pp. 85–96). Washington, DC: American Psychological Association.

Kronborg, L., & Meyland, J. (2003). Changes in postgraduate teachers' opinions about gifted students and their education. In *Proceedings for the 15th world conference for gifted education – gifted 2003: A celebration down under, Adelaide*, CD Rom (pp. 1–6). Adelaide: World Council for Gifted and Talented Children.

Kronborg, L., & Plunkett, M. (2008). Curriculum differentiation: An innovative Australian secondary school program to extend academic talent. *Australasian Journal of Gifted Education, 17*(1), 19–29.

Kronborg, L., & Plunkett, M. (2012). Examining teacher attitudes and perceptions of teacher competencies required in a new selective high school. *Australasian Journal of Gifted Education, 21*(2), 33–46.

Kronborg, L., & Plunkett, M. (2013). Responding to professional learning: How effective teachers differentiate teaching and learning strategies to engage highly able adolescents. *Australasian Journal of Gifted Education, 22*(2), 52–63.

Kronborg, L., & Plunkett, M. (2015). Providing an optimal school context for talent development: An extended curriculum program in practice. *Australasian Journal of Gifted Education, 24*(2), 61–69.

Lassig, C. (2009). Teachers' attitudes towards the gifted: The importance of professional development and school culture. *Australasian Journal of Gifted Education, 18*(2), 32–42.

Lubinski, D. (2016). From Terman to today: A century of findings on intellectual precocity. *Review of Educational Research, 86*, 900–944.

Lubinski, D., & Benbow, C. (2006) Study of mathematically precocious youth after 35 years: Uncovering antecedents for the development of math-science expertise. *Perspectives on Psychological Science, 1*, 316–345.

Maker, C. J., & Schiever, S. (2010). *Curriculum development and teaching strategies for gifted learners* (3rd ed.). Austin, TX: Pro-ed.

Ministry of Education. (2002). *Initiatives in gifted and talented education*. Wellington, NZ: Author.

Ministry of Education. (2012). *Gifted and talented students: Meeting their needs in New Zealand schools*. Wellington, NZ: Learning Media.

Moltzen, R. (2011). Historical perspectives. In R. Moltzen (Ed.), *Gifted and talented: New Zealand perspectives* (3rd ed., pp. 31–53). Auckland: Pearson.

Parliament of Victoria Education and Training. (2012). *Inquiry into the education of gifted and talented students*. Parliamentary paper no.108 Session 2010–2012: Victorian Government Printer.

Pedersen, F., & Kronborg, L. (2014). Challenging secondary teachers to examine beliefs and pedagogy when teaching highly able students in mixed-ability health education classes. *Australasian Journal of Gifted Education, 23*(1), 15–27.

Plunkett, M. (2002). Impacting on teacher attitudes towards gifted students. In W. Vialle & J. Geake (Eds.), *The gifted Enigma: A collection of articles* (pp. 240–249). Melbourne, VIC: Hawker Brownlow Education.

Plunkett, M., & Kronborg, L. (2007). The importance of social-emotional context: Perceptions of students, parents and teachers regarding an extended curriculum program for students with high abilities. *Australasian Journal of Gifted Education, 16*(2), 35–43.

Plunkett, M., & Kronborg, L. (2011). Learning to be a teacher of the gifted: The importance of examining opinions and challenging misconceptions. *Gifted and Talented International, 26*(1–2), 31–46.

Preckel, F., Matheis, S., & Kronborg, L. (2015, August). *Pre-service teachers attitudes and beliefs about the gifted: A cross-cultural comparison study*. Paper session presented at the WCGTC Conference, Odense, Denmark.

Renzulli, J. (1986). The three ring conception of giftedness: A developmental model for creative productivity. In R. J. Sternberg & J. E. Davidson (Eds.), *Conceptions of giftedness* (pp. 53–92). New York, NY: Cambridge University Press.

Renzulli, J. S. (2002). Expanding the conception of giftedness to include co-cognitive traits and to promote social capital. *Phi Delta Kappan, 84*, 33–58.

Riley, T. (2000). *Equity with excellence: Confronting the dilemmas and celebrating the possibilities*. Paper presented at Teaching and Learning: Celebrating Excellence, Hamilton, New Zealand.

Riley, T., & Bicknell, B. (2013). Gifted and talented education in New Zealand Schools: A decade later. *APEX: The New Zealand Journal of Gifted Education, 18*(1). Retrieved from www.giftedchildren.org.nz/apex

Roberts, J. L. (2006). Teachers of secondary gifted students: What makes them effective? In A. Dixon & S. Moon (Eds.), *Handbook of secondary gifted education* (pp. 567–580). Waco, TX: Prufrock Press.

Schroth, S. T., & Helfer, J. A. (2009). Practitioners' conceptions of academic talent and giftedness: Essential factors in deciding classroom and school composition. *Journal of Advance Academics, 20*, 384–403.

Senate References Committee (Employment, Workplace Relations, Small Business and Education). (2001). *The education of gifted children*. Canberra: Commonwealth of Australia.

Steenbergen-Hu, S., Makel, M., & Olszewski-Kubilius, P. (2016). What one hundred years of research says about the effects of ability grouping and acceleration on K – 12 students' academic achievement. *Review of Educational Research, 86*, 849–899.

Tannenbaum, A. J. (2003). Nature and nurture of giftedness. In N. Colangelo & G. A. Davis (Eds.), *Handbook of gifted education* (3rd ed., pp. 45–59). Boston, MA: Allyn and Bacon.

VanTassel-Baska, J., & Johnsen, S. (2007). Teacher education standards for the field of gifted education. *Gifted Child Quarterly, 51*, 182–205.

VanTassel-Baska, J., MacFarlane, B., & Feng, A. X. (2006). A cross-cultural study of exemplary teaching: What do Singapore and the United States secondary gifted class teachers have to say? *Gifted and Talented International, 21*(2), 38–47.

VCE School Ranking. (2016). *Victorian Certificate of Education (VCE) School ranking*. Retrieved from https://bettereducation.com.au/results/vce.aspx

7

DESIGNING AND ADAPTING CURRICULUM FOR ACADEMICALLY GIFTED STUDENTS

Jane M. Jarvis

Guiding Questions

- What are elements of effective curriculum for academically gifted students?
- What is the relationship between curriculum that is appropriate for academically gifted students and curriculum that is appropriate for all students?
- What is the evidence base that supports specific curriculum models and teaching practices for gifted students?
- What are some key avenues for future research into curriculum and teaching practices for academically gifted students, with a focus on the Australian and New Zealand contexts?

Key Ideas

- Effective, well-designed curriculum and teaching practices are fundamental to the success of any gifted education program, regardless of its specific setting or grouping configuration.
- High-quality curriculum for gifted learners is grounded in high-quality curriculum for all learners; learning experiences can then be adjusted for pace and level of complexity, and to provide opportunities for gifted learners to develop specific strengths and interests.
- Gifted students are diverse, and therefore curriculum that is suitable for gifted students will also be varied and flexible in response to learner differences.

- Decisions about curriculum design, content, and delivery should be guided by contextualised goals for gifted education.
- There is international research evidence to support the use of several curriculum models with gifted students, but systematic research is needed to assess their applicability and effectiveness in Australian and New Zealand contexts.

Introduction

> The heart of effective programming for gifted students lies in the integration of advanced curricula with effective instructional strategies to develop learning activities that will enhance student learning outcomes.
>
> (Callahan, Moon, Oh, Azano, & Hailey, 2015, p. 137)

The focus of this chapter is on the content of education for gifted or advanced students, and the organisation and delivery of that content at the classroom level. This includes curriculum and pedagogy for gifted students in mainstream, heterogeneous classrooms as well as for those within selective classes, programs, or schools. As reflected in the opening quote, curriculum occupies a central place in gifted education. Regardless of structural elements such as grouping configuration, program model, or site, the quality of gifted education ultimately depends upon learners' consistent access to engaging, challenging curriculum that nurtures specific talents and interests, allows for different rates of progress, and is sensitive to individual and cultural differences.

Despite curriculum's prominent role in gifted education, there have been relatively few comprehensive, methodologically rigorous efficacy studies involving gifted learners, particularly in Australian and New Zealand settings. This is perhaps not surprising, given the complexity and cost of conducting large-scale, randomised control (or even quasi-experimental) intervention studies in the field of education, let alone in the smaller field of gifted education. Indeed, researchers have noted the low percentage of experimental studies in gifted education more generally (e.g., Dai, Swanson, & Cheng, 2011; Jolly & Kettler, 2008; Plucker & Callahan, 2014). These limitations notwithstanding, it is important for program designers, teachers, researchers, and other decision makers to understand the research support for widely advocated practices for gifted learners and to acknowledge gaps in the current evidence base.

Curriculum for gifted students

Kettler (2016) delineates four levels of curriculum, reflecting its concurrent nature as (a) a *course of study*, (b) a set of *defined standards* for content mastery and student

Designing and adapting curriculum **97**

achievement, (c) a sequence of *learning experiences* designed by teachers to enable student engagement with defined content, and (d) a process of *authentic engagement* by students in a field of study. In considering how these complementary levels can be leveraged to develop educational experiences for gifted learners, the question arises: when does a curriculum become a *gifted education* curriculum? Any response to this question embodies assumptions about the nature of giftedness and the identity of gifted education as a field of scholarship and practice, including its relationship to the broader field of education.

Early advocates recommended discrete, specialised learning experiences for students identified as gifted (typically through superior performance on tests of general intellectual ability). Usually delivered in selective classes, these learning experiences were designed to address common intellectual characteristics of gifted students. By implication, this approach of designating a separate 'gifted' curriculum assumes that learning experiences for gifted students are not appropriate for 'non-gifted' students (Hertberg-Davis & Callahan, 2013).

Practitioners such as Stedman (1924) and Hollingworth (1926) were among the first to define special educational opportunities for gifted learners. Hollingworth's recommendations for curricular enrichment (engaging with topics not usually offered in the school curriculum) and extension (completing more advanced work related to the regular curriculum) included to reduce repetition or 'drill'; emphasise group work and the relationships between disciplinary elements through the 'project method'; employ a seminar style of teaching, with opportunities for questioning and sharing ideas; provide access to advanced resources and reference materials; encourage students to share and explore their own special interests; encourage independence; include the study of biographies of eminent individuals; encourage the study of a foreign language; focus on the history of civilizations, to prepare gifted students to make original contributions to society; and foster "the development of industrious habits" (1926, p. 334) so that gifted students learn to engage deeply with content and do not expect learning to be effortless. Hollingworth's recommendations can be understood in their historical context as a response to the predominantly teacher-directed, drill-based teaching methods of her time. However, the emphasis on enriching curriculum through access to topics not ordinarily studied, project-based learning, high-level questioning, and encouraging students' personal interests has endured in gifted education.

Scholars have continued to build upon and adapt the foundations of Hollingworth's work. Contributions such as (but not limited to) those from Ward (1961), Passow and Tannenbaum (1978), Renzulli (1977), and Kaplan (1979) helped to define and refine a set of principles and practices for crafting curriculum for gifted students. These include a focus on in-depth, interest-based study; promoting higher-order thinking skills through engagement with abstract concepts; the development of products that are original and challenge existing ideas; exposure to enrichment activities not ordinarily included in the curriculum; and the development of research and thinking skills that can be applied to engagement with 'real-world' problems.

98 Jane M. Jarvis

Despite ongoing support for core principles of curriculum design, VanTassel-Baska (2009) points out that the misapplication of these principles (particularly those concerning enrichment and differentiation) has sometimes resulted in questionable, or even counterproductive, practices in the name of gifted education. Examples include curriculum for gifted students that has been (a) selected solely on the basis that it includes topics not offered through the regular classroom curriculum (e.g., "computer programming, moral and ethical dilemmas, and foreign language," p. 266); (b) focussed on providing special privileges for gifted students, such as excursions or special projects, that are not available to others; and/or (c) concerned with teaching general skills of critical and/or creative thinking, which are now considered to be essential for all students. Tomlinson (2009) further notes that in practice, curriculum and learning experiences for gifted students have often stemmed from the personal interests of a gifted education teacher or coordinator, without a comprehensive scope and sequence across topics or years. Without a clear understanding of its own 'instructional identity' (Tomlinson, 1996) and relationship to broader educational goals and practices, gifted education remains open to well-documented charges of elitism.

In a study of gifted education practices in South Australian schools, Jarvis and Henderson (2012) found evidence of the seemingly arbitrary selection of curriculum topics and lack of planned scope and sequence for pull-out classes noted earlier; some participants explained these choices in terms of working within available resources, while others appeared to suggest that the content of pull-out classes was secondary to the benefits gifted students would gain simply from being with others of similar ability. The practice of grouping gifted students together has received consistent support in the literature, and can certainly have social and affective benefits for gifted learners (e.g., Rogers, 2007). However, researchers caution that simply grouping gifted students together without providing appropriately challenging work does little to encourage meaningful collaboration (Diezmann & Watters, 2001) and adds little value to student learning. In other words, the grouping configuration is not an end in itself, but should serve the purpose of enabling access to appropriately challenging learning experiences.

Curriculum for gifted students or curriculum for all students?

In Australia and New Zealand, the formal identification of gifted students and the development of specialised learning opportunities are not mandated. While a small percentage of highly able students may attend selective schools, most are educated in mainstream, mixed-ability classrooms. In both countries, national curriculum documents refer to gifted students in the context of broader statements about learner diversity and inclusive practices, and articulate the expectation that teachers will use a common curriculum framework as a basis for designing and adapting learning experiences for the full range of learners (Australian Curriculum, Assessment & Reporting Authority [ACARA], 2014a; Ministry of Education,

2007, 2008). These documents reflect a shift in the broader educational discourse towards a rights-based concern with inclusion (Moltzen, 2011). In this context, it is particularly important to consider the relationship between curriculum for gifted students and curriculum suitable for all students.

Many principles and practices that originated from gifted education are now considered non-negotiable for a broader student population (e.g., Hertberg-Davis & Callahan, 2013; Hockett, 2009). These include the teaching of higher-order thinking skills, inquiry learning approaches, and the development of skills and competencies associated with creative productivity (Renzulli, 2012). In the current educational climate, the development of 21st-century skills is touted as a central goal of schooling for all students, who must be prepared to live and work within a flexible, technology-rich, globalised world in jobs that do not yet exist. These broad aims are reflected in the Australian Curriculum framework, which gives prominence to critical and creative thinking capabilities across disciplines (ACARA, 2014b). In New Zealand, the National Education Goals similarly include the "development of the knowledge, understanding and skills needed by New Zealanders to compete successfully in the modern, ever-changing world" (Ministry of Education, 2015, para. 4).

Highlighting the contemporary congruence between gifted education and general education, Hockett (2009) synthesised principles of quality curriculum recommended by experts and researchers in both fields. These include:

- Based around key concepts
- Focussed on essential skills, ideas, and principles of the discipline
- Flexible in response to student differences
- Moves students progressively towards higher levels of expertise within a discipline
- Emphasises student outcomes, including deep conceptual understanding
- Relevant and engaging to students
- Integrative, maintaining a balance between depth and breadth

Similarly, in outlining the foundations for the Parallel Curriculum Model (PCM), Tomlinson et al. (2002, 2009) defined principles of quality curriculum for all learners, including those showing advanced performance or high potential. These principles emphasise the organisation of content around essential facts and skills, as well as deeper conceptual understandings. They also promote guided opportunities for students to solve problems and create products that are purposeful and useful, to make personal connections to the content, to make choices, to collaborate in meaningful ways, and to be mentally and affectively challenged and supported (Tomlinson et al., 2002, 2009). Notably, the PCM deliberately amalgamated elements from several established curriculum models in gifted education into a single framework, namely Kaplan's (1979, 2014) Depth and Complexity, Renzulli's Enrichment Triad (1977) and Multiple Menu (Renzulli, Leppien, & Hays, 2000) models, and Tomlinson's (2001, 2014) differentiated instruction. The PCM therefore embodies best-practice principles from gifted education but is presented as a flexible model that

100 Jane M. Jarvis

can be applied for a diverse range of learners, including through the "ascending intellectual demand" component, which allows for increasingly complex learning experiences as students progress through a discipline.

If practices that were once considered uniquely appropriate for gifted learners are now germane to the education of all learners, does gifted education have a unique identity? Or, is curriculum for gifted students 'just good curriculum'? Some commentators warn against subsuming learning experiences for gifted students under general headings of 'good teaching' or 'good curriculum' (e.g., Kaplan, 2007). For example, it has been noted that while the term "differentiation" originally described a qualitatively different approach to curriculum and pedagogy for academically gifted students, it has since been 'commandeered' by mainstream education as an approach suitable for all learners (e.g., Jolly, 2016). This has obvious potential benefits, including an enhanced focus on addressing learner diversity in all classrooms. However, the drawback is that a very general differentiated approach may dilute any focus on the specific needs of gifted students. That is, mandating a differentiated approach will not automatically engender appropriate curriculum and teaching for gifted students in heterogeneous classrooms, especially without targeted, ongoing professional development and support for teachers (Hertberg-Davis, 2009). Research has also suggested that even with access to challenging, concept-based curriculum (such as through International Baccalaureate and Advanced Placement courses), many gifted students still require differentiated learning experiences and additional provisions to address their learning needs (Hertberg-Davis & Callahan, 2008). These include opportunities to build background knowledge, to work with content in a variety of ways, and to explore individual areas of interest; students who are traditionally underrepresented in advanced classes, such as twice-exceptional students and those from low socio-economic backgrounds, may especially benefit from additional supports and tailored learning opportunities (Hertberg-Davis & Callahan, 2008). Within any curricular framework, it is essential to acknowledge that gifted students are diverse, and there is no single curriculum for "the gifted" that will suit all students' needs at all times (Kaplan, 2009).

How then can curriculum that is suitable for gifted students be distinguished from simply 'good curriculum'? An early method to address this question was proposed by Passow (1982) through his "would, could, should" rule of thumb to evaluate learning experiences designed for gifted students. Passow suggested that we consider: (a) *Would* other students choose to participate in this learning experience if given the choice? (b) *Could* other students be successful in the program given appropriate support? and (c) *Should* all students have the opportunity to participate in this learning opportunity? If the answer is 'yes' to any of these questions, then the curriculum or program may not be defensible as uniquely appropriate for gifted students.

Tomlinson (2005) takes a different, albeit related, route to defining the distinction, suggesting that curriculum that is appropriate for gifted students must be firmly grounded in quality curriculum for all learners, which can then be differentiated through (a) planned variations in pacing, (b) adjustments to the level of complexity with which content is studied (to provide appropriate levels of challenge), and (c) opportunities to study advanced areas of interest in more intensive ways than might otherwise be offered. For example, highly able students may be challenged to work with professional-level resources, learn specialised terminology, or engage with more complex questions in small-group discussion while studying the same key concepts as students working at grade level (Jarvis, 2017). Thus, while all students require access to important concepts and ideas, they benefit from engaging with that content at a pace and level of complexity that is commensurate with their current knowledge and skill (readiness), and they are likely to experience greatest engagement when they are able to draw upon and expand their personal interests; therefore, the difference between good general curriculum and good curriculum for gifted students can be understood as a matter of degree. The degree of adjustment and the selection of specific elements to modify will differ depending on individual learner need.

For school-based educators, contemporary gifted education can perhaps be characterised as having three interrelated goals: (a) to respond to students who already display advanced academic performance, (b) to nurture potential in students who might be currently underperforming for a range of reasons, and (c) to raise the standard of curriculum and teaching for all learners through the integration of gifted education pedagogies and a focus on development towards higher levels of expertise (Jarvis, 2009; Jarvis & Henderson, 2014). A school-wide response addressing all three goals will necessarily be multi-faceted, but the starting point must be high-quality curriculum and teaching for all learners. Several contemporary gifted education program models have been developed around the assumption that many 'gifted' practices can be integrated at the foundational layer of enriched curriculum for all learners, which enables subsequent layers of more targeted, intensive opportunities for students who display high levels of interest, motivation, and ability; examples include the Schoolwide Enrichment Model (Renzulli & Reis, 1985, 2010) and Levels of Service (Treffinger, Young, Nassab, Selby, & Wittig, 2008). These and other multi-tiered approaches are conceptually consistent with contemporary intervention models in special education, behavioural support, and mental health (Jarvis, 2017), suggesting an opportunity to align gifted education with other whole-school initiatives.

Curriculum design in context

Callahan and Hertberg-Davis (2013) maintain that, while there is no single 'right' way to design exemplary services for gifted students, there are multiple 'wrong' ways that are unlikely to result in effective learning outcomes. These include assuming that all the answers for all gifted students are known; botching together the individual components of educational philosophy, definitions of giftedness, program design, and curriculum in a way that results in misalignment; choosing services and curriculum based on what other schools use, without appreciating the opportunities and complexities of the local context; and making choices based on "either the charismatic speaker or attractive, easy-to-use but inappropriate curricular materials" (p. xii). These are important caveats when considering curriculum and teaching practices for gifted students. Rather than, "What curriculum and teaching practices are effective for gifted learners?", a wiser question may be, "*For which groups of gifted students* does a particular curriculum or set of teaching practices have demonstrated effectiveness, *in what setting/s* and *under what conditions?*" For educators and school leaders, a related question should be, "Which evidence-based curriculum provides the best fit for our students, program goals, and available resources?" This more nuanced questioning is important to ensure that the choice of a particular curriculum model or set of materials is defensible, sustainable, and likely to result in worthwhile learning outcomes.

Herewini, Tiakiwai, and Hawksworth (2012) provide a particularly insightful account of how one Māori school in New Zealand sought to negotiate a definition, set of goals, identification process, and model of curriculum and teaching that arose from and were owned by the Māori community, while simultaneously being informed by predominantly Western practices. Considerations of curriculum and pedagogy were closely aligned with deeper values of the local community, which contributed to the perceived success of this program. Similarly, in his account of the Wii Gaay ('clever child') program for gifted Aboriginal students in New South Wales, Merrotsy (2006) explains how the curriculum incorporated cultural and relationship-building activities led by Aboriginal community leaders, and engagement with cultural and academic mentors and role models, in addition to integrated approaches to building essential academic skills through interest-based investigations. Involvement by Aboriginal community leaders at all stages of planning and implementation ensured that curricular content was culturally relevant and engendered a sense of shared ownership of the gifted program.

Beyond (albeit related to) issues of local community context, the choice of curriculum and teaching approaches depends upon a perception of the underlying goals of gifted education (VanTassel-Baska, 2013). For example, Olszewski-Kubilius and Calvert (2016) propose that curriculum aimed at talent development (with future high performance or eminence in a specific talent domain as the end goal) will have a different focus than where the goal is advanced academic performance, or where the aim is to address the immediate learning needs of individual students in the context of F–12 classrooms. An evidence-based understanding of curriculum for talent development is still evolving, but since the goal is to identify and develop domain-specific abilities, curriculum design should emphasise opportunities to develop and nurture domain-specific interests through enrichment (Hertzog, 2017), to master advanced domain-specific content, to access appropriate mentors and coaches, and to foster relevant non-cognitive factors associated with high-level engagement and performance (Olszewski-Kubilius & Calvert, 2016). Curriculum is tailored to the individual in different ways at different stages in the talent development process, and may look qualitatively different across domains.

By contrast to the talent development model, an 'advanced academics' approach to gifted education seeks to ensure that students' academic needs are addressed through consistently engaging, challenging curriculum across the school years (Peters & Matthews, 2016). Accordingly, decisions about curriculum design and differentiation are made within (rather than beyond) the framework of general school curriculum. From a research perspective, this approach assumes that:

> it may be difficult or impossible to conduct research on curriculum effectiveness in gifted education considering the diverse nature of the gifted population. Perhaps more fruitful avenues of research include studies of interventions designed to alleviate academic need fostered by the mismatch between student ability and the curriculum.
>
> *(Peters & Matthews, 2016, p. 67)*

The long-running U.S. Study of Mathematically Precocious Youth (SMPY) provides a good example of the synergy between program purpose and curriculum design. A key focus of this project is on identifying and nurturing precocious intellectual ability, predominantly in the areas of mathematics and science (Lubinski & Benbow, 2006). This body of research confirms that while a constellation of factors predict future success, ongoing access to accelerated content and targeted domain-relevant experiences significantly enhance the likelihood that intellectually precocious children (as measured by tests of quantitative and spatial reasoning) will go on to make high-level contributions in maths and science fields.

Curriculum models in gifted education

There has been limited robust research into the effectiveness of different curriculum and teaching approaches advocated in gifted education, particularly in Australia and New Zealand. For example, while enrichment – providing access to topics not ordinarily covered in the standard, year-level curriculum – is regularly touted as appropriate for gifted students, research evaluating enrichment opportunities for academically gifted students is far from comprehensive (Subotnik, Olszewski-Kubilius, & Worrell, 2011). VanTassel-Baska (2003) groups the range of evidence-based approaches to curriculum and instruction for academically gifted students into three types: (a) *content mastery* (approaches that enable students to move through content at a faster pace, with adjustments for complexity), (b) *process-product* (opportunities that focus on the development of inquiry skills, often applied to content of interest to individuals or small groups of students), and (c) *conceptual or epistemological* (where curriculum is designed to promote deep understanding of transferable concepts, applied across disciplines). Each of these general approaches has been the subject of research supporting its effectiveness for specific groups of gifted learners, under certain conditions.

VanTassel-Baska and Brown's (2007) review of research into the effectiveness of various curriculum models in gifted education, with studies selected based on a set of criteria, including a framework for curriculum design and development, transferability across contexts and year levels, differentiated features for gifted students,

104 Jane M. Jarvis

clear relationship to national standards and school-based curriculum, evidence of scope and sequence considerations, and longitudinal evidence of effectiveness with gifted students. The authors found that, from an initial pool, only 11 studies met the criteria, and none included student populations from Australia or New Zealand. Selected research-based curriculum models are discussed in the following sections, as a representative sample of research in this field.

Integrated Curriculum Model (ICM)

Among the most extensively researched curriculum models for gifted or advanced students is the Integrated Curriculum Model (ICM) developed by VanTassel-Baska and colleagues in the U.S. (VanTassel-Baska & Wood, 2009). The ICM aims to address the academic needs of gifted students through the inter-related dimensions of (a) advanced content, (b) higher-order reasoning and production (the process–product dimension), and (c) in-depth study of key disciplinary (and interdisciplinary) concepts and issues.

While the ICM provides a framework to guide curriculum design by teachers, researchers have developed and evaluated a series of units and supporting resources across multiple learning areas and age groups, over a period of several decades. For example, a series of studies illustrated that in classrooms implementing researcher-developed ICM science units, gifted students outperformed those in comparison classrooms on tests of scientific knowledge (Kim et al., 2012), scientific reasoning, and application of the scientific method (Feng, VanTassel-Baska, Quek, Bai, & O'Neill, 2005). Studies have also shown specific learning gains for gifted students studying ICM units in English (VanTassel-Baska, Bracken, Feng, & Brown, 2009; VanTassel-Baska, Zuo, Avery, & Little, 2002) and Social Studies (Little, Feng, VanTassel-Baska, Rogers, & Avery, 2007). Notably, research supporting the ICM highlights the key role of teachers in implementing the units with fidelity and underscores the need for professional development and support to help teachers understand and apply the model (Little et al., 2007). This is consistent with other research on the faithful implementation of researcher-developed curriculum (e.g., Misset & Foster, 2015).

CLEAR curriculum model

A more recent curriculum model (the "CLEAR" model) was developed by U.S. researchers based on a synthesis of elements from Tomlinson's (2001, 2014) differentiated instruction, the Schoolwide Enrichment Model (Renzulli & Reis, 1985), and Kaplan's (1979, 2014) Depth and Complexity model. A series of primary English units based on the CLEAR model was implemented in a large-scale research study involving students in over 100 classrooms across different states (Callahan et al., 2015). Students who engaged with the CLEAR units significantly outperformed students in comparison classrooms on researcher-developed assessments and performance assessments, after controlling for entry-level achievement

(Callahan et al., 2015). Currently, researchers are investigating the use of CLEAR curriculum units with gifted students in rural settings (Azano, Callahan, Broodersen, & Caughey, 2017).

Another large study evaluated history curriculum units based on many of the same design elements as both ICM and CLEAR (Stoddard, Tieso, & Robbins, 2015). These units were implemented with a deliberately diverse range of students and school settings, including schools in low socio-economic areas, students from diverse cultural and linguistic backgrounds, and students with identified special needs. In comparison to students who were taught their regular history curriculum, students who engaged in these units showed significantly greater gains on standardised assessments (Stoddard et al., 2015). The findings from this study affirm the principle that supported engagement with rich curriculum can be an important catalyst for some students' talents to come to the fore, particularly those who have lacked consistent access to rich learning experiences and who may not be identified as gifted through traditional, achievement-oriented identification processes (Jarvis, 2009; Walsh, Kemp, Hodge, & Bowes, 2012).

Projects M^3 and M^2

While the format differed from the CLEAR units, another group of researchers similarly designed units according to a framework that incorporated aspects of existing curriculum models in gifted education. Project M^3 involved the development and implementation of maths curriculum units for gifted and promising primary mathematics students across diverse school sites (Gavin et al., 2007). Aspects of curriculum design included the opportunity to engage like practicing professionals in a field, to apply the tools and methods of a discipline, and to make connections across disciplines. The units also incorporated a focus on advanced mathematical concepts, complexity of content, depth of mathematical understanding, differentiated instruction, and supported a nurturing classroom environment. Researchers found significant differences between the treatment and comparison groups on standardized and researcher-developed maths measures (Gavin, Casa, Adelson, Carroll, & Sheffield, 2009).

In subsequent studies, Project M^2 involved the design of challenging measurement and geometry units for junior primary students, based on the framework used in Project M^3 (Gavin, Casa, Firmender, & Carroll, 2013). The curriculum exposed students to further advanced, challenging mathematics than were normally encountered at that year level. While there were no significant differences on a traditional, standardised measure of maths knowledge, the treatment group significantly outperformed the comparison group on the open-response assessment, which relied upon deeper mathematical understanding (Gavin, Casa, Adelson, & Firmender, 2013). In a further study with kindergarten students, the treatment group outperformed comparison groups on both sets of measures (Casa, Firmender, Gavin, & Carroll, 2016).

106 Jane M. Jarvis

Australian and New Zealand research

In Australia and New Zealand, there have been no large-scale, multi-site research studies evaluating particular curriculum models for diverse gifted students across subject areas, age groups, and settings. Such research would be in line with calls for systematic studies to evaluate current practices and provisions in gifted education, to inform national policy (e.g., Moltzen, 2003).

The most commonly researched topic related to curriculum and teaching for gifted students in Australia and New Zealand has been acceleration. Depending on how it is implemented, acceleration could be considered a model of programming or provision rather than a curriculum model per se, but it does reflect VanTassel-Baska's (2003) description of the content mastery element of curriculum for gifted students. In recent years, most discussions of acceleration have cited Hattie's (2009) estimate of its strong effect size ($d = 0.88$) in relation to student achievement. Hattie's conclusion that acceleration represents one of the strongest influences on student achievement of all school-level practices was based on two meta-analyses (Kulik & Kulik, 1984; Kulik, 2004) that did not include research from Australia or New Zealand. However, research in both countries has affirmed the overall positive social, affective, and academic outcomes for gifted students who experience some form of acceleration (see Vasilevska & Merrotsy, 2011, for an annotated bibliography of Australian research on acceleration).

In terms of differentiation and enrichment of curriculum for gifted students, Australian and New Zealand research has primarily involved descriptions of curriculum or special learning opportunities (e.g., Aldous, Barnes, & Clark, 2008; Riley, MacIntyre, Bicknell, & Cutler, 2010); studies of teachers' practices, beliefs, and attitudes related to curriculum and teaching strategies for gifted students (e.g., Kronborg & Plunkett, 2013; Smith, 2015) and research on gifted students' social and affective experiences of engaging with challenging curriculum (e.g., Bate, Clark, & Riley, 2013; Eddles-Hirsch, Vialle, McCormick, & Rogers, 2012; Kronborg, Plunkett, Kelly, & Urquhart, 2008). Other studies have focussed on curriculum or instruction for a specific population of gifted students, such as those from Indigenous backgrounds (e.g., Chaffey & Brown, 1999), pre-school children (e.g., Walsh & Kemp, 2012) or twice-exceptional learners (e.g., Clark, 2016), or on specific curriculum areas such as maths (e.g., Diezmann & Watters, 2001).

This body of research has contributed important insights into the nature and role of appropriate curriculum and teaching approaches for gifted learners. However, there remains a need for a coherent, comprehensive evidence base about the effectiveness of specific curriculum models and teaching strategies for a diverse range of gifted students. In particular, few studies have included robust measures of student learning outcomes; consequently, there is little research systematically investigating the relationship between curriculum approaches and student learning. Furthermore, few studies have included a comparison group of similar-ability students not engaged in the curricular intervention that is the subject of the research, or have compared learning outcomes for gifted students with those not identified as gifted. Most studies have not incorporated multiple outcome measures or included students across diverse sites. A body of well-designed research on the effectiveness of curriculum approaches suitable for gifted students, including large-scale, multi-site studies where possible, is likely to be particularly beneficial to inform policy makers, teacher educators, and stakeholders. This is a priority for future gifted education research in Australia and New Zealand, despite the challenges inherent in developing such an evidence base.

Discussion Questions

- Consider a curriculum unit that is familiar to you. What opportunities might there be to adjust elements of the unit so that some students can work through content at a faster pace or engage with concepts at a higher level of complexity?
- Why is local context important when making decisions about designing and adapting curriculum for gifted students?
- How would you define the relationship between good curriculum for all students and good curriculum for gifted students?
- Why is it important to include measures of student learning outcomes in the design of research studies on curriculum for gifted students?

References

Aldous, C., Barnes, A., & Clark, J. (2008). Engaging excellent Aboriginal students in science: An innovation in culturally inclusive schooling. *Teaching Science, 54*(4), 35–39.

Australian Curriculum, Assessment and Reporting Authority (ACARA). (2014a). *Student diversity advice*. Retrieved from www.australiancurriculum.edu.au/studentdiversity/student-diversity-advice

Australian Curriculum, Assessment and Reporting Authority (ACARA). (2014b). *General capabilities*. Retrieved from www.australiancurriculum.edu.au/generalcapabilities/overview/introduction

Azano, A. P., Callahan, C. M., Broodersen, A. V., & Caughey, M. (2017). Responding to the challenges of gifted education in rural communities. *Global Education Review, 4*(1), 62–77.

Bate, J., Clark, D., & Riley, T. (2013). Gifted kids curriculum: What do the students say? *Kairaranga, 13*(2), 23–28.

Callahan, C. M., & Hertberg-Davis, H. L. (Eds.). (2013). *Fundamentals of gifted education: Considering multiple perspectives*. New York, NY: Routledge.

Callahan, C. M., Moon, T. R., Oh, S., Azano, A. P., & Hailey, E. P. (2015). What works in gifted education: Documenting the effects of an integrated curricular/instructional model for gifted students. *American Education Research Journal, 52*, 137–167.

Casa, T. M., Firmender, J. M., Gavin, M. K., & Carroll, S. R. (2016). Kindergarteners' achievement on geometry and measurement units that incorporate a gifted education approach. *Gifted Child Quarterly, 61*, 52–72.

Chaffey, G., & Brown, D. (1999). Developing potential in Aboriginal children. *Education in Rural Australia, 9*(2), 57–63.

Clark, T. R. (2016). *Exploring giftedness and autism: A study of a differentiated educational program for autistic savants.* London: Routledge.

Dai, D. Y., Swanson, J. A., & Cheng, J. (2011). State of research on giftedness and gifted education: A survey of empirical studies published during 1998–2010. *Gifted Child Quarterly, 55,* 126–138.

Diezmann, C. M., & Watters, J. J. (2001). The collaboration of mathematically gifted students on challenging tasks. *Journal for the Education of the Gifted, 25,* 7–31.

Eddles-Hirsch, K., Vialle, W., McCormick, J., & Rogers, K. (2012). Insiders or outsiders: The role of social context in the peer relations of gifted students. *Roeper Review, 34,* 53–62.

Feng, A. X., VanTassel-Baska, J., Quek, C., Bai, W., & O'Neill, B. (2005). A longitudinal assessment of gifted students' learning using the integrated curriculum model (ICM): Impacts and perceptions of the William and Mary language arts and science curriculum. *Roeper Review, 27,* 78–83.

Gavin, M. K., Casa, T. M., Adelson, J. L., Carroll, S. R., & Sheffield, L. J. (2009). The impact of advanced curriculum on the achievement of mathematically promising elementary students. *Gifted Child Quarterly, 53,* 188–202.

Gavin, M. K., Casa, T. M., Adelson, J. L., Carroll, S. R., Sheffield, L. J., & Spinelli, A. M. (2007). Project M3: Mentoring mathematical minds – A research-based curriculum for talented elementary students. *Journal of Advanced Academics, 18,* 566–585.

Gavin, M. K., Casa, T. M., Adelson, J. L., & Firmender, J. M. (2013). The impact of challenging geometry and measurement units on the achievement of Grade 2 students. *Journal for Research in Mathematics Education, 44,* 478–509.

Gavin, M. K., Casa, T. M., Firmender, J. M., & Carroll, S. (2013). The impact of advanced geometry and measurement curriculum units on the mathematics achievement of first-grade students. *Gifted Child Quarterly, 57,* 71–84.

Hattie, J. A. C. (2009). *Visible learning: A synthesis of over 800 meta-analyses relating to achievement.* London: Routledge.

Herewini, L., Tiakiwai, S., & Hawksworth, L. (2012). Gifted and talented. *Set, 2,* 41–48.

Hertberg-Davis, H. L. (2009). Myth 7: Differentiation in the regular classroom is equivalent to gifted programs and is sufficient: Classroom teachers have the time, the skill, and the will to differentiate adequately. *Gifted Child Quarterly, 53,* 251–253.

Hertberg-Davis, H. L., & Callahan, C. M. (2008). Gifted students' perceptions of advanced placement and international baccalaureate programs. *Gifted Child Quarterly, 52,* 199–216.

Hertberg-Davis, H. L., & Callahan, C. M. (2013). *Fundamentals of gifted education: Considering multiple perspectives.* New York, NY: Routledge.

Hertzog, N. B. (2017). Designing the learning context in school for talent development. *Gifted Child Quarterly, 61,* 219–228.

Hockett, J. A. (2009). Curriculum for highly able learners that conforms to general education and gifted education quality indicators. *Journal for the Education of the Gifted, 32,* 394–440.

Hollingworth, L. S. (1926). *Gifted children: Their nature and nurture.* Oxford: Palgrave Macmillan.

Jarvis, J. M. (2009). Planning to unmask potential through responsive curriculum: The 'famous five' exercise. *Roeper Review, 31,* 234–241.

Jarvis, J. M. (2017). Supporting diverse gifted students. In M. Hyde, L. Carpenter, & S. Dole (Eds.), *Diversity, inclusion and engagement* (3rd ed.). Port Melbourne, VIC: Oxford University Press.

Jarvis, J. M., & Henderson, L. (2012). Current practices in the education of advanced learners in South Australian schools. *Australasian Journal of Gifted Education, 21*(1), 5–22.

Jarvis, J. M., & Henderson, L. (2014). Defining a coordinated approach to gifted education. *Australasian Journal of Gifted Education, 23*(1), 5–14.

Jolly, J. L. (2016). Differentiated curriculum: Learning from the past and exploring the future. In T. Kettler (Ed.), *Modern curriculum for gifted and advanced academic students* (pp. 23–36). Waco, TX: Prufrock Press.

Jolly, J. L., & Kettler, T. (2008). Gifted education research 1994–2003: A disconnect between priorities and practice. *Journal for the Education of the Gifted, 31*, 427–446.

Kaplan, S. N. (1979). *Inservice training manual: Activities for developing curriculum for the gifted and talented.* Los Angeles, CA: National/State Leadership Training Institute on the Gifted and Talented.

Kaplan, S. N. (2007). Differentiation: Asset or liability for gifted education? *Gifted Child Today, 30*(3), 23–24.

Kaplan, S. N. (2009). Myth 9: There is a single curriculum for the gifted. *Gifted Child Quarterly, 53*, 257–258.

Kaplan, S. N. (2014). Depth and complexity. In C. M. Callahan & H. L. Hertberg-Davis (Eds.), *Fundamentals of gifted education: Considering multiple perspectives* (pp. 277–286). New York, NY: Routledge.

Kettler, T. (2016). Curriculum design in an era of ubiquitous information and technology: New possibilities for gifted education. In T. Kettler (Ed.), *Modern curriculum for gifted and advanced academic students* (pp. 3–22). Waco, TX: Prufrock Press.

Kim, K. H., VanTassel-Baska, J., Bracken, B. A., Feng, A., Stambaugh, T., & Bland, L. (2012). Project Clarion: Three years of science instruction in Title I schools among K-third grade students. *Research in Science Education, 42*, 813–829.

Kronborg, L., & Plunkett, M. (2013). Responding to professional learning: How effective teachers differentiate teaching and learning strategies to engage highly able adolescents. *Australasian Journal of Gifted Education, 22*(2), 52–63.

Kronborg, L., Plunkett, M., Kelly, L., & Urquhart, F. (2008). Student attitudes towards learning in differentiated settings. *Australasian Journal of Gifted Education, 17*(2), 23–32.

Kulik, J. A. (2004). Meta-analytic studies of acceleration. In N. Colangelo, S. G. Assouline, & M. U. M. Gross (Eds.), *A nation deceived: How schools hold back America's brightest students* (Vol. II, pp. 13–22). Iowa City, IA: Connie Belin and Jacqueline N. Blank International Center for Gifted Education and Talent Development.

Kulik, J. A., & Kulik, C. C. (1984). Effects of accelerated instruction on students. *Review of Educational Research, 54*, 409–425.

Little, C. A., Feng, A. X., VanTassel-Baska, J., Rogers, K. B., & Avery, L. D. (2007). A study of curriculum effectiveness in social studies. *Gifted Child Quarterly, 51*, 272–284.

Lubinski, D., & Benbow, C. P. (2006). Study of mathematically precocious youth after 35 years, uncovering antecedents for the development of science expertise. *Perspectives on Psychological Science, 1*, 316–345.

Merrotsy, P. (2006, November). *The Wii Gaay project: Gifted Aboriginal students.* Paper presented at the 12th Aboriginal Studies Association Conference, Sydney, NSW.

Ministry of Education. (2007). *The New Zealand curriculum for English-medium teaching and learning in years 1–13.* Wellington, NZ: Learning Media.

Ministry of Education. (2008). *Te Marautanga o Aotearoa.* Wellington, NZ: Learning Media.

Ministry of Education. (2015). *The national education goals.* Retrieved from https://education.govt.nz/ministry-of-education/legislation/negs

Missett, T. C., & Foster, L. H. (2015). Searching for evidence-based practice: A survey of empirical studies on curricular interventions measuring and reporting fidelity of implementation published during 2004–2013. *Journal of Advanced Academics, 26,* 96–111.

Moltzen, R. I. (2003). Gifted education in New Zealand. *Gifted Education International, 18*, 139–152.

Moltzen, R. I. (2011). Inclusive education and gifted and talented provision. In G. Richards & F. Armstrong (Eds.), *Teaching and learning in diverse and inclusive classrooms: Key issues for new teachers* (pp. 102–112). London: Routledge.

Olszewski-Kubilius, P., & Calvert, E. (2016). Implications of the talent development framework for curriculum design. In T. Kettler (Ed.), *Modern curriculum for gifted and advanced academic students* (pp. 37–54). Waco, TX: Prufrock Press.

Passow, A. H. (1982). *Differentiated curricula for the gifted and talented: Committee report to the National/State leadership training institute on the gifted and talented.* Ventura County, CA: Office of the Superintendent of Schools.

Passow, A. H., & Tannenbaum, A. J. (1978). *Differentiated curriculum for the gifted and talented: A conceptual model.* Rockville, MD: Office of Projects for the Gifted and Talented Montgomery County Schools.

Peters, S., & Matthews, M. S. (2016). An advanced academics approach to curriculum building. In T. Kettler (Ed.), *Modern curriculum for gifted and advanced academic students* (pp. 55–68). Waco, TX: Prufrock Press.

Plucker, J. A., & Callahan, C. M. (2014). Research on giftedness and gifted education: Status of the field and considerations for the future. *Exceptional Children, 80,* 390–406.

Renzulli, J. S. (1977). The enrichment triad model: A plan for developing defensible programs for the gifted and talented. *Gifted Child Quarterly, 21,* 227–233.

Renzulli, J. S. (2012). Re-examining the role of gifted education and talent development for the 21st Century: A four-part theoretical approach. *Gifted Child Quarterly, 56,* 150–159.

Renzulli, J. S., Leppien, J. H., & Hays, T. (2000). *The multiple menu model.* Storrs, CT: Creative Learning Press.

Renzulli, J. S., & Reis, S. M. (1985). *The schoolwide enrichment model: A comprehensive plan for educational excellence.* Mansfield, CT: Creative Learning Press.

Renzulli, J. S., & Reis, S. M. (2010). The schoolwide enrichment model: A focus on student strengths and interests. *Gifted Education International, 26*(2–3), 140–157.

Riley, T., MacIntyre, B., Bicknell, B., & Cutler, S. (2010). Diving in and exploring curricular frameworks: The New Zealand Marine Studies Centre Programme. *Gifted Education International, 26,* 234–238.

Rogers, K. B. (2007). Lessons learned about educating the gifted and talented: A synthesis of the research on educational practice. *Gifted Child Quarterly, 51,* 382–396.

Smith, S. (2015). A dynamic differentiation framework for talent enhancement: Findings from syntheses and teachers' perspectives. *Australasian Journal of Gifted Education, 24*(1), 59–72.

Stedman, L. M. (1924). *Education of gifted children.* Yonkers-On-Hudson, NY: World Book Company.

Stoddard, J. D., Tieso, C. L., & Robbins, J. I. (2015). Project CIVIS: Curriculum development and assessment of underserved and underachieving middle school populations. *Journal of Advanced Academics, 26,* 168–196.

Subotnik, R. F., Olszewski-Kubilius, P., & Worrell, F. C. (2011). Rethinking giftedness and gifted education: A proposed direction forward based on psychological science. *Psychological Science in the Public Interest, 12,* 3–54.

Tomlinson, C. A. (1996). Good teaching for one and all: Does gifted education have an instructional identity? *Journal for the Education of the Gifted, 20,* 155–174.

Tomlinson, C. A. (2001). *How to differentiate instruction in mixed-ability classrooms.* Alexandria, VA: Association for Supervision and Curriculum Development.

Tomlinson, C. A. (2005). Quality curriculum and instruction for highly able learners. *Theory into Practice, 44,* 160–166.

Tomlinson, C. A. (2009). Myth 8: The "patch-on" approach to programming is effective. *Gifted Child Quarterly, 53*, 254–256.

Tomlinson, C. A. (2014). *The differentiated classroom: Responding to the needs of all learners* (2nd ed.). Alexandria, VA: Association for Supervision and Curriculum Development.

Tomlinson, C. A., Kaplan, S. N., Renzulli, J. S., Purcell, J., Leppien, J., & Burns, D. (2002). *The parallel curriculum model: A design to develop high potential and challenge high-ability learners.* Thousand Oaks, CA: Corwin Press.

Tomlinson, C. A., Kaplan, S. N., Renzulli, J. S., Purcell, J., Leppien, J., Burns, D., Strickland, C. A., & Imbeau, M. B. (2009). *The parallel curriculum model: A design to develop high potential and challenge high-ability learners* (2nd ed.). Thousand Oaks, CA: Corwin Press.

Treffinger, D. J., Young, G. C., Nassab, C. A., Selby, E. C., & Wittig, C. V. (2008). *The talent development planning handbook: Designing inclusive gifted programs.* Thousand Oaks, CA: Corwin Press.

VanTassel-Baska, J. (2003). Content-based curriculum for high-ability learners: An introduction. In J. VanTassel-Baska & C. Little (Eds.), *Content-based curriculum for high-ability learners* (pp. 1–24). Waco, TX: Prufrock Press.

VanTassel-Baska, J. (2009). Myth 12: Gifted programs should stick out like a sore thumb. *Gifted Child Quarterly, 53*, 266–268.

VanTassel-Baska, J. (2013). Matching curriculum, instruction and assessment. In J. A. Plucker & C. M. Callahan (Eds.), *Critical issues and practices in gifted education* (pp. 377–385). Waco, TX: Prufrock Press.

VanTassel-Baska, J., Bracken, B., Feng, A., & Brown, E. (2009). A longitudinal study of enhancing critical thinking and reading comprehension in title I classrooms. *Journal for the Education of the Gifted, 33*, 7–37.

VanTassel-Baska, J., & Brown, E. F. (2007). Toward best practice: An analysis of the efficacy of curriculum models in gifted education. *Gifted Child Quarterly, 51*, 342–358.

VanTassel-Baska, J., & Wood, S. (2009). The integrated curriculum model. In J. S. Renzulli, E. J. Gubbins, K. S. McMillen, R. D. Eckert, & C. A. Little (Eds.), *Systems and models for developing programs for the gifted and talented* (2nd ed., pp. 655–691). Storrs, CT: Creative Learning Press.

VanTassel-Baska, J., Zuo, J. L., Avery, L. D., & Little, C. A. (2002). A curriculum study of gifted student learning in the language arts. *Gifted Child Quarterly, 46*, 30–44.

Vasilevska, S., & Merrotsy, P. (2011). Academic acceleration in Australia: An annotated bibliography. *TalentEd, 27*, 75–126.

Walsh, R. L., & Kemp, C. R. (2012). Evaluating interventions for young gifted children using single-subject methodology: A preliminary study. *Gifted Child Quarterly, 57*, 110–120.

Walsh, R. L., Kemp, C. R., Hodge, K. A., & Bowes, J. M. (2012). Searching for evidence-based practice: A review of the research on educational interventions for intellectually gifted children in the early childhood years. *Journal for the Education of the Gifted, 35*, 103–138.

Ward, V. S. (1961). *Educating the gifted: An axiomatic approach.* Columbus, OH: Merrill.

8

SCHOOL PROGRAMS AND STRATEGIES FOR GIFTED LEARNERS

Lesley Henderson and Tracy Riley

Guiding Questions

- What are the key elements of program design for gifted and talented students?
- How do programs for gifted students align with whole-school values and practices?
- What can the research tell us about the principles of effective and sustainable programs for gifted students?
- Why is it important to evaluate programs for gifted and talented students?

Key Ideas

- Gifted and talented students require qualitatively different learning opportunities extending beyond what can be provided in the regular classroom.
- There should be a continuum of provisions for gifted students within the school and broader community.
- Both enrichment and acceleration should be available as options for gifted and talented students to ensure that they have positive learning and developmental outcomes.
- Gifted programs should align with the school vision and articulate with other programs and services so that gifted programs are integral to the whole school's educational mission.
- No single program will suit all students in all contexts – educators and parents need to consider principles, purposes, and research evidence of program design in making informed decisions.

- High-quality programs are designed with evaluation in mind and are strengthened by what is learned through evaluation processes.
- Additional evaluation and systematic research needs to be undertaken in the Australian and New Zealand contexts.

Programs for gifted and talented students: essential considerations

There is no single provision that will meet the needs of all gifted and talented students in all contexts all of the time. A variety of program models and options can be considered to address the academic and affective needs of gifted and talented students – albeit with limited empirical support for their effectiveness in Australia and New Zealand. The intention of this chapter is not to summarise the range of program options nor to describe a few good programs, but instead to consider the factors that contribute to the development, management, and evaluation of sustainable, high-quality gifted programs that are effective in meeting the needs of gifted and talented students. When considering program options, instead of asking "which program should I implement?" decision makers are instead encouraged to ask "for which students in what context might this program be effective?" or, as Long, Barnett, and Rogers asked, "what are the factors that ultimately contribute to the scope and quality of gifted programs?" (2015, p. 121).

Clarification of terms

The term *gifted program* is used in this chapter to refer to a planned set of services and provisions designed for gifted and talented students within the student population of any school or centre. One provision on its own is unlikely to suffice, but neither will a number of disparate and disconnected provisions necessarily be effective. The scope of gifted programs will be described as being multi-dimensional with all elements "combined in thoughtful ways into a spectrum of services" (Hertberg-Davis & Callahan, 2013, p. 161) that determine a school or centre's entire approach to the education of its gifted and talented students. The quality of a gifted program will be indicated by the appropriateness of the services and provisions for whom they are designed and the effectiveness of their implementation as determined by ongoing review and evaluation processes. The sustainability of a gifted program will depend on the level of priority assigned to the program, the resources invested, the professional development provided for all staff, and the degree to which the program is owned and embraced by the whole school (Jarvis & Henderson, 2014). Gifted program evaluation will also be considered in this chapter, as it is integral to the process of design, review, and redesign of gifted programs and the determination of their effectiveness and impact on whole-school improvement. No single definition of giftedness and talent is provided in this chapter, because adopting or developing a definition will be an initial step taken in developing a gifted program. Whichever definition is applied, the expectation is that gifted programs will provide educational challenges and supports that are required by highly able students in order for them to learn, achieve, and experience healthy well-being.

The purpose of the gifted program

Giftedness on its own is no guarantee of successful academic outcomes, so how a school provides for its gifted students is critical to their development (Gagné, 2013). Gifted students often learn new material at a faster pace and are capable of engaging with more complex and advanced curriculum than are their age peers. In response to these characteristics, teachers need to provide daily intellectual challenge in the gifted learner's area or areas of strength and opportunities to work at a faster pace, ideally with like-minded peers (Rogers, 2007).

Where educational policies and documents enshrine the entitlement of *all* students to an appropriately challenging and rigorous education (e.g., ACARA, 2017), teachers, schools, and centres become responsible to meet this obligation. In emphasising the need for gifted programs, advocates can appeal to the individual student's entitlement to an education that meets their needs and enables them to flourish.

Seen in this light, gifted education is positioned inclusively, but this can be somewhat problematic. For example, although the New Zealand Education Review Office reports that 80% of schools are 'mostly inclusive', the evidence shows that gifted learners often remain excluded from funding, policies, and opportunities for specialist provisions. In August 2016, the New Zealand Ministry of Education announced that it was strengthening inclusive education and modernising its delivery of services. The Ministry has adopted the term 'learning support' rather than special education, discarding language that accentuates differences and barriers. Despite the change in language from special to inclusive education, the policies do not go far enough to include gifted – this would require changes in funding and infrastructure. Schools are responsible for gifted students, as mandated in New Zealand's National Administration Guidelines. Without significant investment to enable capability and capacity, inclusive education is often exclusive, even somewhat elusive, when it comes to the needs of gifted and talented students. Gifted and talented students, it can be argued, have not faced marginalisation or exclusion in terms of their access to or participation in local schools or age-appropriate settings, but they may have been excluded from learning in these environments (Kearney, Bevan-Brown, Haworth, & Riley, 2008).

A gifted program should be aligned with the school's vision, strategic plan, and teaching and learning plan for all students, and thereby supported by the school community and promoted by the school's leadership. With student cohorts comprising diverse students with wide-ranging needs, the gifted program articulates how the school or centre's stated purposes are achieved for the gifted and talented students in that population. Ongoing evaluation will provide evidence of the program's effectiveness. And the gifted program is ideally encompassed within a policy that is reviewed and revised regularly to ensure that the intended learning outcomes are being achieved in the planned ways, and that the gifted program remains relevant to the school or centre's priorities. Longitudinal studies indicate that students who participate in high-quality gifted programs not only benefit personally but are also more likely to make high-level contributions to society in their chosen talent domains (Freeman, 2001; Gross, 2006; Lubinski, Webb, Morelock, & Benbow, 2001; Simonton, 1999).

The scope of gifted programs

The scope of gifted programs "refers to the range of provisions offered, the identification procedures associated with these provisions and the administration and management of such provisions, including professional development for staff" (Long, Barnett, & Rogers, 2015 p. 120). Responding to learner differences by way of programming demonstrates the inter-relatedness of how we conceptualise gifted education, with the learning and behavioural characteristics seen in gifted students, formal and informal identification, a continuum of programs, and, ultimately, evaluations to determine effectiveness. These interrelated factors have been depicted by the New Zealand Ministry of Education (2012) as shown in Figure 8.1, acting as

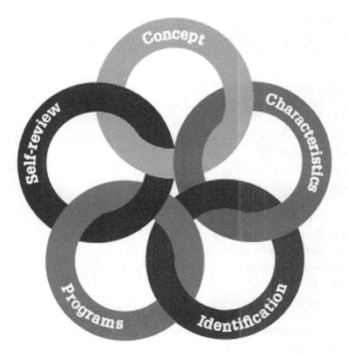

FIGURE 8.1 The interrelationships among concept, characteristics, identification, programs, and self-review

Source: New Zealand Ministry of Education (2012, p. 9)

guidance for schools in designing, developing, and reviewing programs for gifted students.

This figure is a reminder that no element of gifted education should be viewed in isolation; rather, all components are dynamic and interrelated. How a school community defines giftedness will influence the learning and behavioural characteristics typically recognised, in turn influencing identification methods, programs, and review or evaluation mechanisms (McAlpine, 1996; New Zealand Ministry of Education, 2012).

Some elements of gifted programs, such as definitions, identification, and classroom provisions, are addressed in other chapters within this book, so the focus of this chapter is on the provisions, resources, and systems within the school and community that provide enrichment and acceleration opportunities beyond the differentiated classroom program for identified students.

In their research in Northern Ireland, Mcgarvey, Marriott, Morgan, and Abbott (1997) found that successfully implemented programs had the following defined elements:

- A clear and consistent definition of giftedness
- An overarching philosophy
- Identification criteria and procedures that were consistent with their philosophy and definition of giftedness
- Clear program goals and objectives
- Differentiated curriculum
- Professional learning for school personnel and parents (a point also confirmed by Chessman, 2007; Lassig, 2009)
- Program personnel with a clear position statement
- A budget and allocation of resources
- A system for program evaluation

The list of elements highlights that the scope of successfully implemented programs is comprehensive and well-considered.

Reis and Gubbins (2017) framed the design of gifted programs in terms of seeking answers to the following six questions:

1 Who will be served?
2 How will students be identified?
3 What program model will be used?
4 What types of learning opportunities will be provided?
5 Where will service options be offered?
6 When will services be offered? (p. 59)

In the process of addressing these questions, Reis and Gubbins emphasised that a number of factors need to be considered, "including funding, the availability of trained personnel, and the level of challenge and depth of the regular curriculum" (2017, p. 59).

Differentiation in inclusive classrooms as the foundation for gifted programs

With identification serving as a mediating link between conceptualisations of giftedness and programs, effective identification methods unveil students' special abilities, qualities, and interests, with the aim of differentiation being to further develop, enhance, and build those strengths. Gifted learners are not a homogenous group; they bring with them different learning preferences, skills, abilities, motivation, expectations, and experiences, which differentiation may be able to respond to through "doing different kinds of things, not simply more of the same things" (New Zealand Ministry of Education, 2012, p. 55). Therefore, differentiation requires a vital set of competencies for teachers in today's classrooms of learners with cultural and linguistic diversity, varying cognitive abilities, different learning preferences, and wide-ranging socio-economic backgrounds.

The notion of differentiation has "become a mainstream concept in education, considered key to raising student performance and closing the achievement gap" (Pappano, 2011, p. 3). In particular, differentiated curriculum, delivered in more flexible and responsive learning environments, provides an important way to support *all* learners and minimise barriers to learning.

For gifted students, daily engagement in high-quality learning tasks that are differentiated to provide appropriate challenge in the regular classroom is the foundation upon which the gifted program is grounded. High-quality differentiated curriculum is a way that previously unidentified students may be identified. For example, Walsh (2014) found that only when young children were asked open-ended higher-order questions did they provide evidence of advanced thinking and reasoning capacities in their responses.

Gifted programs as a continuum of approaches

Supported by an effectively differentiated regular classroom, the gifted program can then apply the principles of enrichment and acceleration through the provision of a continuum of approaches in a range of learning environments matched to the gifted individuals' strengths and interests, as shown in Figure 8.2. The range of options available to students should mirror the range and intensities of different abilities and qualities, and the available resources within any school or centre. These options can extend beyond the classroom and school context into online and local communities.

The research evidence for both *acceleration* and *enrichment* options is strong. Hattie (2009) ranked academic acceleration as fifth based on his meta-analyses of educational interventions that positively impact on learning and achievement, with an effect size of 0.88. His analysis of enrichment was less favourable, ranked at 68th with an effect size of 0.39. However, Kim's (2016) meta-analysis of the effects of enrichment programs on gifted students found that the effect size was much higher at 0.96, and concluded that "enrichment programs had a positive impact on both gifted students' achievement . . . and socio-emotional development" (p. 1).

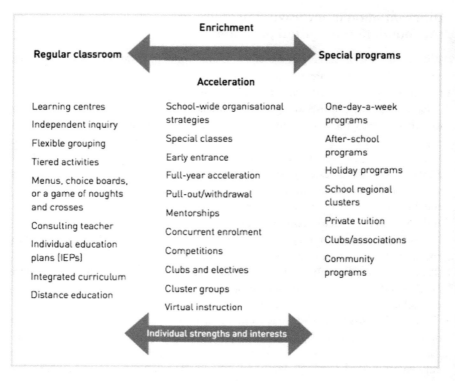

FIGURE 8.2 A continuum of approaches
Source: New Zealand Ministry of Education (2012, p. 61)

There are at least 18 forms of acceleration, including early entry into school or university, subject or grade acceleration, and curriculum compacting or telescoping (Munro, 2012). Acceleration enables students to move through the curriculum at a pace that matches their ability to learn and at a level that provides appropriate intellectual challenge. Sometimes this can be achieved within the regular classroom, but often it requires provisions beyond the regular classroom. Gross (1999) affirmed that

> well-planned programs of acceleration enhance these students' self-esteem, their love of learning, their acceptance of themselves and their gifts, and their capacity to form warm and supportive friendships. For many gifted students, acceleration replaces discord with harmony.
>
> (p. 1)

Acceleration is possibly the most widely researched, the most academically effective, and yet the most under-utilised educational intervention for gifted students, with "considerable variation between education sectors, systems and individual schools" in its implementation (Gross, Urquhart, Doyle, Juratowitch, & Matheson, 2011, p. 5).

Enrichment can also take many forms. Academic enrichment "refers to the provision of learning opportunities that give depth and breadth to the curriculum in line with students' interests, abilities, qualities and needs" (NZ Ministry of Education, 2012, p. 59). Enrichment can be an individual provision or combined with grouping procedures to provide gifted pull-out programs or cluster group activities. Well-designed enrichment activities can incorporate the kind of qualitative difference that gifted students need in their learning, building on the use of higher-order creative and critical thinking skills, ethical reasoning, and authentic problem-solving within the disciplines, in addition to the application of strategies that take into account a student's learning profile and preferences. Renzulli's Enrichment Triad Model, originally developed in 1977, has continued to be an influential gifted program model (Maker & Schiever, 2005), in addition to its extension into the Schoolwide Enrichment Model (Renzulli & Reis, 1985), based upon the underlying philosophy that the "rising tide lifts all ships" (Renzulli, 1998, p. 105).

The quality of gifted programs

Dai and Chen (2014) identified the conundrum that arises when there are so many options from which to choose and few guidelines to inform that choice:

> There is no consensus . . . as to what constitutes effective gifted programming . . . (and) such a wide range of programming choices could be a mixed blessing to stakeholders. On the one hand, a large repertoire of program and strategy options provides the vehicle for flexible adoptions and adaptions. On the other hand, however, how to determine the appropriateness and effectiveness of a given program and service in specific situations becomes a challenge.
>
> *(p. 113)*

Given the range of possible provisions that can be combined within the gifted program, and the diversity of schools and sites that design and implement gifted programs, advice relating to quality should focus on the key elements rather than on the description of the program itself. Delcourt and Siegle (1995) stated that

> a successful program for the gifted does not necessarily depend on the type of programming arrangement (within-class program, pull-out program, separate class, special school). While one type of arrangement may be more beneficial for a particular child, it is the way the program is implemented that determines its impact.
>
> *(para. 2)*

What matters is what happens within those arrangements – the quality of the learning opportunities and the richness of gifted students' experiences. Exemplary programs share common elements that emerge from a review of the literature on gifted programs and their evaluation (Callahan, 2004, 2017; Eckert & Robins, 2017; Maker, 1986; Renzulli, 1975; VanTassel-Baska & Brown, 2007). The essential elements are clarity, relevance (including cultural relevance), challenge, supports, coherence, and validity. These elements and their contribution to the quality of the gifted program are outlined in the following sections.

Clarity

Clear program goals, transparency of identification processes, and justification of resource allocation are of prime importance in a high-quality gifted program. All stakeholders should have a clear understanding of the need for the program, who it intends to serve, and its aims and supports, and a carefully articulated description of program elements (Eckert & Robins, 2017).

Relevance

Gifted programs are designed for gifted students, so one of the key markers of quality is the degree to which the program meets these students' needs, is appropriate for them, relevant to them, and valued by them. If the students are gifted in mathematics, an effective provision would provide appropriately challenging learning opportunities in mathematics. All aspects of the program, including identification measures, arrangements, and evaluation, should be appropriate for and relevant to the students selected for the program. The content of any curriculum-based provisions should be highly relevant to the discipline and represent significant knowledge and skills that are valued by professionals working in that field. Programs are also implemented within a specific school, address a specific purpose, and have constraints related to budget and time allocation, so the degree to which the program is appropriate for the context should also be considered in order that the design of the program is feasible (Maker, 1986). Schools and centres in rural and remote areas will have specific considerations relating to relevance (Plunkett, 2012; Stambaugh & Wood, 2015).

Cultural responsiveness

Relevance also extends to cultural responsiveness: does the program embrace and provide options that respect and promote what is culturally valued? While some principles upon which gifted programs can be built are universal, perhaps unique in the Australian and New Zealand context is the attention ascribed to culturally responsive principles, particularly for Indigenous peoples. Culturally responsive programs are described as holistic and developed through engagement with students, their families, and communities (Bevan-Brown, 2009). Bevan-Brown (2005) described four elements of a culturally responsive environment in Aotearoa New Zealand:

1   Teachers who value diversity generally and Māori culture specifically
2   Programs that incorporate cultural content, including knowledge, skills, customs, traditions, and language

School programs and strategies **121**

3 Programs that incorporate cultural values, beliefs, attitudes and behaviours
4 Teaching and assessment that reflects culturally preferred ways of learning

Culturally responsive programs require teachers to look firstly at their own values and beliefs and secondly at their practices (Ladsen-Billings, 1995). Bevan-Brown (2009) outlined how provisions for gifted students can be made more culturally responsive. She explained that content needs to be both culturally inclusive and interwoven in specialist provisions: "encouraging and extending children in their Māoritanga goes hand-in-hand with the development of their giftedness" (p. 15); see Bevan-Brown (2009) for examples of culturally responsive practices.

Challenge

One of Rogers' (2007) "lessons learned" about appropriate provisions for gifted students was their need for daily challenge. The appropriate level of challenge, sophistication, and complexity of learning should always be relative to the students' existing level of knowledge, skills, and understanding. It follows that the use of assessment information is significant in any gifted program. Masters (2014) would say that assessment has only one purpose: to ascertain what a student already knows in order to determine what they need to know next, and therefore to ensure that learning tasks are appropriately challenging. The use of higher-order thinking and problem-solving and principles of deep learning provide guidance in developing intellectually challenging learning opportunities, and the pace of learning for gifted students should match the speed at which they are capable of learning.

Social support

Gifted programs provide selected students with opportunities to work with similarly able peers with whom they can feel accepted and supported, and adults who are likely to understand and value them. If gifted programs operate from a physical location, they can also provide safe havens where gifted students can go to feel they belong, such as a dedicated classroom or area within the school (Farrall & Henderson, 2015). The affective needs of gifted students are well-documented (Hébert, 2016; Neihart, Pfeiffer, & Cross, 2016; Smith, 2017). Schools that foster the social and emotional development of students have been found to also improve students' academic achievement (Slee et al., 2009), so it is important to both challenge students and also support them holistically as highly able learners.

Bailey et al. (2012) found that "social interaction underlies effective strategies for gifted and talented students" (p. 43), citing several studies that evaluated gifted provisions based on social interactions. One of their conclusions was that "most forms of provision for gifted and talented students occur in social settings and students' abilities to deal with such contexts are likely to be important factors in academic success and personal motivation" (p. 44). Counselling for some gifted students as needed may also be an important component of gifted programs to support their social and emotional development and well-being (Vialle, 2012).

Coherence

One danger in providing multiple approaches within the program for gifted and talented students is when these become fragmented or add-on approaches, sometimes described as part-time solutions to full-time problems. In New Zealand, for example, in efforts to be inclusive of many different types of gifted learners, schools will sometimes provide an array of part-time, temporary, even one-off, enrichment activities (Riley et al., 2004). This type of approach does not promise a coherent learning program and can be exacerbated by a lack of specialised curriculum. Therefore, the markers of coherent gifted programs are a scope and sequence of provision, including high-quality differentiated curriculum. Ensuring that all elements within the gifted program work towards the same goals also helps to provide coherence: different options for different students in different learning areas can still all be linked by the aims of the program into a unified continuum of approaches.

Validity

With limited resources and almost unlimited needs in schools, a gifted program cannot exist or continue to exist without evidence that it makes a difference for the gifted students. In addition, data must be collected and analysed to demonstrate that the program goals have been achieved, or at least progress has been made towards achieving those goals. Any program should be grounded in research-based theories and informed by current findings about what works in practice. Monitoring the constant interplay between intention and implementation ensures that evaluation is used in a dynamic and informative way. Maker wrote that "not only must we supply evidence for the validity of individual programs, but we must, as a group, prove that the idea of special education for gifted students is a valid one" (1986, p. 347).

Professional development for personnel

Where there is agreement that gifted children have special needs and require specialised programs, by implication they are likely to require specialist personnel to lead and manage these programs (VanTassel-Baska, 2005). This is true not only of the program coordinator and the specialist teachers whose expertise in an area of learning can be applied to an enrichment activity but also classroom teachers. Gifted programs build from what the inclusive and differentiated classroom provides, so professional learning about gifted education for all staff is essential if teachers are to know how to recognise and provide for gifted students (Chessman, 2007; Henderson & Jarvis, 2016; Lassig, 2009). In addition, certain provisions require specific professional learning in order for staff to effectively implement the provision. For example, a philosophy program can only be taught by a teacher who has strong critical thinking skills and a depth of knowledge and understanding in the discipline. VanTassel Baska (2005) emphasised that "teachers of gifted students need in-depth preparation through an endorsement or certification program of studies at a university. Sustained professional development is also necessary in areas of program delivery" (p. 96).

Sustainability of gifted programs

While gifted programs require staff with gifted education backgrounds, programs need to be "bigger" than the personnel if they are to be sustainable. In a study of gifted education coordinators in South Australian schools, several participants commented that no one else could take over their role, and one remarked that "everything I do is in my head" (Henderson & Jarvis, 2017). While these gifted education practitioners may have been instrumental in establishing high-quality gifted programs in their schools, when the program is perceived to be the domain of the coordinator and dependent on their personal expertise, the program is likely to fail when that person leaves the school. This dependence on one person for gifted programs is also reported in New Zealand case studies (e.g., Riley & Moltzen, 2010; Russell & Riley, 2011), but these studies showed that over time and with professional learning, a larger number of staff "demonstrated growth in their understandings of theory and research, and this was demonstrated in their practice" (Riley & Moltzen, 2010, p. 103). This type of growth is one way of potentially ensuring sustainability, but only if coupled with high-quality gifted programs that:

- Are consistent with the school's philosophy and visions for successful student outcomes
- Are supported by the school's principal/leadership team (Long et al., 2015; Moon & Rosselli, 2000)
- Are systemically embedded in the whole school culture and approach to teaching and learning
- Exist independently of the specialised personnel
- Are supported by evaluation data and evidence that they are effective in meeting their goals and improving outcomes for gifted and talented students

In an evaluation of Ministry of Education–funded programs in New Zealand, Riley and Moltzen (2010) concluded that the key elements for sustainable gifted programs are documentation, professional learning and development, ongoing evaluation, and a secure source of funding. They reported that these factors enabled "sustainability, and potentially transferability, with some degree of certainty" (p. 144).

Importantly, the case study programs incorporated the following processes of evaluation, which may have positively influenced program sustainability through accountability:

- Systems to determine the needs of stakeholders. As the programs were being implemented and evaluated, the systems were refined in an attempt to better match the program to stakeholders' needs
- Commitment to ongoing data collection to determine program effectiveness

- Responsiveness to evaluation processes, both internal and external, as shown in cyclical program change and improvement
- Program evolution leading to a more effective program that was more closely aligned with its intended outcomes and goals (Riley & Moltzen, 2010, p. 102)

Program evaluation

A gifted program is a purposeful investment of resources and, in order to justify its continuance, there needs to be accountability for its effectiveness. Program evaluation is also a means for continual improvement as the program is reviewed, revised, and renewed (Riley et al., 2004). Table 8.1 provides questions designed for an evaluation of gifted programs (Riley & Moltzen, 2010), which could be applied to an investigation of schools' or centres' provisions for gifted and talented students.

Few rigorous, systematic, and objective evaluations of gifted programs have been reported in the Australian and New Zealand research literature. This may be due to a lack of time for evaluation on the part of school-based coordinators (Jarvis & Henderson, 2012), or a lack of priority placed on evaluation, or a lack of knowledge about the evaluation processes. It may be that gifted program coordinators seldom consider the evaluation of the program to be of equal importance to the design and implementation of the program (Callahan, 2004, 2017; Riley et al., 2004). In cases where gifted programs are evaluated, it appears that program coordinators commonly use surveys of student and parent satisfaction as evidence of the program's effectiveness (Braggett & Moltzen, 2000; Freeman, Raffan, & Warwick, 2010). However, Moon (2017) reflected that "not all evidence is equal or should be given equal weight in decision making – particularly when considering programmatic or policy decisions" (p. 240). Criticisms of gifted programs arise when there is no documented evidence of any improvement in learning outcomes or achievement for the intended students, or no evidence that the program provides a level of challenge and complexity beyond what could be achieved through the regular curriculum.

Program evaluation should be considered from the outset of the gifted program's inception so that the design process has a built-in set of success criteria that can be monitored in an ongoing manner. The design of clearly articulated program goals is needed so that the achievement of those goals can inform the evaluation process. Because quality gifted programs are designed to be comprehensive in nature, multiple evaluation tools and strategies should be applied at different stages of the program.

Riley et al. (2004) found evaluating gifted programs difficult when the evaluation process was imposed as an add-on to the program, rather than being an integral component. Riley and Moltzen (2010) recommended using an action research approach as it "provides the flexibility and fluidity needed for parallel evolution of the program and the evaluation" (p. 29). Their recommendations included:

1   Using a team approach, which is inclusive of stakeholders from within the school community, but also professionals external to the school who may have expertise

School programs and strategies **125**

TABLE 8.1 Gifted program evaluation questions (Riley & Moltzen, 2010)

What is going on?	*Is it working?*	*How do we know?*
How were decisions around the program design arrived at? Who was involved in the decision-making process? How has the process impacted upon the sustainability of the program?	How appropriate were the identification procedures, curriculum adaptations, and forms of assessment in relation to the program goals?	How comprehensive are provider-initiated student and program monitoring and evaluations?
What changes in climate and philosophy have been required for the successful implementation of this program?	What aspects of curriculum differentiation have been designed specifically to meet the major objectives of the program?	How do the findings of the monitoring or evaluation inform the program?
How have professional leaders approached the task of climate change, how were these changes managed, and how were changes in practice achieved?	To what extent has this specific program design contributed to improved student outcomes?	What is the evidence for improved student learning and social, emotional, or cultural outcomes as a result of participation in the program?
How appropriate were the identification procedures, curriculum adaptations, and forms of assessment in relation to the program goals?		How have resources and personnel impacted on the success or otherwise of the program?
What aspects of curriculum differentiation have been designed specifically to meet the major program objectives?		What role has staff professional development played in achieving program goals?
		How well has the program planning occurred in regard to sustainability? What has the impact of the program been on the whole organisation?

2   Carefully matching the evaluation purposes with the methods of data collection
3   Developing trust and clarifying roles of all those involved in the evaluation process
4   Using the results of evaluation for program improvement; this requires gathering practical information by asking practice-driven questions

Tailoring gifted programs for specific contexts

Bailey et al. (2012) found that "it is difficult to draw clear conclusions about generalisable pedagogies due to the large number of variables that can affect students, teachers, and learning environments" (p. 45). Contextual, philosophical, and personal variables are identified by Moon and Rosselli (2000) as pervasive influences on the design and effectiveness of gifted programs. They used the term "situated program development" (p. 506) to refer to the process whereby all aspects of program design, implementation, and evaluation retain a clear focus on specific needs and complexities within the local context. What is needed, according to Dai and Chen (2014), "is more process-oriented, context-sensitive research that answers important questions of how a practical model works, rather than merely whether it works" (p. 35). They suggested that design-based research

> is more sensitive to valued goals, resources, and constraints of a program or service. Rather than merely determine whether a program is effective, design-based research asks further questions, such as:
>
> - How it is made more effective, and for what outcomes?
> - What are the trade-offs in achieving its valued goals?
> - What constraints should be satisfied for its success?
>
> *(p. 35)*

The ELEVATE program in New South Wales (Hoekman, 2016) and the ChallenGE Project in South Australia are two examples of the application of design thinking to program development, implementation, and evaluation in an attempt to improve outcomes for gifted students in the independent schools sector. Design thinking "privileges the user's subjective perspective" (Yeager et al., 2016, p. 375) and therefore is sensitive to and respectful of gifted students. The process of program design in the ELEVATE and ChallenGE projects using this approach begins with the participating schools collecting data in their own context about stakeholders' goals and analysing that data to identify existing promising practices and areas for change. Practitioners are then guided to design and implement a prototype intervention, which is subsequently reviewed, revised, and scaled up to the whole school. In this way, the unique character of the school context, the students, and personnel are at the forefront of the program design; the program is developed organically and tailored to meet the specific needs of each context and cohort.

The ChallenGE Project, currently operating in partnership with Flinders University in Adelaide, has a parallel research component in progress. The research component is using design-based research methodology to investigate characteristics of effective provisions, personnel, and environments. It is hoped that this research will provide some local answers to Dai and Chen's questions about the critical characteristics of innovative, context-specific, purposeful programs and contexts for enhancing outcomes for gifted students.

Implications for research

Schools across Australia and New Zealand vary in their approaches to the education of gifted students. Several studies have attempted to determine current programs and provisions in specific geographic areas (Jarvis & Henderson, 2012; Riley et al., 2004; Walker & Barlow, 1990). A clearer picture of the nature and scope of gifted education programs would help to establish current practices and use of resources and identify areas of need. In addition, research is needed in Australia and New Zealand that provides evidence of the effectiveness of gifted programs and optimal contexts for the development of giftedness, to build a stronger understanding of best practice for gifted students across all levels of education. Bailey et al.'s (2012) systematic review of research studies examining gifted and talented classroom interventions concluded that, "If research in the field of gifted and talented education is to influence practice then it is essential that the quality of research design and reporting be improved" (p. 45). Advocacy for the establishment, resourcing, and maintenance of gifted programs in schools is dependent on strong evidence that gifted programs are effective in improving student outcomes; the design of gifted programs is dependent on sound research evidence.

Conclusion

For teachers and leaders who are contemplating the establishment of a gifted program, this chapter is intended to provide a framework of principles reflecting best practice. Advice to anyone in the early stages of program design is to start small, review, revise, and scale up as the evidence becomes clear that program elements are achieving their intended outcomes. For teachers and school leaders with responsibility for existing gifted programs, the principles discussed in this chapter may inform a review of existing approaches with a view to strengthening what is effective and making changes as appropriate. All coordinators of gifted programs are encouraged to be mindful of their own well-being, to be realistic about what can be achieved within the time and resources allocated, to seek support from colleagues within the school and professional gifted education networks, and to establish an advisory group of stakeholders who are invested in the gifted program and can help to ensure its viability, effectiveness, and sustainability. With the publication of more program evaluation research, the evidence that gifted programs are an essential part of an inclusive educational landscape can be strengthened.

Discussion Questions

- Applying the principles of program design, evaluate a current program in your school or centre. In what ways might the program be changed and adapted to reflect the stated principles and meet the needs of your specific context?

- Thinking about a particular gifted child or group of gifted children, design a program to enrich or accelerate their learning. Ensure that you address all elements of effective program design.
- "Gifted programs are often used by schools for marketing purposes or to keep parents happy." Discuss the implications of this statement for the design and implementation of programs for gifted students.

References

ACARA. (2017). *Student diversity advice*. Retrieved from www.australiancurriculum.edu.au/studentdiversity/student-diversity-advice

Bailey, R., Pearce, G., Smith, C., Sutherland, M., Stack, N., Winstanley, C., & Dickenson, M. (2012). Improving the educational achievement of gifted and talented students: A systematic review. *Talent Development and Excellence, 4*(1), 33–48.

Bevan-Brown, J. M. (2009). Identifying and providing for gifted and talented Māori students. *APEX: The New Zealand Journal of Gifted Education, 15*(4), 6–20.

Braggett, E. J., & Moltzen, R. I. (2000). Programs and practices for identifying and nurturing giftedness and talent in Australian and New Zealand. In K. A. Heller, F. J. Monks, R. J. Sternberg, & R. F. Subotnik (Eds.), *International handbook of giftedness and talent* (pp. 779–798). Oxford: Elsevier.

Callahan, C. M. (2004). *Program evaluation in gifted education*. Thousand Oaks, CA: Corwin Press.

Callahan, C. M. (2017). Developing a plan for evaluating services provided to gifted students. In R. D. Eckert & J. H. Robins (Eds.), *Designing services and programs for high-ability learners: A guidebook for gifted education* (2nd ed., pp. 225–238). Thousand Oaks, CA: Corwin Press.

Chessman, A. (2007). *Catering for difference: Institutionalising a program for gifted students in a NSW comprehensive high school*. Sydney, NSW: Australian Government, New South Wales Department of Education and Training.

Dai, D. Y., & Chen, F. (2014). *Paradigms of gifted education: A guide to theory-based, practice-focused research*. Waco, TX: Prufrock Press.

Delcourt, M. A. B., & Siegle, D. (1995). *What educators and parents need to know about elementary school programs in gifted education: Practitioners' Guide A9508* [Brochure]. Retrieved from http://nrcgt.uconn.edu/online_resources/

Eckert, R. D., & Robins, J. H. (Eds.) (2017). *Designing services and programs for high-ability learners: A guidebook for gifted education* (2nd ed.). Thousand Oaks, CA: Corwin Press.

Farrall, J., & Henderson, L. C. (2015). *Supporting your gifted and talented child's achievement and well-being: A resource for parents*. Adelaide, SA: AISSA.

Freeman, J. (2001). *Gifted children grown up*. London: David Fulton Publishers.

Freeman, J., Raffan, D., & Warwick, I. (2010). *Worldwide provision to develop gifts and talents: An international survey*. Reading, UK: CfBT Education Trust.

Gagné, F. (2013). The DMGT 2.0: From gifted inputs to talented outputs. In C. M. Callahan & H. L. Hertberg-Davis (Eds.), *Fundamentals of gifted education: Considering multiple perspectives* (pp. 56–68). New York, NY: Routledge.

Gross, M. U. M. (1999). *From "the saddest sound" to the D Major chord: The gift of accelerated progression*. Retrieved from www.hoagiesgifted.org/d_major_chord.htm

Gross, M. U. M. (2006). Exceptionally gifted children: Long-term outcomes of academic acceleration and non acceleration. *Journal for the Education of the Gifted, 29*, 404–429.

Gross, M. U. M., Urquhart, R., Doyle, J., Juratowitch, M., & Matheson, G. (2011). *Releasing the brakes for high-ability learners: Administrator, teacher and parent attitudes and beliefs*

School programs and strategies **129**

that block or assist the implementation of school policies on academic acceleration. Sydney, NSW: GERRIC.

Hattie, J. A. C. (2009). *Visible learning: A synthesis of over 800 meta-analyses relating to achievement.* Abingdon, Oxon: Routledge.

Hébert, T. P. (2016). *Understanding the social and emotional lives of gifted students* (2nd ed.). Waco, TX: Prufrock Press.

Henderson, L. C., & Jarvis, J. M. (2016). The gifted dimension of the Australian Professional Standards for Teachers: Implications for professional learning. *Australian Journal of Teacher Education, 41*(8), 60–83.

Henderson, L. C., & Jarvis, J. M. (2017). *The role of the gifted education coordinator in South Australian schools.* Manuscript in preparation.

Hertberg-Davis, H. L., & Callahan, C. M. (2013). Contexts for instruction: An introduction to service delivery options and programming models in gifted education. In C. M. Callahan & H. L. Hertberg-Davis (Eds.), *Fundamentals of gifted education: Considering multiple perspectives* (pp. 161–163). New York, NY: Routledge.

Hoekman, K. (2016, October). *Applying disciplined design to unleash the brilliance of Australia's high potential learners: ELEVATE Program partnerships and communities.* Paper presented at the AAEGT National Gifted Conference: Beyond the boundaries, Sydney, NSW.

Jarvis, J. M., & Henderson, L. C. (2012). Current practices in the education of gifted and advanced learners in South Australian Schools. *Australasian Journal of Gifted Education, 21*(1), 5–22.

Jarvis, J. M., & Henderson, L. C. (2014). Defining a coordinated approach to gifted education. *Australasian Journal of Gifted Education, 23*(1), 5–14.

Kearney, A. C., Bevan Brown, J. M., Haworth, P. A., & Riley, T. L. (2008). Inclusive education: Looking through the kaleidoscope of diversity. In A. St. George, S. Brown, & J. O'Neill (Eds.), *Facing the big questions in teaching: Purpose, power and learning* (pp. 109–120). Melbourne, VIC: Cengage Learning.

Kim, M. (2016). A meta – analysis of the effects of enrichment programs on gifted students. *Gifted Child Quarterly, 60*, 102–116.

Ladsen-Billings, G. (1995). Toward a theory of culturally relevant pedagogy. *American Educational Research Journal, 32*, 465–491.

Lassig, C. J. (2009). Teachers' attitudes towards the gifted: The importance of professional development and school culture. *Australasian Journal of Gifted Education, 18*(2), 32–42.

Long, L. C., Barnett, K., & Rogers, K. B. (2015). Exploring the relationship between principal, policy and gifted program scope and quality. *Journal for the Education of the Gifted, 38*, 118–140.

Lubinski, D., Webb, R. M., Morelock, M. J., & Benbow, C. P. (2001). Top 1 in 10,000: A 10-year follow-up of the profoundly gifted. *Journal of Applied Psychology, 86*, 718–729.

Maker, C. J. (Ed.) (1986). *Critical issues in gifted education: Defensible programs for the gifted.* Salem, MA: Aspen Publishers.

Maker, C. J., & Schiever, S. W. (2005). *Teaching models in education of the gifted* (3rd ed.). Austin, TX: Pro-Ed.

Masters, G. N. (2014). *Assessment: Getting to the essence.* Retrieved from www.acer.edu.au/files/uploads/Assessment_Getting_to_the_essence.pdf

McAlpine, D. (1996). The identification of children with special abilities. In D. McAlpine & R. Moltzen (Eds.), *Gifted and talented: New Zealand perspectives* (pp. 63–90). Palmerston North, NZ: Massey University E.R.D.C. Press.

Mcgarvey, B., Marriott, S., Morgan, V., & Abbott, L. (1997). Planning for differentiation: The experience of teachers in Northern Ireland primary schools. *Journal of Curriculum Studies, 29*, 351–364.

Moon, S. P., & Rosselli, H. (2000). Developing gifted programs. In K. A. Heller, F. J. Monks, R. J. Sternberg, & R. F. Subotnik (Eds.), *International handbook of giftedness and talent* (2nd ed., pp. 499–521). Oxford: Elsevier Science.

Moon, T. (2017). Using scientifically based research to make decisions about gifted education programs, services, and resources. In R. D. Eckert & J. H. Robins (Eds.), *Designing services and programs for high-ability learners: A guidebook for gifted education* (2nd ed., pp. 239–255). Thousand Oaks, CA: Corwin Press.

Munro, J. (2012, August). *Effective strategies for implementing differentiated instruction.* Paper presented at the Australian Council for Educational Research Conference 2012, New South Wales, Australia.

Neihart, M., Pfeiffer, S. I., & Cross, T. L. (2016). *The social and emotional development of gifted children: What do we know?* (2nd ed.). Waco, TX: Prufrock Press.

New Zealand Ministry of Education. (2012). *Gifted and talented students: Meeting their needs in New Zealand schools.* Retrieved from http://gifted.tki.org.nz/For-schools-and-teachers

Pappano, L. (2011). Differentiated instruction re-examined. *Harvard Education Letter, 27*(3), 3–5. Retrieved from http://hepg.org/hel-home/issues/27_3/helarticle/differentiated-instruction-reexamined_499

Plunkett, M. M. (2012). Justice for rural gifted students. In S. Nikakis (Ed.), *Let the tall poppies flourish: Advocating to achieve educational justice for all gifted students* (pp. 37–49). Melbourne, VIC: Heidelberg Press.

Reis, S. M., & Gubbins, J. (2017). Comprehensive program design. In R. D. Eckert & J. H. Robins (Eds.), *Designing services and programs for high-ability learners: A guidebook for gifted education* (2nd ed., pp. 58–75). Thousand Oaks, CA: Corwin Press.

Renzulli, J. S. (1975). *A guidebook for evaluating programs for the gifted and talented.* Ventura, CA: Office of the Ventura County Superintendent of Schools.

Renzulli, J. S. (1998). A rising tide lifts all ships. *The Phi Delta Kappan, 80,* 104–111.

Renzulli, J. S., & Reis, S. M. (1985). *The schoolwide enrichment model: A comprehensive plan for educational excellence.* Mansfield Center, CT: Creative Learning Press.

Riley, T. L., Bevan Brown, J. M., Bicknell, B. A., Carroll Lind, J., & Kearney, A. C. (2004). *Gifted and talented education in New Zealand.* Wellington, NZ: Ministry of Education.

Riley, T. L., & Bicknell, B. (2013). Gifted and talented education in New Zealand schools: A decade later. *APEX: The New Zealand Journal of Gifted Education, 18*(1), 1–16. Retrieved from www.giftedchildren.org.nz/apex/v18no1.php

Riley, T. L., & Moltzen, R. (2010). *Enhancing and igniting talent development initiatives: Research to determine effectiveness profile* [Commissioned Report] Wellington, NZ: Ministry of Education.

Rogers, K. M. (2007). Lessons learned about educating the gifted and talented: A synthesis of the research on educational practice. *Gifted Child Quarterly, 51,* 382–396.

Russell, V., & Riley, T. L. (2011). Personalising learning in secondary schools: Gifted education leading the way. *APEX: The New Zealand Journal of Gifted Education, 16*(1[JJ1]–[JJ2]). Retrieved from www.giftedchildren.org.nz/apex/v16art02.php

Simonton, D. K. (1999). Talent and its development: An emergenic and epigenetic model. *Psychological Review, 106,* 435–457.

Slee, P. T., Lawson, M. J., Russell, A., Askell-Williams, H., Dix, K. L., Owens, L., Skrzypiec, G., & Spears, B. (2009). *Kids matter primary evaluation: Final report.* Adelaide, SA: Centre for Analysis of Educational Futures, Flinders University of South Australia.

Smith, S. (2017). Responding to the unique social and emotional learning needs of gifted Australian students. In E. Frydenberg, A. Martin, & R. J. Collie (Eds.), *Social emotional learning in Australasia and the Asia-Pacific* (pp. 147–166). Singapore: Springer Social and Behavioural Sciences.

Stambaugh, T., & Wood, S. M. (Eds.) (2015). *Serving gifted students in rural settings*. Waco, TX: Prufrock Press.

VanTassel-Baska, J. (2005). Gifted programs and services: What are the non-negotiables? *Theory into Practice, 44*, 90–97.

VanTassel-Baska, J., & Brown, E. F. (2007). An analysis of the efficacy of curriculum models in gifted education. *Gifted Child Quarterly, 51*, 342–358.

Vialle, W. (2012). The role of school counsellors in fostering giftedness: The Australian experience. In A. Ziegler, C. Fischer, H. Stoeger, & M. Reutlinger (Eds.), *Gifted education as a life-long challenge* (pp. 265–278). Berlin: LIT-Verlag.

Walker, R., & Barlow, K. (1990, November). *The provision of education for gifted and talented children in private primary schools: A critical examination.* Paper presented at the annual conference of the Australian Association for Research in Education, Sydney, NSW.

Walsh, R. L. (2014). *Catering for the needs of intellectually gifted children in early childhood: Development and evaluation of questioning strategies to elicit higher order thinking* (Doctoral thesis). Macquarie University, NSW.

Yeager, D. S., Romero, C. S., Paunesku, D., Hulleman, C. S., Schneider, B., Hinojosa, C., . . . Dweck, C. S. (2016). Using design thinking to improve psychological interventions: The case of the growth mindset during the transition to high school. *Journal of Educational Psychology, 108*, 374–391.

9

GIFTEDNESS IN SCIENCE, TECHNOLOGY, ENGINEERING, AND MATHEMATICS

James J. Watters

Guiding Questions

- What general principles inform the education of students gifted in the domains of Science, Technology, Engineering, and Mathematics (STEM)?
- What is the status of research on experiences and programs that support gifted students in the Australian and New Zealand contexts?
- What are the challenges confronting the engagement of gifted students in STEM?

Key Ideas

- STEM and related domains of knowledge are important in advancing economic development and ensuring a sustainable society; preparing students for key vocational and professional careers; and developing competencies in scientific literacy and numeracy that are essential for all citizens.
- Gifted students, including those gifted in STEM domains, require accelerated, challenging instruction in core subject areas that match their special aptitudes.
- Gifted students benefit from opportunities to work with other gifted students; they are also more likely to engage in challenging learning experiences when grouped together with like-minded peers.
- Gifted students require highly competent teachers who both understand the nature and needs of these students and are deeply knowledgeable in the content they teach, in order to foster interests and engagement.

Introduction

> "Our best future is a future that builds on technology, innovation, ideas and imagination. It is a future with STEM."
>
> —Alan Finkel, Australian Chief Scientist

Although STEM and related domains of knowledge are important in advancing economic development and ensuring a sustainable society, they also play a significant role in almost all daily activities. At a vocational level, many contemporary trades demand sophisticated mathematical and scientific understandings (Watters & Christensen, 2013). However, scientific and technological literacy and numeracy are just as important as essential attributes of responsible citizens. An important outcome of STEM education is a general appreciation and understanding of the role that scientific evidence and logical reasoning play on a daily basis in social and political debate (Eilks, Nielsen, & Hofstein, 2014; Zeidler, 2016). Therefore, STEM education opportunities for all students, gifted or otherwise, are important so that students can engage in meaningful learning in scientific and mathematical domains.

Teaching students gifted in STEM domains

Successful approaches for extending gifted students in mathematics and science incorporate advanced and integrated content (VanTassel-Baska, 2015; VanTassel-Baska, Bass, Ries, Poland, & Avery, 1998), curriculum compacting (whereby teachers adjust the curriculum by replacing content that individual students have already mastered with new content or enrichment opportunities), and acceleration (whereby students are able to progress through content at a faster rate, including through grade-skipping or early entrance to school or university). Whether in mainstream classes or in pull-out programs, the quality and challenge of learning tasks and expertise of the teachers are paramount. For example, Tyler-Wood, Mortenson, Putney, and Cass (2000) demonstrated that students who engaged in a 2.5-hour course twice a week over 2 years, which was designed by a team of science and maths teachers and delivered through a team teaching model, significantly outperformed students in streamed classes. The teachers realigned the regular curriculum, implementing compacting principles and integrating mutually reinforcing concepts from maths and science. Students spent more mathematics and science classroom time doing hands-on activities in the pull-out classrooms as opposed to the comparison classrooms. Examples such as this highlight the significance of challenging tasks, homogeneity in grouping, and competent teachers. The approach also highlights the role of collaborative planning by specialists and teachers. Competent teaching developed through effective professional development is a fundamental requirement (Lassig, 2009; Watters, 2010).

There are many other examples in the literature where strategies like pre-testing and compacting, which focus on rich and integrated content provide challenging and valued experiences for students. Gallagher (2000) drew the distinction between

134 James J. Watters

token action and substantial action. For a few hours a week, the gifted child's needs might be met by a gifted education specialist or mentor who visits the classroom or withdraws the child for enrichment. For the rest of the time, the child's world is the regular classroom, where hopefully the teacher has the knowledge and skills to engage him or her. A similar situation can be seen where schools offer extracurricular programs such as Future Problem Solving or Tournament of the Minds, which offer a focus for gifted students but ultimately fail to provide substantial, long-term educational experiences. Considering the needs of gifted students is core business of a school.

The Australian and New Zealand contexts

Research on gifted education and related fields in Australia and New Zealand has burgeoned in the last two decades. The methodological approaches to researching gifted students has also changed during this period, with greater emphasis on qualitative designs that seek to understand how and why gifted behaviours manifest in particular ways. However, analysis of publications reported in peer-reviewed journals indicates the dominant area of research relates to the affective domain, such as studies of self-concept, self-esteem, motivation, self-perceptions, and other dimensions of socioemotional behaviour. The knowledge domain most researched has been mathematics, with approximately 15% of overall publications focussed on mathematics, representing papers with topics ranging from neurobiological studies of the brains of gifted mathematicians to educational practices such as acceleration and identification. Rigorous studies of experiences of students gifted in science, technology, or engineering are sparse. The following section focusses on programs and strategies and where appropriate highlights accompanying research.

Science

There are many initiatives targeting students with an interest in science, mostly for the purpose of encouraging them to pursue careers in science. Sponsored by Australian National University, The Australian Science Innovations coordinates competitions such as *The Big Science Competition* and *The Australian Science Olympiad* and conducts a camp for females in Years 8 and 9, which promotes a range of state-based talent searches or competitions. The Gifted Education Research, Resources, and Information Centre (GERRIC) has provided a range of holiday programs, many of which focus on scientific topics for gifted students. Other science-oriented resources are provided by the Commonwealth Scientific and Industrial Research Organisation through its Double Helix Club. These programs provide an extracurricular opportunity for gifted students to experience advanced topics.

Despite the wide range of science initiatives in Australia and New Zealand, few have been rigorously evaluated. Diezmann and Watters (2000) developed an enrichment program for children aged 5–7 years, who attended a 10-week series of workshops comprising groups of 15 in which the teacher scaffolded the development of science-related reasoning skills and knowledge construction in a social context that encouraged discourse and argument. The goal was to foster student autonomy whereby individuals were encouraged to deal with novelty, adopt a sceptical disposition towards existing ideas, and generate creative products. Selection was based on profiles provided by teachers, parents, and a student portfolio. Preservice teachers were recruited as mentors to assist students on their projects. This program was based on a pull-out model in science and continued for 10 years.

Poncini and Poncini (2000) described the engagement of a small group of high school students in school-based research projects in Tasmania. Their motive was to provide gifted students with an extracurricular learning experience that simulated real scientific investigations and exposed them to the frustrations and complications of research. Mentored by a skilled practitioner of science, students were exposed to concepts of hypothesis generation and rigorous testing, and learned skills of experimentation. The sessions were run during lunch times, and students were selected based on their level of interest. Some dropped out early, leading Poncini and Poncini to argue that interest was a decisive factor, as the students who persisted experienced the ultimate reward of their projects being published. All but one of the students progressed to university to study science or a science-related course.

Reform conducted a decade ago in New Zealand saw the science curriculum shift from an exclusively content-driven approach to a more inclusive, learner-centred approach. Coll (2007) reported a number of examples where teachers allowed students to design their own projects. Flexibility in the curriculum was a catalyst for establishing programs to support the scientifically gifted. Choice, autonomy, and negotiated curricula are recurring themes identified in successful programs (e.g., Lüftenegger et al., 2015).

The Australian Science and Mathematics school on the Flinders University Campus in Adelaide is a non-selective school for students in Years 10–12 who have an interest in science and mathematics, and allows for engagement in challenging science curricula that emphasise interdisciplinary problem solving. The school incorporates open-plan flexible learning spaces supported by a pedagogy designed on principles of flexibility, adaptability, interactivity, and collaboration (Oliver & Fisher, 2015). Students explore topics that include nanotechnology, biotechnology, forensic science, satellite mathematics, and photonics, and the curriculum emphasises the application of science and mathematics in industry. Other specialist schools in science include the John Monash Science School (Victoria) and the Queensland Academy for Science, Mathematics, and Technology.

One potentially innovative formal subject offered in the Queensland system is Science-21, which enables students in Years 11 and 12 to explore scientific themes in real-world contexts. This interdisciplinary science course is designed to broaden students' understanding of relevant science in today's scientific and technological age and represents a challenging and rigorous course of study.

Technology

The role of technology in gifted education can take two broad forms. Technology can be a focus of learning and a tool for learning. Advocacy for the use of technology with gifted students in the Australian context tracks back to Knight and Knight (1994), who noted uptake of technology was slow but saw avenues for supporting gifted students through word processing, access to databases, desktop publishing, simulations, and games. They advocated for students to learn programming languages, which is a contemporary focus in education. Many have argued that technology as a tool can facilitate individualised learning by delivering interactive learning materials differentiated for the gifted (McVey, 2008). Autonomous access to databases, resources, and online projects provides challenge and motivation and can facilitate the building of relationships among like-minded students. While there are encouraging examples of the use of technology to enhance learning for gifted students, the lower participation rates of girls and Indigenous students in technology subjects, as in all STEM domains, remains a challenge (e.g., Google & Gallup, 2016).

Nicholas and Ng (2009) reported on a two-phase program involving internet technologies to extend the learning of a group of interested or highly able 13- to 15-year-old students. The first phase was a four-day camp in Victoria where 32 students drawn from multiple schools engaged in a range of activities related to sun and space science. The second phase (involving 50% of camp participants) occurred when students returned to their respective schools and joined an online learning community (via Moodle). Students were encouraged to investigate a range of topics including social and ethical issues, with facilitators available to help students complete topics. Based on the follow-up data, researchers reported that eight students were active in contributing to discussion forums. As the school term progressed, the frequency of logging into the system and posting dropped off. Most students completed their projects; however, the researchers concluded that competition with regular school commitments and the reliance on ongoing scaffolding by mentors were constraints.

In a small-scale case study, Knights (2017) drew upon activity theory to analyse the approach used by three gifted boys in a Year 6 class who were able to engage with science topics using laptops. His findings included evidence that laptops provide an opportunity for gifted students to customise learning and increase engagement through self-efficacy and management, and that laptops were a tool providing gifted students with the means for greater autonomy and self-regulation of their learning.

An application of technology that dominates school practices is the programming of robots. Whilst robotics involves physics and design engineering skills, the computer programming aspect has become popular in schools, as evidenced by participation in competitions such as Robocup (Gregor, 2005).

A promising area of significance in contemporary society is the study of codes. Cryptology is the study of making (cryptography) and breaking (cryptanalysis) codes. Several institutions, including the John Hopkins Center for Talented Youth and the North Carolina School of Science and Mathematics in the U.S. are providing opportunities for gifted students to engage in coding. Summer courses teach students both the essential mathematics and history behind the codes and ciphers and how to break the codes using programming languages such as Python. After-school coding clubs and competitions are beginning to appear in Australia (e.g., CodingKids, CoderDoJo, and CodingHour). These initiatives are in their infancy, and to date there have been no substantial independent evaluations. The significance of coding has been recognised in the Australian Digital Technologies curriculum, which mandates the teaching of coding for all students from Years 3–8. The New Zealand curriculum on digital technologies is in the process of being updated to incorporate coding.

Engineering

In Australia, engineering education is captured through Design and Technologies curriculum, which incorporates areas such as Engineering Principles and Systems, Food and Fibre Production, and Materials and Technologies, and topics including Computer-Aided Design. This emphasis is the design process of identifying a problem, creating a plan, and making the product. A case study of Year 6 females engaged in engineering design (Ginns, Stein, McRobbie, & Swales, 2000) is one of very few studies on the involvement of gifted students in engineering. In the case study class, lessons focussed on structured and guided activities involving the construction and demonstration of self-propelled model boats and small-group construction of self-propelled model cars. The researchers followed gifted student Rita through this extended unit of work. Despite being described by her classroom teachers as quiet and shy, Rita displayed advanced thinking and was able to talk in-depth about the design process. The level of autonomy provided by the teacher enabled Rita to describe and explore her own ideas, argue and debate those ideas, and critically analyse the contributions of others. The researchers noted that while shyness and a lack of confidence might be interpreted as a lack of ability in some females compared to their male classmates, providing opportunities for students to collaborate in meaningful, challenging learning opportunities in engineering can bring advanced abilities to the fore.

Mathematics

An extensive review of Australian and New Zealand research on exceptional mathematics students, including gifted students and those with learning difficulties, was published in 2004 by Diezmann, Lowrie, Bicknell, Faraghar, and Putt. A further review approximately a decade later acknowledged an ongoing paucity of research focussing on mathematically gifted students (Diezmann, Stevenson, & Fox, 2012).

Concerns about the educational experiences of mathematically gifted students were identified in an earlier case study of an 8-year-old male named Martin (Diezmann & Watters, 1997). Martin's classroom performance was atypical and of concern to his teacher, who noted that "(he) thinks differently and his interests vary from those of his peers." Martin was repeatedly at odds with the teacher over his non-conformity and adoption of non-standard mathematical algorithms. Although

138 James J. Watters

Martin was passionate about mathematical problem solving, highly motivated to solve problems, and showed advanced reasoning skills, the teacher's insistence that he 'learn' and only use the 'correct' algorithm suggests that Martin's behaviour was seen as problematic. Identification of giftedness in mathematics is challenging and often assessed through students' computational proficiency in applying standard algorithms. The insistence of 'showing your work' potentially inhibits the expression of intuition evident in many gifted mathematicians. Behaviour such as Martin's can be interpreted either as a problem or more perceptively as an indication of giftedness.

A further topic of concern to teachers is the reluctance of gifted students to work collaboratively with others. The common practice of asking gifted students who have finished their set work to help other students is controversial. Although gifted students might initially see this request as acknowledgement of their competence, they may not necessarily learn anything new and, furthermore, the less able student may not benefit. Gifted students think differently and may struggle to understand why other students fail to grasp what appear to be simple ideas. Effective group work is likely to occur through shared discussion of tasks that are appropriately challenging for all group members, allowing for students to collaboratively reach a shared understanding of a complex problem and debate possible solutions. In one study, six mathematically gifted students aged 11–12 were presented with four problems about time, which were designed to vary in complexity (Diezmann & Watters, 2001). Four zones were established in the classroom: teacher zone, quiet zone, chat zone, and work zone, providing choices for students about when to seek teacher direction and when and how to collaborate with classmates. Observation and interview data supported the proposition that the difficulty of the task influenced students' selection of how to work on each problem. When the tasks were appropriately challenging, collaboration had cognitive, metacognitive, and affective benefits for students. The authors concluded that grouping gifted students is only academically beneficial when the tasks are sufficiently challenging. Problematising mathematics tasks were also necessary to sufficiently increase the level of challenge and provide students with more interesting and mathematically worthwhile learning experiences (Diezmann & Watters, 2002).

Vertical curriculum is a form of acceleration in which students are grouped according to levels of readiness rather than according to year level or age. Ryan and Geake (2003) studied the academic progress and achievement of a group of students who were vertically grouped. The students, who nominally should have been in Years 4–7, showed mathematical progress of up to 36 months over a period of one year. In a study involving Year 4 students, a vertical curriculum was introduced in an effort to address poor attitude and a high level of anxiety to learning mathematics (Harrison & Watters, 2004). Reflections by administrators and teachers acknowledged that the approach was an effective way to differentiate the curriculum to meet the needs of both gifted learners and those who struggled with mathematics. Teachers reported that behavioural problems lessened, interest in mathematics increased, and students aspired to improve their performance to gain access to the advanced class. Parental acceptance and support also appeared to be substantial.

Studies of students who are exceptionally gifted in mathematics have been dominated by researchers associated with initiatives launched by Julian Stanley in 1972. Longitudinal analysis of career destinations of students who participated in the Study of Mathematically Precocious Youth (SMPY) and similar programs in the U.S. showed that assessment performance during the selection process predicted future eminence (Lubinski, 2016). The Australian Mathematics Competition (AMC) provides an avenue to assess the long-term achievements of Australian students. The AMC provides medals to approximately one out of every 10,000 students who participate, with 690 medals awarded between 1978 and 2006. In a survey by Leder (2011), medal winners described their interest in the field in terms of the aesthetics, beauty, and logic of mathematics. Forty percent of participants had progressed to a career that required mathematics, while many who saw mathematics as peripheral to their current career acknowledged ways that they regularly applied mathematics, such as through the skills of logic. Qualitative survey responses reflected two themes related to the development of their maths abilities at school: "having sustained periods of time to work relatively independently on challenging tasks," and "opportunities to do advanced work with mathematically talented peers outside the regular school curriculum" (Leder, 2011, p. 37).

Effective provisions for students gifted in STEM domains

Provisions can be made for gifted students at the classroom, whole school, or system levels, and may include acceleration, enrichment, differentiated curriculum, curriculum compacting, pull-out programs, individual education programs, and competitions. There are numerous popular models of curricula advocated for gifted students, mostly emanating from the U.S. (e.g., Hertberg-Davis & Callahan, 2013; Maker & Schiever, 2005; Williams, 1979) and predominantly focussing on the classroom level. An exception is Renzulli's Schoolwide Enrichment Model (Renzulli & Reis, 2010), which combines guidelines for classroom practice with recommended structural organisation of the school, and less-prescriptive approaches including vertical curriculum and streaming.

Acceleration

Although many administrators, teachers, and parents argue that acceleration is harmful from a social and emotional perspective, the evidence from multiple studies over nearly 100 years supports acceleration as an effective practice for gifted students when systematically and thoughtfully implemented (e.g., Steenbergen-Hu, Makel, & Olszewski-Kubilius, 2016; Vasilevska & Merrotsy, 2011). There are few studies of acceleration specifically in STEM areas, but many of the students who have engaged in radical acceleration have shown exceptionality in mathematics (see Gross, 2006).

Grouping strategies

Strategies such as streaming or tracking allocate high-achieving students to a single class and provide a differentiated curriculum. Streaming and other forms of homogenous grouping based on performance are critiqued on the grounds that they perpetuate educational disparities and do not "equalize student outcomes, especially for lower performing students" (Harris, 2011, p. 878). The rationale for streaming draws on the assumption that a more advanced or accelerated curriculum can be provided and that there is less diversity in academic ability in such grouped classes. Rogers' (2002) meta-analysis of ability grouping for mathematics suggests that streaming is highly effective in terms of enhancing academic achievement for high-achieving students. However, this approach and other special programs involving grouping are critiqued on the basis that they disadvantage other students by removing academic role models or impacting negatively on non-gifted students' sense of identity. A broad review of streaming highlights the complexity of the strategy (Johnston & Wildy, 2016).

Streaming in mathematics has been popular in Australia, despite resistance from policy makers at all levels and from some mathematics educators (e.g., Faragher, Hill, & Clarke, 2016). For example, Forgasz (2010) surveyed 44 secondary schools in Victoria and found that 80% of the schools implemented some form of streaming for maths in Years 7–10, with overwhelming support (75%) from teachers. In schools where streaming was not practiced, the majority of teachers supported its introduction. However, specific concerns were reported in terms of student selection processes and management problems in lower streamed classes. A similar picture has emerged in New Zealand, where a survey found that the majority of schools practised some form of ability grouping in mathematics in the first year (Year 9) of secondary school: 35% was grouped according to general ability, 18% had accelerated or advanced classes, and 13% provided some form of mathematics ability grouping (Anthony, Rawlins, Riley, & Winsley, 2002). A more recent study of 15 schools in Christchurch found that all but one used some form of streaming, although this practice might not have been specific to mathematics (Hornby & Witte, 2014).

Few studies of streaming are sufficiently detailed to explore the teaching practices and curriculum modifications implemented in streamed classes. A recent review (Johnston & Wildy, 2016) concluded that "the effects of streaming on students' personal development vary according to the context in which streaming is implemented and that teachers play a key role in mediating the adverse effects of streaming upon students" (p. 54). A positive response to streaming was voiced by students of all abilities, the majority of teachers, and parents in an intensive mixed-methods study of a Queensland school where streaming in mathematics was implemented from Years 8–10 (Watters, 2012). A salient feature was the culture of the school, which acknowledged and addressed the abilities and interests of all students. This allowed specialist teachers to support and provide challenging content to students in higher streamed classes.

Pull-out programs involve removing gifted students at regular intervals from their heterogeneous classes for special support, including enrichment activities or advanced content. The impact of a mathematics-oriented pull-out program for Year 6 students in a New Zealand primary school was reported by Bicknell and Riley (2005). Students were selected on the basis of their performance on the Progressive Achievement Test (mathematics), basic facts knowledge, and a teacher-designed problem-solving test. Selected students attended their regular mathematics class for half of each term before being withdrawn for the pull-out program, which ran for one hour each day of the school week. Participating students reflected that in their regular classrooms, maths was characterised by 'regularity and sameness', with a low level of challenge, and in a way that seemed meaningless, unconnected to the world, and mechanistic. By contrast, they described the pull-out class as far more interesting as it focussed on mathematical investigations related to real problems such as traffic flow. This finding corroborates earlier experiences emphasising the importance of mathematical investigations for gifted students (Diezmann & Watters, 2002). Participants also noted the pull-out teacher's passion, willingness to listen, and ability to relate to them (Bicknell & Riley, 2005).

Teaching strategies

Regrettably, learning areas such as science are rarely taught in ways that typify genuine science and consistently engage gifted students at a level of challenge that is commensurate with their abilities and needs. In school science, problems are well defined; the focus is on content and facts which are reproduced for assessment; there is an assumed right answer to questions; learning occurs in silos termed chemistry, physics, biology; and engagement is driven primarily by extrinsic motivation. In the world of real science, problems are ill-defined, the focus is on knowledge generation, content is integrated and holistic, and engagement is intrinsically driven in a quest for understanding or epistemic curiosity. The lament of many students is that while science is important, school science is irrelevant (Sjøberg, & Schreiner, 2010). Student engagement is predicated on interest; if students find their science learning experience uninteresting, they will disengage (Ainley & Ainley, 2011), and this applies equally to gifted students.

The Collaborative Australian Secondary Science Program (CASSP) was established by the Australian Curriculum Corporation to support effective science teaching programs, characterised by inquiry-based curriculum, formative assessment, and student-centered teaching. In a pilot study supporting the effectiveness of the program (Goodrum, 2006), high-achieving students felt less comfortable than others with an inquiry approach. This finding appears in conflict with widely accepted recommendations for an integrated, inquiry approach to science teaching for gifted students (e.g., VanTassel-Baska et al., 1998). A possible explanation for this finding is that "achieving" relates to those students who are competent at reproducing information and do not exhibit the characteristics indicative of gifted in science, such as intuition, epistemic curiosity, and ability to deal with ambiguity. The case

142 James J. Watters

could also be made that some academically able students lacked the preparation to undertake complex investigations. In the UK, Taber (2007) has noted how national curricula can constrain the adoption of strategies that support the gifted in science. He argues that when the focus of assessment shifts to higher-level cognition, demonstrating creativity, and argumentation, then teachers will be more adventurous in implementing open-ended, inquiry-oriented teaching. Perhaps the challenge of implementing inquiry-oriented science programs in regular schools is the rationale for the establishment of specialist science (and mathematics) high schools.

In fields such as engineering and technology, there are considerable opportunities for teachers to apply open-ended, inquiry-oriented approaches that are likely to engage gifted students. In particular, the broad area of design offers multiple opportunities for students to learn and apply the skills required for complex, creative problem solving. Design thinking is a skill advocated for 21st-century education and captured through the maker movement initiatives and the rise of makerspaces (Martinez & Stager, 2013). Limited research exists on gifted students' approach to the design process, but guidance can be obtained from studies on the comparison of school students or novice engineering undergraduates with expert engineers (Becker & Mentzer, 2015). A central task of engineers is to define and delimit the scope of an engineering problem. The following sequence of steps has been suggested as evident in the process:

1   Identification of a need;
2   Definition of the problem/specifications;
3   Search for information;
4   Generate ideas and possible solutions;
5   Modelling and describing how to implement the design;
6   Feasibility analysis and consideration of constraints;
7   Decide to select optimal solution;
8   Test a prototype and verify the solution; and
9   Communication.

(Childress & Maurizio, 2007, as cited in Mentzer, 2011;
Mentzer, Becker, & Sutton, 2015)

Central to the design process is reflective thinking, which comprises pre-reflective thinking, quasi-reflective thinking, and reflective thinking (King & Kitchener, 1994, 2004), recognising the transition from perceptions of knowledge being certain to one where problems are ill-structured. Studies on engineering thinking of high school students suggest that younger high school students typically apply pre-reflective thinking, whereas seniors develop quasi-reflective thinking (Atman, Chimka, Bursic, & Nachtmann, 1999). Expert engineers and other creative people apply reflective thinking, draw on metacognitive processes to assess what strategies might work, apply a flexible, methodical approach, and consider multiple criteria relevant to the problem. Novice or younger students tend to adopt a single approach to solve a problem and avoid generating and exploring alternatives

Giftedness in STEM **143**

(Atman et al., 1999). Studies such as this can help educators to identify the kinds of open-ended tasks that might encourage expert-like design thinking, and the specific skills and ways of thinking that students can be encouraged to learn and apply. However, there is scope for much more research on how gifted students approach the engineering design process.

In the area of maths, mathematical investigations are loosely defined, engaging problem-solving tasks that allow students to ask their own questions, explore their own interests, and set their own goals (Jaworski, 1994). Implementation in regular Australian primary schools has been shown to be difficult (Marshman, Clark, & Carey, 2015), and teachers require quite specific skills, including encouraging students to explain their reasoning, working from students' ideas, adopting scaffolding approaches, and limiting the level of detail provided to ensure that the task remains open-ended (McCosker & Diezmann, 2009).

Deep learning occurs when problems are posed that are just within students' reach, allowing them to struggle to find solutions. For mathematically gifted students, teachers might need to adapt mathematical problems to ensure that the level of challenge is appropriate. A 'problematised' task is one that has been differentiated to increase its complexity. Figure 9.1 provides an example of a maths task provided to primary students and a problematised version of the task that might be suitable for advanced or gifted learners, with a solution developed by two students.

Another common teaching strategy in maths involves the use of games that require the application of mathematical reasoning and can provide a rich experience for mathematically gifted students. Examples include puzzles, chess, card games, roulette, or Sudoku. Not only are games generally motivating for students, but when used effectively they are a valuable tool to encourage students to learn and discuss mathematical strategies (Ernest, 1986). Sophisticated mathematics underpins the development of some computer-based games, which can provide rich opportunities for gifted students to explore coding (Salen & Zimmerman, 2004; Van Verth & Bishop, 2015). Other popular approaches have been access to websites that provide challenging tasks (Merrotsy, 2004), including sites such as the

Regular Task: Sweets A	Problematised Task: Sweets B
Justin has [1]between 10 and 20 sweets. If he shares all of them [2]among 4 of his friends he will have [3]2 left over. How many sweets could he have had?	What would be the [1]least number of sweets in a bag, if Justin could share his sweets [3]exactly with [2]up to 5 friends?
$\frac{8\ r2}{4\lfloor 10}$ $\frac{3\ r2}{4\lfloor 14}$ $\frac{4\ r2}{4\lfloor 18}$ 10, 14, 18 lollies. (Lisa & Rachel)	60 lollies… It said five friends so you didn't really have to do "1" (Going across the diagram) 2, 3, 4, 5, 6. 2 was divisible by 30 (numbers are inverted but meaning was understood by both) it was 15, then it was 10 (moving across). It didn't work (dividing 30 by 4) so we didn't go any farer (sic) than that … because it didn't work" (meaning not divisible by 4). (Lisa & Rachel)

FIGURE 9.1 A regular task and a problematised task for lower primary students

Source: From Diezmann (2005)

144 James J. Watters

Australian Mathematics Trust or the Khan Academy that provide opportunities for students to learn in a self-paced environment. There is limited research on the specific benefits for gifted students of learning maths through gameplay and using internet-based resources to support their learning.

Finally, involvement in academic competitions is a strategy commonly used to engage gifted students in STEM domains, but this remains under-researched. Many schools participate in programs such as Tournament of the Minds, Future Problem Solving, school maths and science competitions, and programs such as the International Mathematical Olympiad. Australia's Terry Tao came to prominence as the youngest person ever to win a gold medal at the International Olympiad, and has since become one of the 21st century's most creative mathematicians. Seventeen other Australians and one New Zealander have been successful in this competition to date, including Alex Gunning from Melbourne, who has won two gold medals. Engaging with complex problems in competitions often involves considerable commitment and preparation consistent with the kind of training undertaken by elite athletes. Bicknell (2008) has expanded on the potential benefits and the issues that teachers and parents need to consider when gifted students engage with competitions. Attempts to implement complex investigations in science (and probably mathematics) are constrained by the diversity of conceptions that teachers, particularly primary teachers, have of the nature of the inquiry process (Ireland, Watters, Brownlee, & Lupton, 2012, 2014).

Policy impacting STEM

At the turn of the 21st century, Diezmann (2002) argued that there was an apparent zeitgeist in Australia for the mathematically gifted with the convergence of three key factors: (a) strong arguments that the knowledge economy and sustainable economic development will require able and creative mathematical thinkers; (b) educator knowledge about giftedness and supporting gifted students; and (c) greater awareness of the need to improve teacher education both at the pre-service and in-service level to ensure quality teaching. She proposed that the adequacy of programs or initiatives for the mathematically gifted should be evaluated in terms of the extent to which mathematically gifted students engage in (a) creative endeavours, (b) organising meaningful data, and (c) communicating mathematically. She made 10 recommendations for enhancing the education of the mathematically gifted, which are applicable to all STEM domains. Table 9.1 elaborates these recommendations.

Concerns about Australia's performances in STEM, echoed to a lesser extent in New Zealand, has not directly impacted on gifted education policy or practices. In fact, support for gifted students at the policy level has dwindled in the past decade, although professional development is provided by the Ministry of Education in New Zealand to support teachers, students, and parents. The educational needs of gifted students are acknowledged nationally in Australian curriculum documents, but education is a state responsibility, and in most states little attention is

TABLE 9.1 Recommendations for enhancing the education of students gifted in STEM

Recommendation	Explanation
Policy and practice	Although policy can be developed at the governmental level, its implementation rests in the hands of local administrators and teachers. Practice needs to align with policy, and policy development needs to be evidence-based.
Registers of mathematically gifted	Underachievement in the upper levels of primary and in secondary schools is well documented, but teachers are unlikely to recognise underachieving students if records and profiles are not maintained and communicated.
Appropriate assessment	Routine assessment creates a ceiling for the majority of gifted students. Substantial evidence suggests above level testing is necessary. Furthermore, assessment should provide opportunities for students to demonstrate knowledge production and creativity.
Peer learning communities	Students gifted in STEM need opportunities to be within a community where others share their interests, can understand their ideas, and are prepared to critique their work in a risk-free environment.
Teachers' expertise	The quality of teaching and the knowledge that teachers have in STEM are fundamental. However, teacher personality, willingness to listen, to be flexible, and to acknowledge limits of their own knowledge is just as important.
Teacher training	Education about giftedness in pre-service teacher education courses is almost non-existent in most universities, and where it does exist it is generally an elective. Many of the strategies that teachers need to adopt – compaction, differentiation, assessment – are taught in multiple units, but application to the gifted is given token attention. Challenging stereotypes and myths about the gifted represents one of the greatest challenges for teacher educators.
Parental guidance	Parents are strong supporters of their children, but they may need guidance to recognise the unique characteristics of their children who are gifted in STEM and appreciate effective ways to assist them. The burgeoning homeschool industry is witness to the dissatisfaction many parents have with mainstream schooling.
Community awareness	The media and the public at large frequently ridicules (if not explicitly, at least implicitly in their language, the mathematically bright, the young Einsteins, the geeks and nerds). The achievements of these students will be paramount in the future, so community education about the importance of STEM and the contributions that these students can make should be encouraged.
Research investment	Research on giftedness and the education of gifted students is a low priority. There have been few opportunities to undertake substantial research projects that primarily address the education of these students. Research endeavours have had to capitalise on partnerships with sectors or post-graduate studies, which are rarely followed up in any systematic fashion.
Professional associations	Professional associations play an important role in supporting the educational needs of gifted students, but few of the specialist STEM associations have prioritised actions directed towards supporting teachers of the gifted.

146 James J. Watters

paid to gifted education. Some bright spots appear in the form of three selective STEM schools in Australia, each aligned with a local university. None of these schools explicitly targets gifted students, but instead they all recruit high-achieving, highly interested students. Selection processes potentially exclude underachieving and twice-exceptional students, but pedagogical strategies and curricula are largely consistent with recommended approaches for teaching gifted students. Selective schools and programs exist in other states, but none appear to have a specific STEM focus.

Conclusion

The intention of this chapter was to provide a broad situational analysis of research in gifted education in the domains of science, technology, engineering, and mathematics (STEM) in the Australian and New Zealand contexts. These fields are interrelated in that they capitalise on knowledge about the natural world and they provide essential understandings and skills for contemporary life.

What is the future for students gifted in STEM? The first two decades of the 21st century have not greatly advanced our understanding of this population. Recent research in gifted education in STEM appears to have plateaued in Australia and New Zealand. STEM education research has included participants who are gifted, but their learning or experiences have not been the primary research focus. The reliance on competitions, extracurricular activities, and excursions continues to dominate educational approaches for gifted learners. Professional teacher educators and researchers in the various STEM fields have ignored the issue of giftedness whilst agonising over why students are not pursuing STEM subjects and why entry requirements into many university courses (especially science) have been lowered. This has dire consequences for the standard of industries dependent on STEM graduates. While STEM is seen by most students to be important, the experiences of STEM education in school may be out of touch with the realities of students' lives.

In gifted education, there appears to be an overemphasis among educators on the question of identification at the expense of curriculum and teaching strategies. The proverb "weighing a pig doesn't make it any fatter" can be applied fairly to the field of gifted education. Labelling students as gifted does not contribute to meeting their needs if no sustained and coordinated program of support is implemented. Teachers, parents, and policy makers play an important role in intellectually fattening the gifted. The best recommendation might be to look outside of gifted education to understand learning environments that are clearly differentiated, challenging for advanced students, and establish conditions for long-term engagement, including in the domains of mathematics and science education. Drawing on principles of constructivism and authentic assessment, a Belgian group (De Corte, Verschaffel, & Masui, 2004) has defined a powerful learning environment as follows:

> A powerful learning environment is characterized by a good balance between discovery and personal exploration, on the one hand, and systematic

instruction and guidance, on the other, always taking into account individual differences in abilities, needs, and motivation among learners.

(p. 370)

Powerful learning environments would be characterised by rich conversations, dialogical interactions, negotiated learning and flexibility, and teachers who listen to the needs and interests of students. Such environments would meet the needs of many gifted in STEM and engage others who will need basic STEM literacies to engage with an ever-changing technological world. This can be achieved. For extraordinarily gifted students, the solution may lie in those specialist schools which can provide the environment and expertise to nurture the intellectual elite in much the same way as the Australian Institute of Sport attempts to produce world champions in sport with a budget of $100 million per year.

Discussion Questions

- Gifted students (and indeed, most students) do not see the world in terms of distinct traditional domains of knowledge such as chemistry, calculus, physics, and programming. So why is STEM still taught according to 18th- and 19th-century frameworks of knowledge when transdisciplinary expertise is necessary for the 21st century?
- How can new areas of expertise such as cryptography, nanotechnology, and biomedical science be incorporated into school experiences, including for gifted students?
- Inquiry learning has been presented as a fundamental strategy in STEM education that enables engagement for students of all ability levels. But how can teachers manage inquiry learning in mixed-ability classes to ensure that all students are able to engage at appropriate levels of challenge?

References

Ainley, M., & Ainley, J. (2011). Student engagement with science in early adolescence: The contribution of enjoyment to students' continuing interest in learning about science. *Contemporary Educational Psychology, 36*(1), 4–12.

Anthony, G., Rawlins, P., Riley, T., & Winsley, J. (2002). Accelerated learning in New Zealand secondary school mathematics. *Australasian Journal of Gifted Education, 11*(2), 11–17.

Atman, C. J., Chimka, J. R., Bursic, K. M., & Nachtmann, H. L. (1999). A comparison of freshman and senior engineering design processes. *Design Studies, 20*, 131–152.

Becker, K., & Mentzer, N. (2015, September). *Engineering design thinking: High school students' performance and knowledge*. Paper presented at the International Conference on Interactive Collaborative Learning (ICL), Florence, Italy. Retrieved from www.weef2015.eu/Proceedings_WEEF2015/proceedings/papers/Contribution20.pdf

Bicknell, B. (2008). Gifted students and the role of mathematics competitions. *Australian Primary Mathematics Classroom, 13*(4), 16–20.

Bicknell, B., & Riley, T. (2005). Students' perspectives on a withdrawal program in mathematics. *Australasian Journal of Gifted Education, 14*(2), 27–33.

Coll, R. (2007). Opportunities for gifted science provision in the context of a learner-centred national curriculum. In K. Taber (Ed.), *Science education for gifted learners* (pp. 59–70). London: Taylor & Francis.

De Corte, E., Verschaffel, L., & Masui, C. (2004). The CLIA-model: A framework for designing powerful learning environments for thinking and problem solving. *European Journal of Psychology of Education, 19*, 365–384.

Diezmann, C. (2002). Capitalising on the Zeitgeist for mathematically gifted students. *Australasian Journal of Gifted Education, 11*(2), 5–10.

Diezmann, C. M. (2005). Challenging mathematically gifted primary students. *Australasian Journal of Gifted Education, 14*(1), 50–57.

Diezmann, C. M., Lowrie, T., Bicknell, B., Faragher, R., & Putt, I. (2004). Catering for exceptional students in mathematics. In B. Perry, G. Anthony, & C. Diezmann (Eds.), *Research in mathematics education in Australasia 2000–2003* (pp. 175–195). Flaxton, QLD: Post Pressed.

Diezmann, C. M., Stevenson, M. K., & Fox, J. L. (2012). Supporting exceptional students to thrive mathematically. In B. Perry, T. Lowrie, T. Logan, A. MacDonald, & J. Greenless (Eds.), *Research in mathematics education in Australasia: 2008–2011* (pp. 89–109). Rotterdam: Sense Publishers.

Diezmann, C. M., & Watters, J. J. (1997). Bright but bored: Optimising the environment for gifted children. *Australian Journal of Early Childhood, 22*(2), 17–21.

Diezmann, C. M., & Watters, J. J. (2000). An enrichment philosophy and strategy for empowering young gifted children to become autonomous learners. *Gifted and Talented International, 15*(1), 6–18.

Diezmann, C. M., & Watters, J. J. (2001). The collaboration of mathematically gifted students on challenging tasks. *Journal for the Education of the Gifted, 25*, 7–31.

Diezmann, C. M., & Watters, J. J. (2002). The importance of challenging tasks for mathematically gifted students. *Gifted and Talented International, 17*(2), 76–84.

Eilks, I., Nielsen, J. A., & Hofstein, A. (2014). Learning about the role and function of science in public debate as an essential component of scientific literacy. In C. Bruguière, A. Tiberghien, & P. Clément (Eds.), *Topics and trends in current science education: 9th ESERA conference selected contributions* (pp. 85–100). Dordrecht, The Netherlands: Springer.

Ernest, P. (1986). Games: A rationale for their use in the teaching of mathematics in school. *Mathematics in School, 15*(1), 2–5.

Faragher, R., Hill, J., & Clarke, B. (2016). Inclusive practices in mathematics education. In S. M. Dole, K. Fry, A. Bennison, M. Goos, & J. Visnovska (Eds.), *Research in mathematics education in Australasia 2012–2015* (pp. 119–141). Singapore: Springer.

Forgasz, H. (2010). Streaming for mathematics in Victorian secondary schools. *Australian Mathematics Teacher, 66*(1), 31–40.

Gallagher, J. J. (2000). Unthinkable thoughts: Education of gifted students. *Gifted Child Quarterly, 44*, 5–12.

Ginns, I., Stein, S., McRobbie, C., & Swales, A. (2000). A case study of a gifted female primary school student grappling with a design and technology project. *Australasian Journal of Gifted Education, 9*(2), 43–54.

Goodrum, D. (2006). *Inquiry into science classrooms: Rhetoric or reality.* Paper presented at the ACER Conference Boosting science learning: What will it take? Canberra, ACT. Retrieved from http://research.acer.edu.au/cgi/viewcontent.cgi?article=1013&context =research_conference_2006

Google Inc., & Gallup Inc. (2016). *Diversity gaps in computer science: Exploring the underrepresentation of girls, blacks and Hispanics.* Retrieved from http://goo.gl/PG34aH

Gregor, R. C. (2005). Robotics and the gifted child: What they gain. *Gifted, 135,* 9–11.

Gross, M. U. M. (2006). Exceptionally gifted children: Long term outcomes of academic acceleration and nonacceleration. *Journal for the Education of the Gifted, 29,* 404–429.

Harris, D. M. (2011). Curriculum differentiation and comprehensive school reform: Challenges in providing educational opportunity. *Educational Policy, 25,* 844–884.

Harrison, M., & Watters, J. J. (2004). Vertical timetabling in Year 4 mathematics: Teachers' perceptions and reflections on practice. In E. McWilliam, S. Danby, & J. Knight (Eds.), *Performing educational research: Theories, methods and practices* (pp. 151–169). Flaxton, QLD: Post Pressed.

Hertberg-Davis, H. L., & Callahan, C. M. (Eds.) (2013). *Fundamentals of gifted education.* London: Routledge.

Hornby, G., & Witte, C. (2014). Ability grouping in New Zealand high schools: Are practices evidence-based? *Preventing School Failure: Alternative Education for Children and Youth, 58*(2), 90–95.

Ireland, J. E., Watters, J. J., Brownlee, J., & Lupton, M. (2012). Elementary teacher's conceptions of inquiry teaching: Messages for teacher development. *Journal of Science Teacher Education, 23,* 159–175.

Ireland, J., Watters, J. J., Lunn Brownlee, J., & Lupton, M. (2014). Approaches to inquiry teaching: Elementary teacher's perspectives. *International Journal of Science Education, 36,* 1733–1750.

Jaworski, B. (1994). *Investigating mathematics teaching: A constructivist enquiry.* London: The Falmer Press.

Johnston, O., & Wildy, H. (2016). The effects of streaming in the secondary school on learning outcomes for Australian students: A review of the international literature. *Australian Journal of Education, 60*(1), 42–59.

Lüftenegger, M., Kollmayer, M., Bergsmann, E., Jöstl, G., Spiel, C., & Schober, B. (2015). Mathematically gifted students and high achievement: The role of motivation and classroom structure. *High Ability Studies, 26,* 227–243.

King, P. M., & Kitchener, K. S. (1994). *Developing reflective judgment.* San Francisco, CA: Jossey-Bass.

King, P. M., & Kitchener, K. S. (2004). Reflective judgment: Theory and research on the development of epistemic assumptions through adulthood. *Educational Psychologist, 39,* 5–18.

Knight, B. A., & Knight, C. (1994). Computers in the classroom: Implications for gifted and talented students. *Australasian Journal of Gifted Education, 3*(1), 20–24.

Knights, A. (2017). *Through the LCD glass: Investigating the experiences of gifted students in a one-to-one laptop classroom* (Master of Education thesis). QUT.

Lassig, C. (2009). Teachers' attitudes towards the gifted: The importance of professional development and school culture. *Australasian Journal of Gifted Education, 18*(2), 32–42.

Leder, G. (2011). Mathematics taught me Einstein's old cocktail of inspiration and perspiration: mathematically talented teenagers as adults. *Canadian Journal of Science, Mathematics & Technology Education, 11*(1), 29–38.

Lubinski, D. (2016). From Terman to today a century of findings on intellectual precocity. *Review of Educational Research, 86,* 900–944.

Maker, C. J., & Schiever, S. W. (2005). *Teaching models in education of the gifted* (3rd ed.). Austin, TX: Pro-Ed.

Marshman, M., Clark, D., & Carey, M. (2015, April). The use of mathematical investigations in a Queensland Primary School and implications for professional development. *International Journal for Mathematics Teaching & Learning,* 1–20.

Martinez, S. L., & Stager, G. S. (2013). *Invent to learn: Making, tinkering, and engineering in the classroom.* Torrance, CA: Constructing Modern Knowledge Press.

McCosker, N., & Diezmann, C. (2009). Scaffolding students' thinking in mathematical investigations. *Australian Primary Mathematics Classroom, 14*(3), 27–36.

McVey, S. (2008). Computer technology and the gifted. *Australasian Journal of Gifted Education, 17*(2), 43–48.

Mentzer, N. (2011). *Engineering design thinking and information gathering final report.* Publications Paper 162. Retrieved from http://digitalcommons.usu.edu/ncete_publications/162

Mentzer, N., Becker, K., & Sutton, M. (2015). Engineering design thinking: High school students' performance and knowledge. *Journal of Engineering Education, 104*, 417–432.

Merrotsy, P. (2004). A study of exceptional mathematical ability. *Australasian Journal of Gifted Education, 13*(1), 20–27.

Nicholas, H., & Ng, W. (2009). Engaging secondary school students in extended and open learning supported by online technologies. *Journal of Research on Technology in Education, 41*, 305–328.

Oliver, G., & Fisher, K. (2015). Small footprint, global impact: The Australian science and mathematics school. *Architecture Australia, 104*(1), 60–61.

Poncini, A., & Poncini, L. (2000). A qualitative assessment of gifted and talented students undertaking research science projects. *Australasian Journal of Gifted Education, 9*(1), 41–49.

Renzulli, J. S., & Reis, S. M. (2010). The schoolwide enrichment model: A focus on student strengths and interests. *Gifted Education International, 26*(2–3), 140–156. doi:10.1177/026142941002600303

Rogers, K. B. (2002). *Re-forming gifted education: Matching the program to the child.* Scottsdale, AZ: Great Potential Press.

Ryan, M. J., & Geake, J. G. (2003). A vertical mathematics curriculum for gifted primary students. *Australasian Journal of Gifted Education, 12*(1), 31–41.

Salen, K., & Zimmerman, E. (2004). *Rules of play: Game design fundamentals.* Cambridge, MA: MIT Press.

Sjøberg, S., & Schreiner, C. (2010). *The ROSE project. An overview and key findings.* Retrieved from http://roseproject.no/network/countries/norway/eng/nor-Sjoberg-Schreiner-overview-2010.pdf

Steenbergen-Hu, S., Makel, M. C., & Olszewski-Kubilius, P. (2016). What one hundred years of research says about the effects of ability grouping and acceleration on K – 12 students' academic achievement. *Review of Educational Research, 86*, 849–899.

Taber, K. S. (2007). *Science education for gifted learners.* Abingdon, Oxon: Routledge.

Tyler-Wood, T. L., Mortenson, M., Putney, D., & Cass, M. A. (2000). An effective mathematics and science curriculum option for secondary gifted education. *Roeper Review, 22*, 266–269.

Van Verth, J. M., & Bishop, L. M. (2015). *Essential mathematics for games and interactive applications: A programmer's guide* (3rd ed.). London: CRC Press.

VanTassel-Baska, J. (2015). The integrated curriculum model. In H. E. Vidergor & C. R. Harris (Eds.), *Applied practice for educators of gifted and able learners* (pp. 169–197). Dordrecht, NL: Sense Publishers.

VanTassel-Baska, J., Bass, G., Ries, R., Poland, D., & Avery, L. D. (1998). A national study of science curriculum effectiveness with high-ability students. *Gifted Child Quarterly, 42*, 200–211.

Vasilevska, S., & Merrotsy, P. (2011). Academic acceleration in Australia: An annotated bibliography. *TalentEd, 27*, 75–126.

Watters, J. J. (2010). Career decision making among gifted students: The mediation of teachers. *Gifted Child Quarterly, 54*, 222–238.

Watters, J. J. (2012). *School ability grouping – streaming: Student voices – There is more to grouping than academic self-concept.* Paper presented at the 13th International ECHA Conference on Giftedness across the Lifespan, Münster, Germany.

Watters, J. J., & Christensen, C. (2013). Vocational education in Science, Technology, Engineering and Maths (STEM): Curriculum innovation through school industry partnerships. In C. P. Constantinou, N. Papadouris, & A. Hadjigeorgiou (Eds.), *10th conference of the European science education research association: Science education research for evidence-based teaching and coherence in learning* (Vol. 1, pp. 89–110). University of Cyprus: European Science Education Research Association.

Williams, F. E. (1979). Assessing creativity across Williams "cube" model. *Gifted Child Quarterly, 23,* 748–756.

Zeidler, D. (2016). STEM education: A deficit framework for the twenty first century? A sociocultural socio scientific response. *Cultural Studies of Science Education, 11*(1), 11–26.

10

EARLY CHILDHOOD ENVIRONMENTS AND EDUCATION

Kerry Hodge and Anne Grant

Guiding Questions

- What sources of information guide identification of giftedness in the years before formal schooling?
- How is giftedness expressed in very young children, and what does this tell us about their learning needs?
- How does a child-centred, play-based approach to education in the first five years of life relate to recommended practice for young gifted children?
- What policies or resources exist to guide early childhood teachers?

Key Ideas

- The educational needs of gifted children have become visible in Australian policy in early childhood education; in New Zealand, recognition is currently less explicit. In both countries, teachers need professional development in early gifted education.
- Characteristics observed by parents and teachers are used more than formal assessments to identify giftedness in the early years.
- Given a limited evidence base, recommended practice for gifted children relies on modifications to a play-based curriculum with broad learning outcomes, usually in inclusive settings.
- The holistic development of young gifted children appears to be nurtured better when teachers work in partnership with families and *whānau* (roughly translated in Māori as 'tribe') and when they pay attention to

Early childhood environments and education **153**

> differences in learning approaches between children's environments during transitions, such as between home and early childhood settings, and from these settings to school.

Introduction

The first five years of life are a time of significant development that is critical for outcomes in later education (Sylva et al., 2014). The importance of this period for all children and for the significant adults in their lives is reinforced by *Te Whariki*, the curriculum for New Zealand's early childhood settings:

> [Early childhood is] . . . a period of momentous significance for all people growing up in [our] culture. . . . By the time this period is over, children will have formed conceptions of themselves as social beings, as thinkers, and as language users, and they will have reached certain important decisions about their own abilities and their own worth.
>
> *(Donaldson, Grieve, & Pratt, 1983, p. 1,*
> *as cited in the Ministry of Education, 1996)*

What does this mean for children who are gifted? In this chapter we will present what is known about gifted children during their first five years of development and the implications in Australia and New Zealand for their education, their sense of self and their families, and teachers. While the field lacks a definition of giftedness in the early years (Koshy & Robinson, 2006; Margrain & Farquhar, 2012), the frequent quoting of Harrison's (2003) proposed working definition suggests wide support in Australia:

> A gifted child is one who performs or has the potential to perform at a level significantly beyond his or her age peers and whose unique abilities and characteristics require special provisions and social and emotional support from the family, community and educational context.
>
> *(p. 8)*

This definition aligns with Gagné's (2003) Differentiated Model of Giftedness and Talent in its focus on advanced natural (inherited) abilities and the potential for development of systematically developed skills or performance that are exceptional (talents). Although Harrison has not mentioned relevant areas of development, the domains of natural ability in Gagné's model are highly relevant to early childhood education, and the "unique abilities and characteristics" of very young children are more likely to be evident in these domains, rather than in advanced skills. Harrison's indication of the importance of adults' support aligns with the role of Gagné's environmental catalysts in the developmental process. Harrison's inclusion of the need

154 Kerry Hodge and Anne Grant

for social and emotional support reinforces the focus in early childhood education on the whole child – not just the intellectual domain – and coincides with research on the social and emotional needs of older gifted children (Neihart, Pfeiffer, & Cross, 2016).

Young gifted children have been a neglected topic in research literature and in educational practice (Koshy & Robinson, 2006; Margrain & Farquar, 2012; Robinson, 2008; Walsh, Hodge, Bowes, & Kemp, 2010), and there is general consensus that these children are at educational risk if they are not identified early and have their learning needs met (Gross, 1999; Koshy & Robinson, 2006; Sankar-DeLeeuw, 2006). Reasons proposed by Robinson (2008) for this neglect include concerns about the reliability of early identification and whether children identified early will exhibit advanced abilities.

Identifying giftedness early

Are the preschool years too early for children to be reliably identified as gifted? In the years before school, 'emerging' (Koshy & Robinsons, 2006) or 'potential' giftedness (Gross, 1993) may be more appropriate descriptions of advanced development, as Harrison's (2003) definition suggested. Even from infancy, gifted children have demonstrated longer attention spans and greater goal-directedness. Exploring early signs of giftedness after children's IQ tests at age 8, researchers found that 20 of the 107 children were gifted and that differences in language development were evident as early as 18 months. These differences persisted into adulthood (Gottfried, Gottfried, & Guerin, 2006).

Researchers have investigated teachers' and others' experience with young gifted children and views on whether giftedness can, and should, be identified in the early years. Although generalisations from these self-selected samples are cautioned against, the studies provide information where none existed previously. Surveys of teachers in prior-to-school settings across New South Wales (n = 80) (Hodge, 2015b) and New Zealand (n = 137) (Wong, 2015) revealed that the majority of teachers believed that they had taught a gifted preschooler. Hodge (2015b) found a strong consensus that giftedness can be identified in the years before school and in any community. An additional survey of 125 respondents found the majority of respondents supported efforts to identify giftedness in young children (Margrain & Farquar, 2012).

While little is known about the accuracy of teachers' ability to identify giftedness in early childhood (Robinson, 2008), identification by parents has been well established for decades as generally reliable (Robinson, 2008). For example, three studies from the United States employed parent nomination of their child as precocious in general or in specific abilities (at ages ranging from 18 months to 6 years) along with standardised assessment of the children's development. For the studies using IQ subtests, the descriptions or ratings of their children's behaviours by more than half of the parents were aligned with scores in the top 2% for their age (Robinson,

Abbott, Berninger, & Busse, 1996; Robinson & Robinson, 1992). For the third study, parents' descriptions of precocious language at home related well to language samples collected during free play sessions in the laboratory (Robinson, Dale, & Landesman, 1990). Although some overestimation occurs, parents' descriptions of their young child's advanced abilities should be taken seriously and explored.

Characteristics of young gifted children

Numerous studies of young children in their homes and early childhood environments have identified consistent intellectual and social-emotional characteristics of giftedness, although individuals possess different clusters and express them uniquely (e.g., Harrison, 2005; Hodge & Kemp, 2000; Margrain, 2010; Sankar-DeLeeuw, 2004). Koshy and Robinson (2006) suggest the following characteristics:

- Intense curiosity
- Rapid learning and easy recall
- Keen observation and generalisation to other contexts
- A long attention span and persistence when interested
- Language that is sophisticated and usually develops early
- Interests and knowledge that are intense or broad and demonstrate moral awareness or a tendency to question the status quo
- Early mastery of symbolic representation through drawing, reading, or writing
- Exceptional interest and skill in numbers or spatial abilities
- Preference for older companions, including adults
- Seeking and enjoyment of challenge or avoidance of risking a non-expert result
- Frustration occurring because of asynchronies among a child's intellectual and physical abilities and emotional regulation

Cultural differences

There has been no published research on cultural differences in the ways very young children reveal their giftedness or how their parents view their advanced abilities, although Bevan-Brown (2009) suggested that routine interactions and discussions with a very familiar and trusted teacher are likely to enable Māori parents to share information about their child without considering themselves to be 'boasting'.

In an overview of Indigenous Australian views about giftedness, Webber (2016) described a number of characteristic perceptions of giftedness. Giftedness is traditionally associated with leadership that honours spiritual alignment with ancestors. Core values guiding development of giftedness are the importance of kinship, knowledge of cultural ways and ceremony, as well as connection, respect, and responsibility to the land. Elders particularly value, and mentor, behaviours that demonstrate high linguistic and spatial ability. In essence, giftedness is not 'a gift' for the individual; it belongs to everyone in the community.

156 Kerry Hodge and Anne Grant

Methods for identifying giftedness in the early years

A variety of information sources are recommended for the early identification of giftedness (Robinson, 2008). In Australia and New Zealand, early childhood teachers may identify giftedness through their usual approach of assessing all children holistically, such as compiling narratives (also called learning stories) or portfolios based on observations of learning (Hodge, 2015b; Margrain, 2011). These approaches, as well as use of the following identification methods, assume that teachers have some knowledge of giftedness in young children. Providing sufficiently challenging experiences can allow children to reveal unexpected abilities (Hodge & Kemp, 2002; Sutherland, 2008). The practice of frequent informal discussion between teachers and parents also contributes the important family perspective on a child's strengths and interests (Margrain, 2011; Margrain & Farquar, 2012). Bevan-Brown (2009) encouraged teachers to adopt a culturally appropriate lens when interpreting any observations.

Rating scales based on known characteristics of giftedness can help focus observations (Margrain, 2011), but few have been validated. The Giftedness in Early Childhood Scale (Allan, 1999, cited in Allan, 2002) was developed for systematic, focussed observations in New Zealand early childhood settings and included 'negative' behaviours and behaviours valued by Māori *whānau*. During its trial by teachers, gifted children were identified and feedback suggested the scale was relevant in early childhood education. However, there have been no published reports of its subsequent use, nor have there been reports of use in Australia or New Zealand of the Gifted Rating Scales-Preschool (Pfeiffer & Jarosewich, 2003), for which selected scales have been validated against IQ scores (Pfeiffer & Petscher, 2008).

Norm-referenced tests, while useful, are not routinely given to preschoolers in Australia and New Zealand and have limitations (Hodge & Kemp, 2000; Margrain, 2011). In general, very early developmental assessments tend to be unstable (Robinson, 2008). Young children's responses to test items can be influenced by non-cognitive factors such as fatigue or lack of motivation to give their best performance, especially to a stranger (Gross, 1999), although when children appear motivated their scores can be considered credible (Robinson & Robinson, 1992). If families are able to afford the cost (Margrain, 2011), testing below age 6 is recommended when children appear extremely advanced so that interventions can be planned (Gross, 1999). Gathering of observations from people who know the young child well – teachers, family, *whānau* – is especially important when the reliability of formal assessment is in doubt (Hodge & Kemp, 2000).

Stability of early advancement

Robinson (2008), citing longitudinal studies in the United States, addressed concerns about whether children whose early development is advanced continue to perform above their age peers in later years. Pletan, Robinson, Berninger, and Abbott (1995) found that children nominated as having advanced mathematical abilities when aged 5–6 years remained advanced and even increased their advancement over their age peers two years later, while Robinson and Robinson (1992) reported high correlations between gifted children's general ability scores at ages 2–5 and their scores up to four years later, with a rise for the group as a whole. An Australian study of preschoolers nominated by their parents as possibly gifted and followed into school for up to three years had similar findings. Characteristics described by their parents were generally confirmed by ability and achievement test scores at the ages of 3 or 4 years (Hodge & Kemp, 2000), and most children continued to perform at significantly advanced levels in the early years of school (Hodge & Kemp, 2006).

Learning needs

Accepted understandings of the learning needs of young gifted children are based on the characteristics of giftedness already discussed in this chapter. Some additional aspects of the development of young gifted children are explored further.

Holistic development

A guiding principle in early childhood education is that all areas of learning – intellectual, social, emotional, and physical – are interrelated, and that learning and development occur in a holistic way (Berk, 2003). There is evidence that, in a young gifted child, these interactions across areas of learning can occur more quickly or be more significant than in a child whose development is age-typical (Grant, 2013; Harrison, 2005). Harrison (2005) identified a need for complexity and connection across both intellectual and social domains.

High levels of intellectual stimulation

A child's intellectual giftedness is inevitably associated with an intense need for a high level of intellectual stimulation, which in turn creates a need for appropriate experiences that may be unusual for the child's age. For instance, an infant may explore surroundings for extended lengths of time, a gifted toddler may require longer or more varied play sessions and constant undivided attention from a 'play partner', or a preschooler may seek extended conversations with an older child or adult on complex topics (Harrison, 2005) if his/her age peers cannot satisfy this need for stimulation.

Interactions with children of similar intellectual ability are recommended as providing both satisfying stimulation and social connection (Gross, 1999; Harrison, 2005). However, others have reported that the nature of social connections between young gifted children and others is a more complex notion than suggested by the description 'like minds' (Farrent & Grant, 2005; Sankar-DeLeeuw, 2004; Wilson, 2015). Social play opportunities with 'like minds' were found to provide satisfying play situations for some young gifted children, but not for all and not all the time.

With intellectual advancement comes an early capacity for higher-order thinking (Harrison, 2005) – the capacity to apply, analyse, and synthesise information, evaluate it, and use it creatively (Anderson & Krathwohl, 2001). Harrison (2005) identified the presence of higher-order thinking in parental observations of their young children's "need to know, to formulate theories and test hypotheses" (p. 94). While such thinking is evident in the play and conversations of young gifted children (Wilson, 2015), it may go unnoticed or be underdeveloped unless there are opportunities to use these higher-level skills (Walsh & Kemp, 2012).

Points of caution

Studies by Harrison (2005), Hodge and Kemp (2000), and Sankar-DeLeeuw (2004) indicated that, in young children, areas of high ability are likely to change and shift as the child gains life experience, knowledge, and skill. Also, levels of learning can be very uneven, with peaks and troughs, stops and starts – asynchronies. When some areas of learning are advanced significantly above age-typical expectations, such unevenness can be more pronounced, leading to a misguided focus only on less developed areas of learning (Grant, 2013), especially if coupled with domains of delayed development (Chamberlin, Buchanan, & Vercimak, 2007).

Reports from parents, teachers, and researchers about interactions with young gifted children describe a wide variety of areas of advanced knowledge, skill, and interest. Examples are extensive levels of knowledge about plants or a deep engagement with the Māori legends of a child's community (Dean, Sampson, Preston, & Wallace, 2015). Amongst this group of young gifted children, some will show advanced levels of academic learning and others will not (Hodge & Kemp, 2000).

Whatever the area of knowledge, skill, and interest, it is important that current advanced levels of learning are supported and extended at the same time as learning is supported in areas that may be more age-typical. All levels of learning require an educational response.

Responding to the learning needs of young gifted children

While behaviours indicating advanced ability can be apparent at a very early age, these children need a variety of experiences and opportunities before they begin to specialise in particular knowledge or skills that may become their area of talent. For instance, extraordinary spatial ability in a young child has the potential to develop into a variety of talents such as athletic ability, dancing, the visual arts, or architecture (Gagné, 2003). Responding to advanced development by focussing too soon on a specific domain may lead to a narrowing of opportunities for development, which could result in potential talent never being fully realised.

As indicated in Gagné's (2003) model, development of inherited natural abilities into skills or performance indicating talent is not automatic but dependent on a number of factors. Early experiences and opportunities within the child's family, in combination with those provided in their early childhood educational setting, are two significant aspects of 'environmental factors' influencing the eventual development of potential of gifted children.

Family responses

Findings from the few studies of family responses to very young gifted children indicate a mutual responsiveness in family interactions (Gottfried et al., 2006; Harrison, 2005; Morrissey, 2011). Such interactions are bi-directional – the child signals a need for high levels of intellectual stimulation and the parent offers matching opportunities.

The literature indicates that parents respond to their children, not in anticipation of potential achievement but in the response to the need for satisfying learning opportunities. These opportunities cover a broad spectrum, from support of high levels of motivation to learn, to holistic learning across social, emotional, physical, and intellectual areas (Margrain, 2010; Sankar-DeLeeuw, 2006). Parents have also preferred their child to be part of a mixed-ability group if there were satisfying intellectual opportunities provided (Grant, 2004).

Parents also report feelings of stress from their children's constant curiosity, continual high level of activity, and intense questioning (Harrison, 2005; Sankar-DeLeeuw, 2006). Some families have sought local programs, such as gifted playgroups, to meet this need and to gain support for themselves (Hodge, 2015a). The New Zealand Centre for Gifted Education's *Small Poppies* program has operated for more than 20 years in selected urban locations (Breen, 2016), but most programs do not endure or are transient in nature.

Parents need to assume the role of educational advocate for their young child and require others' understanding and support (Chellapan & Margrain, 2013). But many parents do find this role lonely and challenging, reporting being unsure what, or how much, is reasonable to request from teachers (Chellapan & Margrain, 2013; Koshy & Robinson, 2006).

All children develop within a social and cultural context that shapes their knowledge, attitudes, beliefs, skills, and even their personality traits (Grace, Hayes, & Wise, 2017). Therefore, contextual perceptions about giftedness will be significant. Among diverse cultural groups, the views of how children develop, how they best learn, and what is important to learn are different (Webber, 2016). Even within one cultural group, family differences – perhaps because of religion or socioeconomic status – can result in different opportunities or expectations about the pathway taken by a gifted child.

Educational policy responses

In the Australian quality framework for early childhood education and care, there is recognition that, like other categories of children with additional needs, children who are "gifted or have special talents . . . require or will benefit from specific considerations or adjustments" (Australian Children's Education and Care Quality Authority, 2013, p. 196). No definition of giftedness is given and no support documents have been published to guide teachers, although the Victorian government has initiated an online resource for parents and teachers of young gifted children (Victoria Department of Education and Early Childhood Development, 2013). In its position statement on inclusion, the peak body of Australia's early childhood sector has included children who are gifted among population groups for whom extra efforts are required to ensure full participation in early childhood education (Early Childhood Australia, 2017).

In New Zealand, the Ministry of Education's policy on gifted education focusses only on primary and secondary education (Ministry of Education, 2012). According to Margrain and Farquar (2012) and Wong (2015), the growing educational response to giftedness in New Zealand has not included sufficient attention to giftedness in the years before school or guidance for early childhood teachers. The Ministry of Education's planned revision of *Te Whāriki* in 2017 offers an opportunity to recognise and respond to very young gifted children. Meanwhile, there is information on early childhood education on the *Gifted and Talented Online* (n.d.) pages of the Ministry's *Te Kete Ipurangi* resource and information website for parents, *whānau*, and teachers.

The interventions of ability grouping and acceleration known to benefit older gifted children (Rogers, 2007) are rarely offered to children in the early years. In both countries, any response to the identified learning needs of gifted children will occur within early childhood settings that are inclusive of all abilities, although some children have had access in university settings to research-based, part-time programs designed for gifted children (e.g., Grant, 2004; Hodge & Kemp, 2002). Policies on access to early enrolment in school vary by jurisdiction, despite evidence, on average, of positive academic effects without negative effects for social and emotional development (Robinson, 2008; Rogers, 2007). Applications for early entry, usually for 6 months before the usual age of entry, are permitted in the Australian Capital Territory, New South Wales, Queensland, South Australia, Tasmania, and Victoria (Gallagher, Smith, & Merrotsy, 2010) but no longer in the Northern Territory (Northern Territory Government, 2016). In each of these jurisdictions, Departments of Education provide strict guidelines for how decisions are made. In New Zealand, children can start school on their fifth birthday, and early entry is not permitted (Ministry of Education, n.d.).

Curriculum responses

The ways in which Australian and New Zealand teachers respond to young gifted children are influenced by their respective policy contexts for early childhood education in general. In each country, the early childhood curriculum is a framework for teachers' decision making, in collaboration with families, based on the strengths, needs, and interests of individual children in their community and cultural contexts. Australia's *Early Years Learning Framework* (Commonwealth of Australia, 2009) and

Early childhood environments and education **161**

New Zealand's *Te Whāriki* (Ministry of Education, 1996) are both pedagogically grounded in the principle of children's play and active exploration of their environment. There are broad learning outcomes or goals rather than prescribed curriculum content. Both frameworks permit a wide range of educational philosophies to inform how implementation occurs in individual early childhood settings (Commonwealth of Australia, 2009; Ministry of Education, 1996).

Some evidence-based guidance for development of early childhood programs for young gifted children can be drawn from programs developed in Australia and New Zealand as specific responses to the need for a high level of intellectual stimulation (Grant, 2004; Hodge & Kemp, 2002; Margrain, Murphy, & Dean, 2015). Given few such reports, recommendations from the international field are helpful (e.g., Hertzog, 2008; Sutherland, 2008). As noted by Walsh, Kemp, Hodge and Bowes (2012), a further limitation is that few programs report empirically based reviews of their efficacy. Consequently, current awareness and suggested best practice inform the following sections on curriculum responses for young gifted children.

General recommendations for very young gifted children have been mostly drawn from accepted principles of curriculum differentiation for older gifted students, according to Maker's (1986) article on principles of curriculum for gifted preschoolers. Broadly speaking, these principles state that learning opportunities for gifted children need to be qualitatively different from those offered to children developing in an age-typical way, and an educational program should be modified in the areas of content, process, product, and learning environment.

Differentiated content

In early childhood programs where the learning activities were based on the current interests of the children and content that would challenge them intellectually (Grant, 2004; Hertzog, 2008; Hodge & Kemp, 2002), activities involved the use of academic skills as tools to support children's investigations. Teachers provided this support according to children's readiness or their requests but not to meet a predetermined learning outcome (Hodge & Kemp, 2002).

While content was always specific to the interests of the children involved, there was a common aim to encourage the following outcomes:

- Complex and abstract thinking, including developing awareness of the fundamental concepts or principles of the topic: for example, exploring physics (Grant, 2004)
- Increasing use of higher-order thinking skills, including analysis, synthesis of ideas, evaluation: for example, through a teacher's questioning (Herzog, 2008; Murphy, 2015)
- Independent learning skills, such as planning, organisation of activity/work, accessing resources, problem solving, concentration, persistence, developing computer and internet skills: for example, exploring reference sources about maps (Hodge & Kemp, 2002).

162 Kerry Hodge and Anne Grant

Social and emotional support was also reported as important. This support needed to go hand in hand with a satisfactory, intellectually stimulating program if holistic learning and development was to be sustained (Grant, 2013; Harrison, 2005; Sankar-DeLeeuw, 2006).

Differentiated processes

Scholars in the area of gifted education advocate play as one means of providing the high levels of intellectual stimulation needed by young gifted children (Harrison & Tegel, 1999; Porter, 2005; Wilson, 2015). Play as a learning strategy is a complex concept (Dockett & Fleer, 2002), observed in children in a variety of forms, such as exploratory play, symbolic play, and play that is rule-governed as in sports, board games, and computer games. These types of play are often seen as a developmental continuum from simple exploratory play through to complex rule-governed play.

Play behaviours observed amongst young gifted children may appear at times to illustrate a simple form of play, but close attention indicates otherwise. Hodge and Kemp (2002) reported that gifted preschoolers enjoyed a range of exploratory forms of play, but these were distinctly complex in nature, such as rearranging collections of objects into multiple sets based on variable characteristics. Another study (Wilson, 2015) found that when advanced materials were offered, high-ability children found opportunities within the various types of play for analytic reasoning, problem solving, and creativity.

Forms of play that provide satisfactory opportunities for high levels of intellectual stimulation are characterised as

- Open-ended
- Socio-dramatic play (symbolic play) supported by adults
- Offering diverse and complex themes
- Providing opportunities to play with like-minded children

(Gibson & Mitchell, 2005; Harrison & Tegel, 1999)

While play is accepted as an appropriate approach to support advanced levels of learning, it is just one of a number of suitable strategies. Hodge and Kemp (2002) described the use of an 'invitational approach' where teacher interaction with the children intentionally prompted more complex play or investigation, including use of higher-order thinking. Other authors described a pedagogical approach of scaffolding children's progress from concrete learning or current thinking to more abstract and complex ideas, following their lead so that the pace matched the children's readiness to learn. These approaches variously involved the synthesis, analysis, evaluation, or creative manipulation of current knowledge and thinking (Gibson & Mitchell, 2005; Dean et al., 2015). The use of disciplinary methods of inquiry and research advocated for older gifted students (Maker & Neilson, 1995) was described by Grant (2004) as a means of encouraging higher-order thinking amongst preschoolers.

Differentiated products

Guidelines for differentiating programs for gifted children state the importance of different expectations for the outcomes, that is, the products of learning activities. For very young gifted children, according to Maker's (1986) recommendations, products should

- Address real problems
- Be directed toward real audiences, not merely the teacher
- Display a transformation of learning – for instance, an original construction or conclusion based on new information, or a dance, or story

Hodge and Kemp (2002) reported the preschoolers in their program enthusiastically embraced this aspect of the program, producing, for instance, a model of a town and a roster to share out popular tasks within their group. Hertzog (2008) described products such as group murals or chair designs that enabled children to share and make visible the learning from their inquiries. Appropriate product differentiation is described by Porter (2005) as enabling young gifted children to create a product that is beyond the level usually achievable by their age-typical peers. This allows further opportunities for the children to engage in a form of learning or skill development that is potentially challenging to them and thus intrinsically satisfying.

Differentiated learning environment

An appropriate learning environment for young gifted children approximates a best-practice environment for all young children. It involves not merely the physical objects and resources that are available to children, but the emotional, social, cultural, and time environment also influence how children will interact with each other and their surroundings. In summary, this is an environment that

- Is child centred and allows choices
- Encourages independence
- Affords opportunities and time for open-ended inquiry, which for advanced children will include relatively complex ideas
- Is rich in print and other resources
- Has authentic learning experiences (those that are real in the children's family or wider community context)
- Makes explicit the language of thinking
- Is accepting of mistakes as well as knowledge and skills not yet learned
(Commonwealth of Australia, 2009; Gibson & Mitchell, 2005; Hertzog, 2008; Hodge & Kemp, 2002; Ministry of Education, 1996)

When the environment was flexible and responsive to children's interests, young gifted children were enthusiastic in pursuing new topics and thinking skills into unexpected areas (Grant, 2004; Hodge & Kemp, 2002).

The 'inquiry approach' as an educational response

While not intended only for gifted children, an inquiry-based approach to learning, such as the Project Approach from the United States and the Reggio Emilia approach from Italy (Katz, Chard, & Kogan, 2014), includes many of these recommendations about a curriculum response for young gifted children. This approach appears, anecdotally, to be increasingly popular in Australia and New Zealand early childhood settings. In particular, it allows gifted children to engage in learning related to their own interests, search for answers to their own questions, and proceed at a pace and depth, as well as towards an outcome, that is satisfying to them (Hertzog, 2008). The level of challenge provided can be determined and supported by the teacher. This allows the interaction between teacher and children to be inclusive of those identified as gifted as well as those who are perhaps not yet identified and those who are more age-typical.

The Reggio Emilia approach to early childhood education is based on children's inquiries (Harrison, 2005; Hertzog, 2008; Lai, 2009). The child is viewed as a rich and powerful learner, and the curriculum is responsive to children's current learning interests as well as incorporating social values, such as the importance of relationships. Its pedagogy is based on very high expectations of children's learning (see Castagnetti & Vecchi, 1997), with the role of the teacher as a co-learner alongside the children. These philosophical views, together with an awareness of the powerful influence of the educational environment, result in products that provide evidence of children's deep and rich thinking and learning (Rinaldi, 2006).

Teachers' preparedness to respond to giftedness

Studies have shown that some teachers appear to identify intellectual advancement and to recognise that this can result in a poor fit intellectually and socially with peers (Allan, 2002; Hodge, 2015b; Wong, 2015). Both the *Early Years Learning Framework* and *Te Whāriki* encourage teachers to assess and respond to individual children's strengths, interests, and needs. Yet greater information or support to respond to the learning needs of gifted children is still needed by teachers. Hodge (2015b) found the majority of her study participants held positive attitudes towards special provision and curriculum changes, but just over half felt confident to provide these supports. New Zealand teachers also reported needing professional development and practical resources in order to respond to young gifted children (Allan, 2002; Margrain & Farquar, 2012; Wong, 2015).

Little is known about teacher support for ability grouping in early childhood settings, although special gifted classes have been suggested (Allan, 2002), perhaps as an alternative to early entry (Margrain & Farquar, 2012). Teachers in Hodge's (2015b) study almost universally supported the idea of a separate 'extension group' for a period during the day for the most capable children, and a majority of teachers provided this at least once or twice a week. While the idea of a regular half-day gifted program had moderate support, few teachers thought it feasible; time, space, and adequate knowledge were identified as impediments.

Early childhood environments and education **165**

The limited Australian research about teacher attitudes toward early entry to school has indicated roughly equal positive and negative (or uncertain) views (Gallagher et al., 2010; Hodge, 2015b). Margrain and Farquar (2012) also found divided opinion about whether gifted children in New Zealand should be allowed to early entry.

Transitions

Transition for children and their families from one educational context to another, including from home to an early childhood setting, is accepted as potentially stressful for all children (Dockett & Perry, 2007). These transitions require a child to form a new sense of self, to adapt to new ways of learning and a new physical environment, as well as to form new relationships with adults and other children. Research has shown that young gifted children face different challenges in making a positive transition than those faced by their age-typical peers.

Grant (2013) reported that differences in approaches to learning between home and the usual early childhood program were likely to be significant for young gifted children. For instance, these children are more likely than age-typical children to establish, within the home context, a highly developed learning approach. This could entail setting their own learning goals in domains in which they have advanced interests, knowledge, and skills, to which their parents respond by providing individualised specialist resources and skills – as in cases of an early interest in reading or robots. When such a child joins a play-based early childhood program, there are potential difficulties, for the teacher and for the child who presumes continuity of this well-established learning approach. However, teachers may not perceive or address this potential difficulty, contributing to stress for the gifted child in trying to bridge such differences with little explanation offered.

According to Whitton's (2005) study, when anticipating starting school, gifted children were primarily focussed on the expectations of new learning opportunities, while their age-typical peers focussed mainly on managing new 'school rules'. In addition, the parents of both groups of children had different expectations about what was important in the new context. Other studies have indicated that teachers were not well informed about the learning needs of young gifted children and orientated their support towards age-typical expectations. This resulted in young gifted children being poorly engaged with the new learning environment and having attendant behaviour difficulties (Grant, 2013; Harrison, 2005; Masters, 2015). Parents and early childhood teachers were both reported as hesitant in identifying advanced development, which created communication barriers about the gifted child's potential learning needs and thus hindered understanding of reasons for difficult behaviours (Grant, 2013; Masters, 2015).

Research directions

There is much to investigate, including how professional development affects early childhood teachers' identification of, and response to, giftedness. Research is needed to build a strong evidence base for appropriate responses to giftedness in the early years, including effective teaching strategies, how teachers and families can work together, and how policies on early entry to school are implemented. Chellapan and Margrain (2013) suggested the need to capture the voices of young gifted children themselves and to know more about how giftedness in very young children is understood in minority cultures.

Conclusion

The unusual strengths and learning needs of gifted children start early and are now receiving some recognition in early childhood education policy documents in Australia and New Zealand. More research is needed, especially about effective interventions and teacher-family partnerships that will nurture the young gifted child's intellectual and social development and sense of self at home and in educational settings. Meanwhile, evidence-based approaches to identifying giftedness and recommended practice in modifying the early childhood curriculum are available to guide much-needed professional development for educators working with gifted children in early childhood settings.

Discussion Questions

- Why might teachers (in preschool or school settings) want to discourage families from exploring the option of early entry to school for their highly competent preschoolers?
- What is an appropriate definition of giftedness or gifted education in the early years? How might it relate to broader definitions or models of giftedness?
- Parents are a child's first teachers, and early childhood curriculum in both Australia and New Zealand promotes partnerships between families and teachers for the well-being of young children. What elements might facilitate or hinder the development of a genuine partnership between teachers and parents when only one party views the young child as gifted?
- An important element of transition is continuity of experience. How might continuity for gifted children and age-typical children be different as they enter new early childhood and school environments?

References

Allan, B. (2002). Identifying and providing for giftedness in the early years. In *The early years research & practice series* (Vol. 1). Palmerston North, NZ: Kanuka Grove Press. Retrieved from http://gifted.tki.org.nz/Early-Childhood-Education-ECE/Identification

Anderson, L., & Krathwohl, D. A. (2001). *Taxonomy for learning, teaching and assessing: A revision of Bloom's Taxonomy of Educational Objectives*. New York, NY: Longman.

Australian Children's Education and Care Quality Authority. (2013). *Guide to the national quality standard*. Sydney, NSW: Author. Retrieved from www.acecqa.gov.au/national-quality-framework/the-national-quality-standard

Berk, L. E. (2003). *Child development* (6th ed.). Boston, MA: Allyn and Bacon.

Bevan-Brown, J. M. (2009). Identifying and providing for gifted and talented Māori students. *APEX, 15*(4), 6–20.

Breen, S. (2016, September). *Lessons learned from 20 years of Small Poppies*. Paper presented at the conference of the New Zealand Association for Gifted Children, Christchurch, NZ. Retrieved from http://conference.giftedchildren.org.nz/wp-content/uploads/2016/09/Sue-Breen-NZAGC-2016-handout.pdf

Castagnetti, M., & Vecchi, V. (1997). *Shoe and meter: Children and measurement: First approaches to the discovery of measurement*. Reggio Emilia, Italy: Reggio Children.

Chamberlin, S. A., Buchanan, M., & Vercimak, D. (2007). Serving twice-exceptional preschoolers: Blending gifted education and early childhood special education practices in assessment and program planning. *Journal for the Education of the Gifted, 30,* 372–394.

Chellapan, L., & Margrain, V. (2013). "If you talk, you are just talking: If I talk is that bragging?" Perspectives of parents with young gifted children in New Zealand. *APEX, 18*(1). Retrieved from www.giftedchildren.org.nz/wp-content/uploads/2014/10/Chellapan-and-Margrain.pdf

Commonwealth of Australia. (2009). *Belonging, being and becoming: The early years learning framework for Australia*. Canberra: Department of Education, Employment and Workplace Relations.

Dean, J., Sampson, C., Preston, A., & Wallace, E. (2015). Looking at learning: Narratives of young gifted children. In V. Margrain, C. Murphy, & J. Dean (Eds.), *Giftedness in the early years: Informing, learning and teaching* (pp. 75–103). Wellington, NZ: New Zealand Council for Educational Research.

Dockett, S., & Fleer, M. (2002). *Play and pedagogy in early childhood: Bending the rules*. South Melbourne, VIC: Thomson.

Dockett, S., & Perry, B. (2007). Children's transition into school: Changing expectations. In A. W. Dunlop & H. Fabian (Eds.), *Informing transitions in the early years* (pp. 92–104). Maidenhead: Open University Press.

Donaldson, M., Grieve, R., & Pratt, C. (1983). *Early childhood development and education: Readings in Psychology*. Oxford: Basil Blackwell.

Early Childhood Australia. (2017). *Position statement on the inclusion of every child in early childhood education and care*. Retrieved from www.earlychildhoodaustralia.org.au/our-work/submissions-statements/

Farrent, S., & Grant, A. (2005). Some Australian findings about the socio-emotional development of gifted pre-schoolers. *Gifted Education International, 19*(2), 142–153.

Gagné, F. (2003). Transforming gifts into talents: The DMGT as a developmental theory. In N. Colangelo & G. A. Davis (Eds.), *Handbook of gifted education* (3rd ed., pp. 60–74). Boston, MA: Allyn & Bacon.

Gallagher, S., Smith, S., & Merrotsy, P. (2010). Early entry: When should a gifted child start school? *Australasian Journal of Gifted Education, 19*(1), 16–23.

Gibson, K. L., & Mitchell, L. M. (2005). Critical curriculum components in programs for young gifted learners. *International Education Journal, 6*(2), 164–169.

Gottfried, A. W., Gottfried, A. E., & Guerin, D. W. (2006). The Fullerton longitudinal study: A long-term investigation of intellectual and motivational giftedness. *Journal for the Education of the Gifted, 29,* 430–450.

Grace, R., Hayes, A., & Wise, S. (2017). Child development in context. In R. Grace, K. Hodge, & C. McMahon (Eds.), *Children, families and communities* (5th ed., pp. 3–25). Melbourne, VIC: Oxford University Press.

Grant, A. (2004). Picasso, physics and coping with perfectionism: Aspects of an early childhood curriculum for gifted preschoolers. *Journal of Australian Research in Early Childhood Education, 11*(2), 61–69.

Grant, A. (2013). Young gifted children transitioning into preschool and school: What matters? *Australasian Journal of Early Childhood, 38*(2), 23–31.

Gross, M. U. M. (1993). *Exceptionally gifted children.* London: Routledge.

Gross, M. U. M. (1999). Small poppies: Highly gifted children in the early years. *Roeper Review, 21*, 207–214.

Harrison, C. (2003). *Giftedness in early childhood* (3rd ed.). Sydney, NSW: GERRIC, University of New South Wales.

Harrison, C. (2005). *Young gifted children: Their search for complexity and connection.* Exeter, NSW: INSCRIPT.

Harrison, C., & Tegel, K. (1999). Play and the gifted child. In E. Dau (Ed.), *Child's play* (pp. 97–109). Sydney, NSW: MacLennan & Petty.

Hertzog, N. (2008). *Early childhood gifted education.* Waco, TX: Prufrock Press.

Hodge, K. (2015a, August). *A supported playgroup for families with young gifted children: Parents' and facilitators' perspectives.* Paper presented at the conference of the World Council for the Gifted and Talented, Odense, Denmark.

Hodge, K. (2015b, August). *Gifted children prior to school: What do their educators believe and do regarding their education?* Paper presented at the conference of the World Council for the Gifted and Talented, Odense, Denmark.

Hodge, K. A., & Kemp, C. R. (2000). Exploring the nature of giftedness in preschool children. *Journal for the Education of the Gifted, 24*, 46–73.

Hodge, K. A., & Kemp, C. R. (2002). The role of an invitational curriculum in the identification of giftedness in young children. *Australian Journal of Early Childhood, 27*(1), 33–38.

Hodge, K. A., & Kemp, C. R. (2006). Recognition of giftedness in the early years of school: Perspectives of teachers, parents, and children. *Journal for the Education of the Gifted, 30*, 164–204.

Katz, L., Chard, S., & Kogan, Y. (2014). *Engaging children's minds: The project approach* (3rd ed.). Santa Barbara, CA: ABC-CLIO.

Koshy, V., & Robinson, N. M. (2006). Too long neglected: Gifted young children. *European Early Childhood Education Research Journal, 14*, 113–126.

Lai, Y. (2009). Reconsidering the education of gifted young children with the Reggio Emilia approach. *Exceptionality Education International, 19*(3), 96–110.

Maker, C. J. (1986). Suggested principles for gifted preschool curricula. *Topics in Early Childhood Special Education, 6*, 62–73.

Maker, C. J., & Neilson, A. B. (1995). *Teaching models in the education of the gifted* (2nd ed.). Austin, TX: PRO-ED.

Margrain, V. (2010). Parent-teacher partnerships for gifted early readers in New Zealand. *International Journal About Parents in Education, 4*(1), 39–48. Retrieved from www.ernape.net/ejournal/index.php/IJPE

Margrain, V. (2011). Assessment for learning with young gifted children. *APEX, 16*(1), 1–12. Retrieved from www.giftedchildren.org.nz/wp-content/uploads/2014/10/v16margrain.pdf

Margrain, V., & Farquar, S. (2012). The education of gifted children in the early years: A first survey of views, teaching practices, resourcing and administration issues. *APEX, 17*(1), 1–13. Retrieved from www.giftedchildren.org.nz/wp-content/uploads/2014/10/margrain.pdf

Margrain, V., Murphy, C., & Dean, J. (Eds.) (2015). *Giftedness in the early years: Informing, learning and teaching.* Wellington, NZ: NZCER Press.

Masters, N. (2015). *"Put your seatbelt on, here we go!" The transition to school for children identified as gifted* (Unpublished doctoral thesis). Charles Sturt University, Wagga Wagga, NSW.

Ministry of Education. (1996). *Te Whāriki early childhood curriculum*. Wellington, NZ: Ministry of Education.

Ministry of Education. (2012). *Gifted and talented students: Meeting their needs in New Zealand schools*. Wellington, NZ: Ministry of Education.

Ministry of Education. (n.d.) *Education in New Zealand*. Retrieved from www.education.govt.nz/home/education-in-nz/#Primary

Ministry of Education. (n.d.). *Gifted and talented online*. Retrieved from http://gifted.tki.org.nz/Early-Childhood-Education-ECE

Morrissey, A-M. (2011). Maternal scaffolding of analogy and metacognition in the early pretence of gifted children. *Exceptional Children, 77*, 351–366.

Murphy, C. (2015). Through the lens of play. In V. Margrain, C. Murphy, & J. Dean (Eds.), *Giftedness in the early years: Informing, learning and teaching* (pp. 38–55). Wellington, NZ: NZCER Press.

Neihart, M., Pfeiffer, S., & Cross, T. (Eds.) (2016). *The social and emotional development of gifted children* (2nd ed.). Waco, TX: Prufrock Press.

Northern Territory Government. (2016). *Guidelines and procedures: Gifted and talented education*. Retrieved from https://education.nt.gov.au/education/policies/gifted-education

Pfeiffer, S. I., & Jarosewich, T. (2003). *Gifted rating scales*. San Antonio, TX: The Psychological Corporation.

Pfeiffer, S. I., & Petscher, Y. (2008). Identifying young gifted children using the gifted rating scales-preschool/Kindergarten scale. *Gifted Child Quarterly, 52*, 19–29.

Pletan, M., Robinson, N., Berninger, V., & Abbott, R. (1995). Parents' observations of Kindergartners who are advanced in mathematical reasoning. *Journal for the Education of the Gifted, 19*, 30–44.

Porter, L. (2005). *Gifted young children: A guide for teachers and parents* (2nd ed.). Sydney, NSW: Allen & Unwin.

Rinaldi, C. (2006). *In dialogue with Reggio Emilia: Listening, researching and learning*. Abingdon, Oxon: Routledge.

Robinson, N. M. (2008). Early childhood. In J. A. Plucker & C. M. Callahan (Eds.), *Critical issues and practices in gifted education: What the research says* (pp. 179–194). Waco, TX: Prufrock Press.

Robinson, N. M., Abbott, R. D., Berninger, V. W., & Busse, J. (1996). The structure of abilities in math-precocious young children: Gender similarities and differences. *Journal of Educational Psychology, 88*, 341–352. Retrieved from www.apa.org/pubs/journals/edu/

Robinson, N. M., Dale, P. S., & Landesman, S. (1990). Validity of Stanford-Binet IV with linguistically precocious toddlers. *Intelligence, 14*, 173–186.

Robinson, N. M., & Robinson, H. (1992). The use of standardized tests with young gifted children. In P. S. Klein & A. J. Tannenbaum (Eds.), *To be young and gifted* (pp. 141–170). Norwood, NJ: Ablex.

Rogers, K. (2007). Lessons learned about educating the gifted and talented: A synthesis of the research on educational practice. *Gifted Child Quarterly, 51*, 382–396.

Sankar-DeLeeuw, N. (2004). Case studies of gifted kindergarten children: Profiles of promise. *Roeper Review, 26*, 192–207.

Sankar-DeLeeuw, N. (2006) Case studies of gifted kindergarten children part II: The parents and teachers. *Roeper Review, 29*, 93–99.

Sutherland, M. (2008). *Developing the gifted and talented young learner*. London: Sage.

Sylva, K., Melhuish, E., Sammons, P., Siraj, I., Taggart, B., Smees, R., & Hollingworth, K. (2014). *Students' educational and developmental outcomes at age 16: Effective Pre-School, Primary and Secondary Education (EPPSE) 3–16* (Research Brief 354). London: Department for Education.

Victoria Department of Education and Early Childhood Development. (2013). *Making a difference for young gifted and talented children*. Retrieved from www.education.vic.gov.au/childhood/professionals/learning/Pages/gtmakedifference.aspx

Walsh, R. L., Hodge, K. A., Bowes, J. M., & Kemp, C. R. (2010). Same age, different page: Catering for young gifted children in prior-to-school settings. *International Journal of Early Childhood*, *42*, 43–58.

Walsh, R. L., & Kemp, C. R. (2012). Evaluating interventions for young gifted children using single-subject methodology: A preliminary study. *Gifted Child Quarterly*, *57*, 110–120.

Walsh, R. L., Kemp, C. R., Hodge, K. A., & Bowes, J. M., (2012). Searching for evidence-based practice: A review of the research on educational interventions for intellectually gifted children in the early childhood years. *Journal for the Education of the Gifted*, *35*, 103–128.

Webber, M. (2016, August). *In search of greatness: Gifted indigenous students and the power of positive racial-ethnic identities*. Paper presented at the conference of the Australian Association for the Education of the Gifted and Talented, Sydney NSW.

Whitton, D. (2005). Transition into school for gifted children. *Australian Journal of Early Childhood*, *30*(3), 27–31.

Wilson, H. E. (2015). Patterns of play behaviours and learning center choices between high ability and typical children. *Journal of Advanced Academics*, *26*, 143–164.

Wong, M. (2015). Social construction of giftedness: What might that mean for early childhood teachers' practice? *APEX*, *19*(1). Retrieved from www.giftedchildren.org.nz/apex/wp-content/uploads/sites/13/2016/02/Social-construction-of-giftedness-What-might-that-mean-for-early-childhood-teachers-practice.pdf

11

GIFTED STUDENTS IN RURAL AND REMOTE SETTINGS

Margaret Plunkett

Guiding Questions

- What might giftedness look like in a rural/remote setting in Australia or New Zealand?
- What are some particular challenges associated with giftedness in terms of living and being educated in a rural/remote setting?
- What strategies have been found to be effective in supporting the development of giftedness in rural and remote communities?

Key Ideas

- The research base from Australia and New Zealand on gifted students in rural locations might be better classified under the broader umbrella of 'regionality'. This is particularly the case in Australia, with the exception of research with Indigenous gifted students, which still largely fits within the confines of rural and remote.
- Despite the documented positives associated with a rural lifestyle, there is a large body of both national and international literature highlighting a set of specific challenges for gifted students living and being educated in such environments.
- Rural schools and communities within Australia and New Zealand need to be more aware of the repercussions of failing to accommodate the needs of their gifted students. There should also be a focus on capitalising on the positive aspects of rurality when devising appropriate responses to the identified challenges.

172 Margaret Plunkett

> • Teacher education and professional learning are key to supporting gifted students in rural/remote communities; this needs to infiltrate even the most remote communities, especially in relation to Indigenous gifted students.

Introduction

> Despite the advances in the education of rural gifted students stretching back a couple of generations, the literature on this particular group of students is still marked by collections of presumed best practices, anecdotal evidence, and conceptual analyses.
>
> (Plucker, 2013, p. 431)

This chapter examines the situation within Australia and New Zealand in relation to the education of gifted students in rural/remote settings. Ten years prior to Plucker (2013) making the above statement, Colangelo, Assouline, Baldus, and New (2003) highlighted the lack of clarity in relation to the definition of 'rural', which continues to impact on the generalisability of research findings (Kettler, Puryear, & Mullett, 2016). It is not surprising that an array of potentially conflicting definitions of rural and rurality exist, with wide-ranging criteria including "population density, economic factors, socio-cultural characteristics and location or remoteness from larger cities" (Stokes, Stafford, & Holdsworth, 2000, p. 11). In an attempt to provide some cohesiveness, the U.S. has adopted a common federal definition of rural, based on proximity to an urban area and involving three degrees: fringe (within 5-mile radius), distant (between 5-and 25-mile radius), and remote (more than 25-mile radius) (Stambaugh, 2010).

Within Australia and New Zealand, a number of measures of rurality continue to be used; these are briefly outlined in this chapter, followed by an examination of the extant literature relating to the provision for gifted students within a rural context. Part of that context involves particular challenges associated with educating gifted students in non-metropolitan settings. However, understanding the rural context also requires questioning the generally accepted deficit view of rural communities, to ensure it does not subsume the less recognised positives.

Giftedness in rural/remote settings in Australia and New Zealand

The Australasian context of rurality

Defining context is an important issue due to the differences in educational outcomes between metropolitan and non-metropolitan students within Australia and New Zealand. According to O'Callaghan (2015), more than 14% of New Zealand's population lives in rural areas. Interestingly, the classification of urban/rural within New Zealand (Pink, 2004) appears to be more straightforward when compared with Australia. In 2004, an 'experimental Urban/Rural Profile' of New Zealand was produced as part of a series of analytical reports based on the 2001 Census, which re-categorised rural areas based on the degree of urban influence (Pink, 2004). Previously, rural areas had been treated as the residual category of urban areas. The 2004 profile involved three levels of classification for urban areas: main urban areas, satellite urban areas, and independent urban areas. Areas were classified as rural with high urban influence, moderate urban influence, low urban influence, or highly rural/remote (Pink, 2004). Following the 2006 Census, another category was added – area outside urban rural profile, to capture any residual areas outside the other categories (Stats NZ, 2017). Figure 11.1 outlines the initial seven categories listed within the 2004 profiles but not including the 2006 addition.

Within Australia, a number of measures have been used over the years to define the concepts of 'rural' and 'remote', with the terms 'region' and 'regionality' receiving more attention as the population and structures have evolved. In terms of classifying a place as rural, remote, or regional, one measure is particularly useful, as it is used for much of the comparative government research – the Remoteness Structure of the Australian Statistical Geography Standard (ASGS). The ASGS brings together in one framework all of the regions, which the Australian Bureau of Statistics (ABS) and other organisations use to collect, release, and analyse geographically classified statistics, through five Remoteness Area (RA) categories including Major Cities, Inner Regional, Outer Regional, Remote, and Very Remote (ABS, 2016).

According to the ABS website (2016), the criteria used for allocation of RAs is based on the Accessibility/Remoteness Index of Australia (ARIA+) and measures remoteness based on the physical road distance to the nearest Urban Centre. Figure 11.2 displays the Remoteness Areas of Australia, which highlights the huge expanse of land that is designated as very remote.

However, while such remote areas exist, the majority of the Australian population (71% of the approximately 24.6 million) tends to be concentrated in major cities, with only 2.2% living in remote or very remote Australia (ABS, 2016). In terms of Indigenous Australians:

> Although 2.4% of Australia's population are Indigenous, their geographic distribution across Australia is quite different. Indigenous people comprise 1% of the population in major cities, 3% in inner regional areas, 6% in outer regional areas, 15% in remote areas and 49% in very remote areas.
>
> *(Baxter, Gray, & Hayes, 2013, p. 2)*

In New Zealand, despite a much smaller overall population of 4.6 million, the Indigenous Māori people make up almost 15% of the population, with another 7% Pasifika people (Stats NZ, 2017).

Based on the high level of both the Australian and New Zealand populations concentrated in main cities, and the very small numbers in remote and very remote

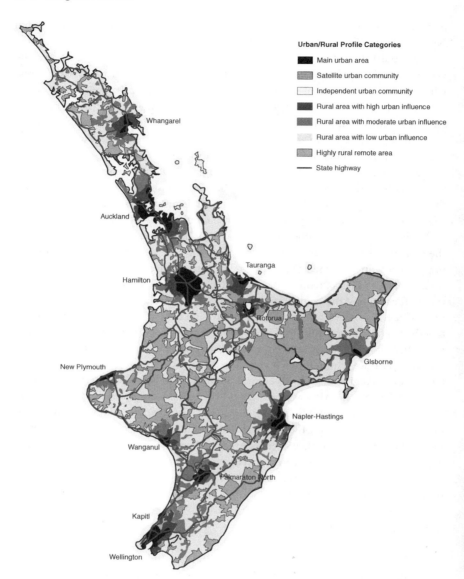

FIGURE 11.1 Urban/rural profile categories of New Zealand

Source: Stats NZ (2017)

settings, it would appear likely that, with the exception of studies of Indigenous gifted students, the term 'rural' has been used quite broadly and could in fact relate to students in outer (and even in some instances, inner) 'regional' areas. This is also possible with some international research, due to the lack of a common measure of rurality within this body of literature. With this in mind, the literature referred

Gifted students in rural and remote settings **175**

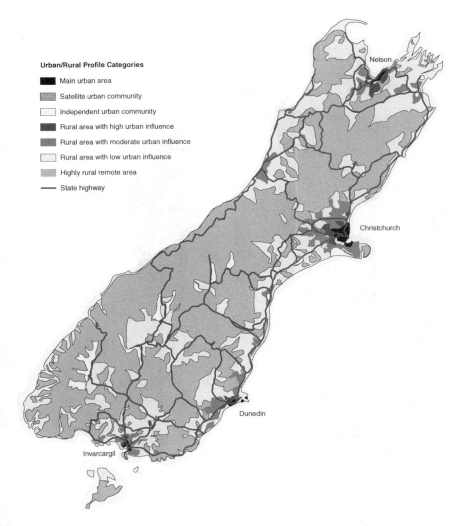

FIGURE 11.1 (Continued)

to and discussed in this chapter will cover situations that might be more accurately described as regional or non-metropolitan, rather than strictly rural or remote. Nonetheless, context is important, due to the impact locale can have on education.

Impact of rurality on educational outcomes

A number of Australian reports have outlined the impact of rurality on educational outcomes, and it could be assumed the rhetoric would apply equally to New Zealand (Riley, Bevan-Brown, Bicknell, Caroll-Lind, & Kearney, 2004; Riley & Moltzen, 2010; Riley & White, 2016). As highlighted by Stokes et al. (2000), in a

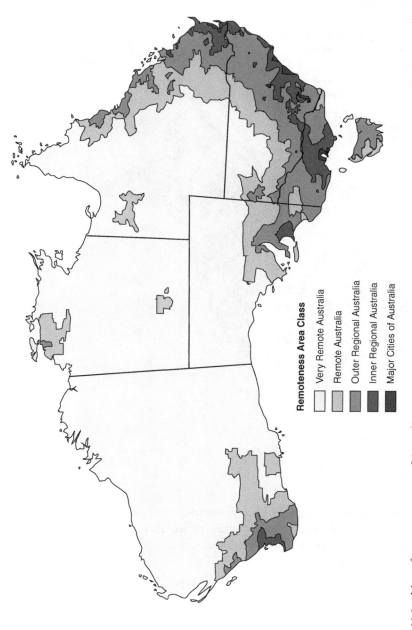

FIGURE 11.2 Map of remoteness areas of Australia

Source: Australian Bureau of Statistics (2016)

Melbourne University report on rural and remote school education, "the quality of education provided in rural and remote Australia is poorer than that provided in urban areas. This has an impact on the overall learning environment of schools and on student achievement" (p. 61). Similarly, the Federal Human Rights Commissioner, Chris Sidoti (2000) argued that just because rural students lived outside the major population centres, they should not have to settle for a second-rate education. Lamb, Rumberger, Jesson, and Teese (2004) found that rurality had an impact on retention, a finding supported in a 2013 Australian Government report showing that students in metropolitan schools were 1.13 times more likely than students in regional schools to complete Year 12 (the final year of schooling) (cited in McLelland, 2013). According to Pegg and Panizzon (2007), educational outcomes in literacy declined with increasing distance from metropolitan centres. Finally, McClelland (2013) found that while retention rates in secondary schools were an indicator of successful education outcomes, metropolitan schools had a much greater retention rate (90%) than did regional schools (70%).

In a recent review of rural education by the Centre for Education Statistics and Evaluation (CESE, 2013), a number of salient points were raised in relation to differing outcomes between urban and rural students. According to the literature review, on an international basis, the Programme for International Student Assessment (PISA) reading assessment performance of rural students is poorer in almost every Organisation for Economic Co-operation and Development (OECD) country, with Australia having one of the largest remoteness gaps (CESE, 2013). The review also highlighted the lower chances of attending university associated with rural residency, particularly for males (CESE, 2013). One important theme to emerge was the impact of low parental aspirations:

> Even from an early age, it appears that rural and remote parents have different expectations for their children's post-school pathways. The Longitudinal Study of Australian Children found that 62% of metropolitan parents of boys aged 8–9 years expected their sons would go on to university, compared with 50 per cent of inner regional parents and 40% of outer regional parents.
>
> *(CESE, 2013, p. 9)*

While these figures relate to the general student population, the impact on gifted students could be even greater, as highlighted in the next section.

Current literature in relation to giftedness in a rural (non-metropolitan) context

Addressing the needs of gifted students is not an easy undertaking in any environment; however, the literature points to specific challenges associated with rurality. Earlier literature tended to reflect what could be described as a deficit interpretation of the experience of being gifted in a rural milieu, possibly as a way of drawing attention to particular challenges. However, some of the more recent literature has

178 Margaret Plunkett

suggested a shift away from a deficit focus to highlight some of the strengths of rural communities and how these might be built upon to provide more effectively for gifted students (Plunkett, 2009; Stambaugh & Wood, 2015; Wood & Zundans-Fraser, 2013). Kettler et al. (2016) note the importance of understanding the context of the place and community that is being investigated, as these are "hallmarks of what we value as rural" (p. 261). A starting point is to examine the body of extant literature on challenges for developing giftedness in a rural context.

Challenges associated with giftedness and gifted education in rural/remote settings

The gifted education literature relating to rural contexts is focussed mainly on the education of gifted students and tends to involve schools, teachers, and students. However, the reality is that everyone associated with giftedness and gifted education, including parents, teacher educators, and researchers, has their own perception about the challenges inherent in addressing the physical, cognitive, and social-emotional needs of gifted children in non-metropolitan areas. Unfortunately, these viewpoints rarely make it into the literature (O'Callaghan, 2015; Plunkett, 2012) and, in general, giftedness in rural settings has not received adequate attention from researchers (Colangelo, 2015).

International research

A particular focus on identifying challenges emerged in international research in the 1980s and 1990s, predominantly in the U.S., with Spicker, Southern, and Davis (1987) classifying problems of size, poverty, non-urban acculturation experiences, and traditional rural values as barriers to rural provision for high-ability students. This group of students has been described as one of the most challenging to reach in terms of educational provision, due to population limitations and/or a lack of resources such as suitable student candidates for special programs; teachers with knowledge or expertise in the area; and adequate support mechanisms and community resources such as museums, libraries, and tertiary facilities (Benbow, Argo, & Glass, 1992). Jones and Southern (1992) found differences between rural and urban settings relating to access and availability rather than service type, suggesting that rural schools often found it more difficult to provide services and experiences common in metropolitan schools, due to the burden of transportation and financial requirements. Meanwhile, Cross and Dixon (1998) suggested that while the opportunities and tribulations associated with giftedness may be shared by rural and urban students, there are particular challenges for rural students accessing advanced courses and academic materials and cultural/educational events due to time and expense.

Understandings about the experience of gifted students in rural environments began to change direction in the 2000s, with researchers such as Howley, Howley, and Pendarvis (2003) highlighting the importance of local knowledge in defining rural areas. Montgomery (2004) also found that the diversity of local knowledge could affect how students learn information and skills for which they do not see real connections, while acknowledging that "accelerated learning of complex and deep information is possible when valued within the sphere of local knowledge" (p. 5).

A review of literature by Howley, Rhodes, and Beall (2009) supported other findings relating to problems associated with distance, accessibility, transportation, and interaction with like-minded peers, but identified the four main challenges facing rural schools as declining populations, persistent poverty, changing demographics, and ongoing accountability requirements. Furthermore, they argued that the relatively strong association between poverty and low academic achievement meant poor rural districts often prioritised remedial education over enrichment (Howley et al., 2009).

Further challenges arise through the forced-choice dilemma often faced by rural students due to a lack of available prospects or resources. That is, rural students are more likely to have to choose between staying to enjoy the rural lifestyle or leaving to partake of educational and employment opportunities (Howley, Howley, & Showalter, 2015; Young & Fisher, 1996). Yet, divergent ideological beliefs and practical reasons relating to post-secondary opportunities may mean that provisions to assist capable students in gaining entry into institutions outside of the region seem illogical or even imprudent. As highlighted by Jones and Southern (1992), there appears to be an implicit assumption in most gifted education programming that participants will pursue advanced or specialised educational careers, despite the lack of career opportunities for students with advanced academic attainments in rural communities. As such, gifted education programs have the potential to be seen as inequitable, as setting a group of students apart, and as siphoning off some of the most capable young persons from the community's future (Jones & Southern, 1992; Stambaugh, 2010).

Lawrence (2009) advocated for the importance of continuing to examine rural giftedness for two main reasons: (1) every child deserves the opportunity to be appropriately challenged, but in addition, (2) communities need to sustain the positive contributions made by gifted students to the economy and culture. She concluded that "rural life in general is neither devoid of meaning nor hostile to gifted students" (p. 467). However, Lawrence (2009) did highlight some of the challenges faced by gifted rural children and their parents, including insufficient services and options. She argued that a number of factors were at play, including a tendency for greater acceptance of the status quo in rural areas and lower levels of support for programming, including through finances, suitably qualified staff, and sufficient numbers of participants. She also contended that the view of rural culture in the U.S. can lead to confusion between "democratic principles and elitism, negative attitudes about giftedness, and a predilection for implementing the easiest but not necessarily the most effective ways to educate gifted students" (Lawrence, 2009, p. 462). Stambaugh (2010) also raised the issue of more limited opportunities in rural areas for academic growth, appropriate role models, advanced materials, and access to suitable extracurricular activities.

180 Margaret Plunkett

In a comprehensive review of research on rural gifted education in the U.S., Plucker (2013) cautioned that rural communities are very diverse and, as such, research findings related to this population need to be interpreted with caution. He summarised nine barriers identified in the literature as impacting gifted education in rural areas:

1 The impact of cohort size, distance, transportation costs, and time on program offerings
2 The relationship between poverty and rurality, which impacts on mobility
3 The lack of norming with rural cohorts in the development of appropriate identification instruments
4 The impact of perceptions of gifted education as a misfit for rural communities
5 The impact of funding disparities between urban and rural schools
6 The impact of perceptions relating to working conditions in rural schools
7 The impact of school consolidation
8 The impact of lack of preparation of rural students for the culture of large universities
9 The impact of gifted students having to leave communities for further education/ careers

While much of the research on giftedness in rural areas has originated in the U.S., many of the identified issues are just as germane to the Australian and New Zealand contexts, as outlined in the next section.

Australian and New Zealand research

Early Australian research by Leonard (1999) argued that attitudes, rather than resourcing, impacted on rural provisions. In his study of a small Australian country high school, he noted a common perception that high-ability students belonged in cities rather than in country areas. The trend for limiting rural gifted education to 'enrichment' or broadening activities was also problematic, as they often lacked challenge and were focussed outside of the immediate environment, further highlighting the suggestion of local inadequacy. Leonard (1999) concluded that rural schools need to approach gifted education from a personal-ideological perspective rather than a deficit-resourcing one. Similar concerns were also highlighted by Plunkett and Harvey (1995), Plunkett, Harvey, and Harvey (2003), Plunkett (2006, 2009, 2012), and in more recent research by Wood and Zundans-Fraser (2013).

Additional challenges identified for high-ability students in rural settings include costs, both social and financial, associated with having to leave a community for education or employment; access difficulties; limited offerings in secondary subjects; and the "early stage at which students' aspirations begin to form" (CESE, 2013, p. 9). In terms of career aspirations, students identify a number of constraining factors, including accessibility to specialist teachers and subjects, teacher turnover, and a lack of suitable high-performing peers to provide competitive benchmarking (CESE, 2013).

Quality teachers are particularly important for rural gifted students, but they require specific knowledge and skills in relation to providing for gifted students in rural environments (CESE, 2013; Plunkett, 2002). The situation for rural teachers is complex, and as acknowledged in the CESE report (2013), possible tensions exist between teachers holding high expectations and their need to sustain positive relationships with the local community, who may have quite different aspirations for their 'best and brightest'. Similarly, teacher education presents some challenges, as very few pre-service teacher programs include courses on gifted education (Fraser-Seeto, Howard, & Woodcock, 2013; Plunkett & Kronborg, 2011), let alone on rural gifted students (Plunkett, 2012). Lawrence's (2009) suggestion for teacher education in the U.S. is similarly pertinent to Australia and New Zealand:

> Universities that prepare teachers of the gifted have a stake in advancing the knowledge base about rural children and youth with special gifts and talents. Reliable information about these students and the supports and constraints provided by their schools and communities will contribute to the establishment of more responsive policies as well as the development of more defensible practices for identifying such students and serving them in public schools of their local rural communities.
>
> *(p. 489)*

Interestingly, a major website developed for rural teacher education in Australia by White, Kline, Hastings, and Lock (2011), called the Renewing Rural and Regional Teacher Education Curriculum website (www.rrrtec.net.au), has many excellent resources relating to rural teacher education, yet makes only one reference to giftedness in a link to a single article on meeting the needs of the gifted in rural areas through acceleration (Benbow et al., 1992).

Indigenous gifted students

Within Australia and New Zealand, there is a growing body of literature on the topic of gifted Indigenous students, which tends to be a subset of the rural gifted literature. While not all Indigenous students live in non-metropolitan settings, within Australia, the vast majority do live outside of major cities (Baxter et al., 2013). Nonetheless, there appears to be another set of specific challenges for gifted Indigenous students over and above the ones identified as applicable to rural gifted students in general. A number of researchers have conducted wide-ranging studies in relation to identification of and provision for giftedness in Australian Aboriginal students (e.g., Chaffey, 2002; Chaffey, Bailey, & Vine, 2003; Christie, 2011; Clark & Merrotsy, 2008; Cronin & Diezmann, 2002; Garvis, 2006; Gibson & Vialle, 2007) and Māori and Pasifika students in New Zealand (e.g., Bevan-Brown, 2011; Faaea-Semeatu, 2011; Miller, 2011; Moltzen, 2004; Webber, 2011). Yet, there is still a long way to go in terms of understanding the complexities of giftedness within an Indigenous context.

According to Garvis (2006), an erroneous belief persists in Australia about the academic capabilities of Aboriginal children, which would be similar in relation to Māori and Pasifika students in New Zealand (Miller, 2011). A culturally specific context to enable gifted Indigenous students to establish a point of reference for their learning and to prevent the creation of "bicultural learning" is important (Garvis, 2006, p. 45). Cronin and Diezmann (2002) highlighted similar issues, suggesting that both identification and achievement of gifted Aboriginal students are impacted "by culture conflict, the lack of knowledge of culturally sensitive identification measures of giftedness, and the anti-intellectual Australian ethos" (p. 12). They concluded that in order for gifted Aboriginal students to achieve their potential, there was a need for culturally sensitive support and guidance in relation to identification, programming, and home-school relationships (Cronin & Diezmann, 2002).

The focus on culturally appropriate practice has also been strongly advocated in the New Zealand context (Riley & Bicknell, 2013), where an inclusive approach to gifted education has been supported since 2000, when the Ministry of Education produced the initial version of a major resource, *Gifted and Talented Students: Meeting Their Needs in New Zealand Schools* (updated by the Ministry of Education, 2012). This resource underpins provision for gifted students in New Zealand, recommending that gifted education programs are:

> culturally responsive and align with relevant research and Ministry of Education policies, such as those outlined in The New Zealand Curriculum, *Ka Hikitia – Managing for Success: The Māori Education Strategy 2008–2012*, the *Pasifika Education Plan 2009–2012*, and in the vision and work programme, *Success for All – Every School, Every Child.*
>
> *(Ministry of Education, 2012, p. 6)*

In terms of culturally sensitive identification, within Australia, the Coolibah Dynamic Assessment strategy (Chaffey, 2002) has shown promising results in terms of identifying academic potential and in raising expectations about the performance of Aboriginal children amongst the children themselves, their teachers, and their communities (Chaffey et al., 2003; Clark & Merrotsy, 2008). In New Zealand, Miller (2011) highlights the need to consider three key factors in identification protocols: the search for personal identity, the conceptions of giftedness held by schools and teachers, and an awareness of the different social and cultural features of Māori and Pacific Islands students' home lives. One resource that is of particular value in this area was developed by the Australian Association for the Education of the Gifted and Talented (AAEGT), with the support of the federal Department of Education, Employment and Workplace Relations (DEEWR), in the form of a book titled, *Giftedness from an Indigenous Perspective* (Vialle, 2011), containing 11 chapters (www.aaegt.net.au/?page_id=946).

In the next section, literature relating to promising practices for overcoming challenges to educating gifted students in regional, rural, and remote settings is presented.

Strategies for addressing giftedness in rural and remote communities

While there may not be a globally agreed-upon definition of rurality, there is little controversy in relation to the idea that similar challenges and possible solutions are faced by all countries with significant populations of rural students (Plucker, 2013). Solutions have tended to be the focus of more recent studies, particularly in the U.S.

International

Recent literature has changed focus to highlight the positive aspects associated with growing up and being educated in rural areas. For example, Howley et al. (2015) advocate "a contrary and largely disparaged position (a position *unusually* appreciative of the educational potential of rural cultures and places); that is, rural life is not limiting and restrictive, but is instead inclusive and generative" (p. 24). Small class sizes, a high level of community involvement, slower pace, close relationships, and less competition for involvement in selective activities are some of the positive aspects that have been associated with a rural lifestyle (O'Callaghan, 2015; Plucker, 2013; Stambaugh, 2010). Stambaugh and Wood (2015) describe this as 'rural essence' and suggest that it provides rural students with a "sense of place, traditions and community pride" (p. 92). While this has not necessarily been shown to translate into positive outcomes (Plucker, 2013), a recent focus of the literature has been on how to capitalise on these positives in terms of identifying appropriate practices that could be incorporated into most rural environments.

In a comprehensive review of major U.S. rural gifted education research, Plucker (2013) outlined a set of promising practices for overcoming challenges outlined in the literature, while capitalising on the associated positive aspects. Howley et al. (2009) had conducted an earlier review and argued for the inclusion of a broader definition of giftedness for rural areas. In the same vein, there have been calls for more appropriate multi-dimensional/multi-faceted identification protocols or strategies, more tailored to the values and characteristics of local environs (Plucker, 2013; Stambaugh, 2015). The use of multiple measures is also supported by Stambaugh (2010), who argued that gifted students in rural areas often display their talents differently, requiring multiple and varied assessments. While the inclusion of non-verbal assessment and creative performance-based assessments and portfolios is recommended, Stambaugh (2010) warned that it would be remiss for rural districts to provide services that prioritise a verbal curriculum for rural students.

In fact, the practice of developing curriculum that is place-based or community-based, building on and connecting with local resources and culture, appears in much of the literature (Azano, 2014; Stambaugh, 2010). Howley et al. (2009) suggest that even if no explicit connection is made between the instructional programs of schools and with the community's economic development, suitable options can still be explored in relation to instructional practices.

Reviews of the extant literature on rural gifted education by both Howley et al. (2009) and Plucker (2013) also include the following as promising practices:

- Development of regional or multi-district partnerships to facilitate resource sharing and shared specialised expertise
- Expanded use of technology and distance education options to facilitate communication for social and intellectual interaction
- Comprehensive support models such as Project Aspire
- Appropriate curriculum practices that infuse an advanced curriculum that incorporates higher-level thinking into the school day as opposed to disjointed extracurricular activities
- In-depth career counseling and exposure to a variety of careers not typically found in the community
- Teacher education and targeted professional development focussing on the characteristics and needs of gifted students

This last point is particularly important, for as Howley et al. (2009) argued, even teachers with some knowledge of giftedness may find it challenging to recognise gifted characteristics in culturally diverse and economically disadvantaged students. As documented within the literature, professional development is important as most initial teacher education programs have very little content on giftedness, and when "combined with traditional rural attitudes towards giftedness, make it unlikely that many rural educators have had much exposure (or motivation to get exposure) to gifted education issues" (Plucker, 2013, p. 431). Stambaugh (2010) recommends that rural teachers of the gifted take into consideration "the belief systems within the community and work to dispel myths regarding gifted education that are antithetical to best practices for these students" (p. 79).

In terms of promising models, the Aspire model (Burney & Cross, 2006) is particularly noteworthy as it acknowledges the necessity of long-term intervention, the need for both psychological and academic support, the critical nature of professional development for sustainable success, and the need to capitalise on the advantages of rural environments, making it "one of the most comprehensive interventions for rural gifted students to date" (Plucker, 2013, p. 431).

Other strategies that have been found to support gifted students have not always been applied effectively in rural areas, with promising practices for accelerative options (Assouline, Flanary, & Nicpon Foley, 2015), flexible grouping (Seward & Gentry, 2015), and use of advanced curriculum (VanTassel Baska & Hubbard, 2015) highlighted in recent literature. One issue is that while promising practices are being identified, the nature of rurality is changing, and rapidly, such that it is difficult to now describe "a prototypical rural community" (Plucker, 2013, p. 431).

Australia and New Zealand

Even taking into consideration Plucker's (2013) caution about the diversity associated with rurality, many of the promising practices outlined in the international research would be suitable in Australia and New Zealand. While New Zealand does have a set of Ministry of Education (2012) Guidelines, there is no national policy or guidelines on gifted education in Australia. As such, each of the Australian states have developed their own way of responding to giftedness in schools. Over the last three decades, state policies and practices have waxed and waned, dependent on the reigning political ideologies (Plunkett & Kronborg, 2007). In Australia, there has been a major dearth of state or federal provisioning, despite rurality being recognised as a major challenge. For example, the 2012 Victorian Parliamentary Inquiry into the education of gifted and talented children made many references to the challenges associated with location; however, this did not translate into any real emphasis on rurality in the recommendations. Similarly, while not specifically referring to giftedness, an article by O'Callaghan (2015) suggests that there are special challenges for teachers and concomitantly students in rural areas in New Zealand.

Flexibility in identification structures for rural students in general appears to be haphazard, so the development of formal guidelines could be worth investigating. A particular issue within Australia has been the lack of funding dedicated specifically to gifted education, either federally or by state governments. As highlighted by Munro (2016), despite most states having some form of policy on gifted education, there is no systemic investment or resources to support the translation of policy into practice. This is particularly pertinent in relation to rural areas, where educational resourcing is even more limited. An exception is recent funding of $80 million by the NSW government to support students in non-metropolitan areas, including gifted students. *The Rural and Remote Education Blueprint for Action* (2013) aims to bridge the gap in educational achievement among rural, remote, and metropolitan schools. One of the key actions was the creation of a virtual secondary school to enable access to a broad range of curriculum opportunities. Other key aims included incentives to attract and retain quality teachers, support for student well-being, and strengthening early childhood education, all of which could potentially have a positive impact on gifted students.

The virtual secondary school is an example of a promising practice involving more creative uses of technology and distance education options. It was initially offered as a unique provision to 120 rural gifted students in the Western Region, to allow them the opportunity of a selective high school experience in their own rural area. Bannister, Cornish, Bannister-Tyrrell, and Gregory (2015) conducted an investigation into the initiative and found very positive outcomes, resulting in the extension of the offering to gifted rural students across NSW. Now called Aurora

College, the virtual school aims to enable students to study specialist subjects not available in their schools and includes selective classes for the study of extension mathematics, science, and engineering studies.

> Aurora College was named after the Aurora Australis, a stunning display of bright light only seen in the southern hemisphere. Providing high performing students in regional areas with the same opportunities as their metropolitan peers will go a long way to closing the gap in educational achievement between city and country students.
>
> *(NSW DEC, 2014, para. 8)*

According to Wood and Zundans-Fraser (2013), rather than focussing on the deficits and what is missing, it is important to examine what is being offered in rural contexts and how it might be improved. They suggest that the following issues need to be addressed in the design and implementation of programs in rural areas:

> the importance of working with like-minds, the need for an extended selection period with multi-faceted data collection, the provision of sufficient lead up time in terms of communication, and the opportunity to share in a celebration of successes in a more public way.
>
> *(Wood & Zundans-Fraser, 2013, p. 48)*

They also point out that rural communities often fear that provision for gifted students in rural settings can result in them being lost to the community, but that programs themselves, if appropriately developed and implemented, can become communities in themselves for the students involved. This sentiment appears to have underpinned much of the direction of gifted education within New Zealand, which unlike Australia does have a national focus on rurality.

Literature from the previous two decades indicates that New Zealand has demonstrated a strong commitment to gifted education in general but has also extended greater effort into ensuring that gifted Māori and Pasifika students, many of whom are living in rural settings, receive appropriate provision. In 2014, Cathcart provided a comprehensive discussion of gifted education in New Zealand, explaining how teachers throughout the country embraced the message in the declaration by Prime Minister Peter Fraser in the 1930s:

> [E]very person, whatever [her or] his level of academic ability, whether [she or] he be rich or poor, whether [she or] he live in town or country, has a right as a citizen, to a free education of the kind for which [she or] he is best fitted and to the fullest extent of [her or] his powers.
>
> *(p. 46)*

New Zealand has its own Centre for Gifted Education (http://nzcge.co.nz), which offers a range of provisions. These include the Mindplus program, which is offered

Gifted students in rural and remote settings **187**

to selected students across New Zealand for one day per week, with approximately 50 schools currently involved. Gifted Online is another initiative, which uses technology to connect gifted children with each other, specialist teachers, and challenging and engaging learning opportunities. Originally designed to provide gifted children from rural New Zealand with access to quality gifted education, Gifted Online is now available to all gifted learners, worldwide.

While the approaches in the U.S., New Zealand, and Australia share some commonalities, there are also contextual differences in terms of research and practices, which would benefit from further exploration, particularly in relation to the key ideas outlined at the beginning of this chapter.

A personal perspective

From personal experience, teaching pre-service teachers to support gifted students in a rural environment requires an initial understanding of the "values, belief systems, and characteristics of their locale before they can understand how these apply to giftedness" (Stambaugh, 2015, p. 98). Professional learning and pre-service teacher education have the potential to make a real difference to understanding giftedness, as echoed in the following comment from a pre-service teacher in one of my gifted education courses:

> I guess I had a different conception about the whole issue of equity prior to doing this subject. It has been quite uncomfortable having my opinions challenged and I am really disappointed that it is only now in my final year, that I've been given the opportunity to grapple with some of the issues. I'd safely assumed that teaching in a rural area, I wouldn't really have to know anything about giftedness but now realise this is just not the case. I am grateful though that I have this new lens to look through in relation to my future students as I really don't think I would've even considered giftedness, twice exceptionality, underachievement etc., unless I had studied this elective. I really think it should be compulsory for everyone to do this before they begin teaching, and even more so for those in rural areas, where we might be the only ones capable of helping gifted students.
>
> *(Anonymous, personal communication)*

While there has not been a significant focus on gifted rural education within Australia or New Zealand, understandings have been developed about key challenges and potential promising responses. The call to reject a deficit focus is a welcome one, and with a direction for future research outlined in Plucker's statement at the beginning of this chapter, it is clear that future rural gifted education research needs to go beyond "presumed best practices, anecdotal evidence and conceptual analyses" (p. 431). More importantly, there needs to be formal recognition of the challenges associated with rural giftedness and practices put in place to positively respond to these, while building on the positives of the 'rural essence'.

As summed up by the guest editors of a special edition on rural giftedness in the *Journal of Advanced Academics*:

> Rural students, like their suburban and urban peers, want to live a life of significance. Too often, however, researchers, the media, politicians, and policy makers fail to provide gifted youth in rural communities the necessary considerations and resources needed for maximizing their potential. As such, we encourage educational researchers to consider rural giftedness as an entry for meaningful scholarship that further addresses opportunity gaps and examines if and how place influences the experiences for talented youth in rural communities.
>
> *(Azano & Besnoy, 2016, p. 244)*

It is hoped that this chapter provides an entry for meaningful scholarship on the topic of rural gifted in an Australian and New Zealand context.

Discussion Questions

- What might a gifted education policy need to include to make it relevant to regional/rural/remote communities in both Australia and New Zealand?
- What role could gifted associations within Australia and New Zealand, such as the AAEGT and NZAGC, play in supporting giftedness in regional/rural/remote settings?
- How can the words 'gifted' and 'gifted rural' be included in the graduate and practicing teaching standards within both Australia and New Zealand to ensure that all teachers understand the concept and are expected to include gifted students in their approach to addressing learner diversity? (At this stage, neither word – gifted or rural – appears in any of these documents.)
- How can teachers in regional/rural/remote areas be enabled to access relevant opportunities for professional development and support in relation to giftedness?

References

Assouline, S. G., Flanary, K., & Foley Nicpon, M. (2015). Challenges and solutions for serving rural gifted students: Accelerative options. In T. Stambaugh & S. M. Wood (Eds.), *Serving gifted students in rural settings* (pp. 135–153). Waco, TX: Prufrock Press.

Australian Bureau of Statistics. (2016). *Map of remoteness areas of Australia*. Retrieved from www.abs.gov.au/websitedbs/D3310114.nsf/home/remoteness+structure

Azano, A. P. (2014). Gifted rural students. In J. Plucker & C. M. Callahan (Eds.), *Critical issues and practices in gifted education: What the research says* (2nd ed., pp. 297–304). Waco, TX: Prufrock Press.

Azano, A. P., & Besnoy, K. (2016). Editorial. *Journal of Advanced Academics, 27*, 243–244.

Bannister, B., Cornish, L., Bannister-Tyrell, M., & Gregory, S. (2015). Creative use of digital technologies: Keeping the best and brightest in the bush. *Australian and International Journal of Rural Education, 25*(1), 52–65.

Baxter, J., Gray, M., & Hayes, A. (2013). *Families in regional, rural and remote Australia: Australian Institute of Family Studies fact sheet.* Retrieved from https://aifs.gov.au/publications/families-regional-rural-and-remote-australia

Benbow, C. P., Argo, T., & Glass, L. (1992). Meeting the needs of the gifted in rural areas through acceleration. *Gifted Child Today, 15*(4), 18–20.

Bevan-Brown, J. (2011). Indigenous conceptions of giftedness. In W. Vialle (Ed.), *Giftedness from an indigenous perspective* (pp. 10–23). Woolongong, NSW: Australian Association for the Gifted and Talented.

Burney, V. H., & Cross, T. L. (2006). Impoverished students with academic promise in rural settings: 10 lessons from Project Aspire. *Gifted Child Today, 29*(2), 14–21.

Cathcart, R. (2014). Will this history have a future? Building gifted provision for New Zealand – and a dilemma for the future. *Australasian Journal of Gifted Education, 23*(2), 45–59.

Centre for Education Statistics and Evaluation (CESE). (2013). *Rural and remote education: Literature review.* Sydney, NSW: Office of Education, Education and Communities.

Chaffey, G. (2002). *Identifying Australian Aboriginal children with high academic potential using dynamic testing* (Unpublished PhD thesis). University of New England, Australia.

Chaffey, G., Bailey, S., & Vine, K. (2003). Identifying high academic potential in Australian Aboriginal children using dynamic testing. *Australasian Journal of Gifted Education, 12*(1), 42–55.

Christie, M. (2011). Some Aboriginal perspectives on gifted and talented children and their schooling. In W. Vialle (Ed.), *Giftedness from an Indigenous Perspective* (pp. 36–42). Woolongong, NSW: Australian Association for the Education of the Gifted and Talented.

Clark, J., & Merrotsy, P. (2008). Gifted Aboriginal students: Making the pathway accessible. In L. Graham (Ed.), *Proceedings of the 'narrowing the gap: Addressing educational disadvantage' conference* (Vol. 1, pp. 84–98). Armidale, NSW: The National Centre of Science, Information and Communication Technology, and Mathematics Education for Rural and Regional Australia (SiMERR), University of New England.

Colangelo, N. (2015). Foreword. In T. Stambaugh & S. M. Wood (Eds.), *Serving gifted students in rural settings* (p. vii). Waco, TX: Prufrock Press.

Colangelo, N., Assouline, S. G., Baldus, C. M., & New, J. K. (2003). Gifted education in rural schools. In N. Colangelo & G. A. Davis (Eds.), *Handbook of gifted education* (3rd ed., pp. 572–581). Boston, MA: Allyn & Bacon.

Cronin, R. P., & Diezmann, C. M. (2002). Jane and Gemma go to school: Supporting young gifted Aboriginal students. *Australian Journal of Early Childhood, 27*(4), 12–17.

Cross, T. L., & Dixon, F. A. (1998). On gifted student in rural schools. *NASSP Bulletin, 82*, 119–124.

Faaea-Semeatu, T. (2011). Celebrating gifted indigenous roots: Gifted and talented pacific island (pasifika) students. In W. Vialle (Ed.), *Giftedness from an indigenous perspective* (pp. 116–122). Woolongong, NSW: Australian Association for the Education of the Gifted and Talented.

Fraser-Seeto, K., Howard, S. J., & Woodcock, S. (2013). Preparation for teaching gifted students: An updated investigation into university offerings in New South Wales. *Australasian Journal of Gifted Education, 22*(2), 45–51.

Garvis, S. (2006). Optimising the learning of gifted Aboriginal students. *International Journal of Pedagogies and Learning, 2*(3), 42–51.

Gibson, K., & Vialle, W. (2007). The Australian Aboriginal view of giftedness. In S. N. Phillipson & M. McCann (Eds.), *Conceptions of giftedness: Sociocultural perspectives* (pp. 169–196). Mahwah, NJ: Lawrence Erlbaum Associates.

Howley, A., Howley, C. B., & Pendarvis, E. D. (2003). Talent development for rural communities. In J. Borland (Ed.), *Rethinking gifted education* (pp. 80–104). New York, NY: Teachers College Press.

Howley, A., Rhodes, M., & Beall, J. (2009). Challenges facing rural schools: Implications for gifted students. *Journal for the Education of the Gifted, 32,* 515–536.

Howley, C. B., Howley, A., & Showalter, D. (2015). Leaving or staying home. In T. Stambaugh & S. M. Wood (Eds.), *Serving gifted students in rural settings* (pp. 23–51). Waco, TX: Prufrock Press.

Jones, E. D., & Southern, W. T. (1992). Programming, grouping and acceleration in rural school districts: A survey of attitudes and practices. *Gifted Child Quarterly, 36,* 112–117.

Kettler, T., Puryear, J. S., & Mullett, D. R. (2016). Defining rural in gifted education research: Methodological challenges and paths forward. *Journal of Advanced Academics, 27,* 245–265.

Lamb, S., Rumberger, R., Jesson, D., & Teese, R. (2004). *School performance in Australia: Results from analyses of school effectiveness.* Retrieved from www.eduweb.vic.gov.au/edu library/public/govrel/reports/schoolperformance-rpt.pdf

Lawrence, B. K. (2009). Rural gifted education: A comprehensive literature review. *Journal for the Education of the Gifted, 32,* 461–494.

Leonard, S. (1999). Approaches to gifted education in rural areas. *TalentEd, 17*(2), 15–18.

McClelland, I. (2013). *Research into education aspiration for regional Victoria report.* Retrieved from www.rdv.vic.gov.au/data/assets/pdf_file/0007/1158631/EducationAspiration_Full Report.pdf

Miller, M. (2011). Gifted and talented Māori and Pasifika students: Issues in their identification and program and pastoral care provision. In W. Vialle (Ed.), *Giftedness from an Indigenous perspective* (pp. 111–115). Woolongong, NSW: Australian Association for the Education of the Gifted and Talented.

Ministry of Education (NZ). (2012). *Gifted and talented students: Meeting their needs in New Zealand schools.* Wellington, NZ: Learning Media. Retrieved from http://gifted.tki.org. nz/For-schools-and-teachers

Moltzen, R. (2004). Underachievement. In D. McAlpine & R. Moltzen (Eds.), *Gifted and talented: New Zealand perspectives* (2nd ed., pp. 371–400). Palmerston North, NZ: Kanuka Grove Press.

Montgomery, D. (2004). Broadening perspectives to meet the needs of gifted learners in rural schools. *Rural Special Education Quarterly, 23*(1), 3–7.

Munro, K. (2016, December 7). Australia's real education problem is the equity gap. *The Sydney Morning Herald.* Retrieved from www.smh.com.au/comment/australias-real-edu cation-problem-is-the-equity-gap-20161206-gt5jwh.html

New South Wales Education. (2014). *State's first virtual high school ready for 2015.* Retrieved from www.dec.nsw.gov.au/about-us/news-at-det/media-releases1/state-s-first-virtual-high-school-ready-for-2015

NSW Education & Communities. (2013). *Rural and remote education: Blueprint for action.* Retrieved from www.det.nsw.edu.au/media/downloads/about-us/our-reforms/rural-and-remote-education/randr-blueprint.pdfO'Callaghan, J. (2015). *Rural NZ schools the 'forgotten group'.* Retrieved from www.stuff.co.nz/national/education/71312397/ rural-nz-schools-the-forgotten-group

Pegg, J., & Panizzon, D. L. (2007). Inequities in student achievement for literacy: Metropolitan versus rural comparisons. *Australian Journal of Language and Literacy, 30,* 177–190.

Pink, G. (2004). *New Zealand: An urban/rural profile report: Statistics New Zealand*. Retrieved from www.stats.govt.nz/browse_for_stats/Maps_and_geography/Geographic-areas/urban-rural-profile.aspx

Plucker, J. A. (2013). Students from rural environments. In C. M. Callahan & H. L. Hertberg-Davis (Eds.), *Fundamentals of gifted education: Considering multiple perspectives* (pp. 424–434). New York, NY: Routledge.

Plunkett, M. (2002). Impacting on teacher attitudes toward gifted students. In W. Vialle & J. Geake (Eds.), *The gifted enigma* (pp. 240–259). Melbourne, VIC: Hawker Brownlow.

Plunkett, M. (2006). *Tales from the pond: Perceptions of grouped and mainstream rural students regarding their distinctive learning environments*. Saarbrücken, Germany: VDM Verlag.

Plunkett, M. (2009). Re-conceptualizing ability grouping within a social justice framework: A student perspective. *Australasian Journal of Gifted Education, 18*(2), 5–16.

Plunkett, M. (2012). Justice for rural gifted students. In S. Nikakis (Ed.), *Let the tall poppies flourish: Advocating to achieve educational justice for all gifted students* (pp. 37–49). Heidelberg, VIC: Heidelberg Press.

Plunkett, M., & Harvey, D. (1995). Accelerated learning programs: Lessons from a country college. *Australasian Journal of Gifted Education, 8*(2), 16–19.

Plunkett, M., Harvey, D., & Harvey, B. (2003). Survived or thrived? Reflections of graduates of an accelerated learning program. *Australasian Journal of Gifted Education, 12*(2), 5–17.

Plunkett, M., & Kronborg, L. (2007). Gifted education in Australia: A story of striving for balance. *Gifted Education International, 23*(1), 72–83.

Plunkett, M., & Kronborg, L. (2011). Learning to be a teacher of the gifted: The importance of examining opinions and challenging misconceptions. *Gifted and Talented International, 26*(1 & 2), 31–46.

Riley, T., Bevan-Brown, J., Bicknell, B., Carroll-Lind, J., & Kearney, A. (2004). *The extent, nature, and effectiveness of planned approaches in New Zealand schools for providing for gifted and talented students. final report*. Wellington: Ministry of Education. Retrieved from www.educationcounts.govt.nz/publications/schooling/5451

Riley, T., & Bicknell, B. (2013). Gifted and talented education in New Zealand Schools: A Decade Later. *APEX: The New Zealand Journal of Gifted Education, 18*(1). Retrieved from www.giftedchildren.org.nz/apex

Riley, T. L., & Moltzen, R. (2010). *Enhancing and igniting talent development initiatives: Research to determine effectiveness*. Wellington, NZ: Ministry of Education. Retrieved from www.educationcounts.govt.nz/publications/schooling/72710

Riley, T., & White, V. (2016). Developing a sense of belonging through engagement with like-minded peers: A matter of equity. *New Zealand Journal of Educational Studies, 51*(2), 211–225.

Seward, K., & Gentry, M. (2015). Grouping and instructional management strategies. In T. Stambaugh & S. M. Wood (Eds.), *Serving gifted students in rural settings* (pp. 111–134). Waco, TX: Prufrock Press.

Sidoti, C. (2000). *The national inquiry into rural and remote school education*. Retrieved from www.hreoc.gov.au/human_rights/rural_education/

Spicker, H. H., Southern, W. T., & Davis, B. I. (1987). The rural gifted child. *Gifted Child Quarterly, 31*, 155–157.

Stambaugh, T. (2010). The education of promising students in rural areas: What do we know and what can we do? In J. L. VanTassel-Baska (Ed.), *Patterns and profiles of promising learners from poverty* (pp. 59–83). Waco, TX: Prufrock Press.

Stambaugh, T. (2015). Celebrating talent. In T. Stambaugh & S. M. Wood (Eds.), *Serving gifted students in rural settings* (pp. 97–110). Waco, TX: Prufrock Press.

Stambaugh, T., & Wood, M. (2015). Part I summary. In T. Stambaugh & S. M. Wood (Eds.), *Serving gifted students in rural settings* (pp. 91–93). Waco, TX: Prufrock Press.

Stats, N. Z. (2017). *Census quick stats about culture and identity*. Retrieved from www.stats.govt.nz/Census/2013-census/profile-and-summary-reports/quickstats-culture-identity/ethnic-groups-NZ.aspx

Stokes, H., Stafford, J., & Holdsworth, R. (2000). *Rural and remote school education: A survey for the Human Rights and Equal Opportunity Commission*. Retrieved from www.hreoc.gov.au/pdf/human_rights/rural_remote/scoping_survey.pdf

VanTassel-Baska, J., & Fischer-Hubbard, G. (2015). Serving the rural gifted child through advanced curriculum. In T. Stambaugh & S. M. Wood (Eds.), *Serving gifted students in rural settings* (pp. 155–177). Waco, TX: Prufrock Press.

Vialle, W. (Ed.) (2011). *Giftedness from an indigenous perspective*. Woolongong, NSW: Australian Association for the Education of the Gifted and Talented. Retrieved from www.aaegt.net.au/?page_id=946

Webber, M. (2011). Look to the past, stand tall in the present: The integral nature of positive racial-ethnic identity for the academic success of Mäori students. In W. Vialle (Ed.), *Giftedness from an Indigenous Perspective* (pp. 100–110). Woolongong, NSW: Australian Association for the Education of the Gifted and Talented.

White, S., Kline, J., Hastings, W., & Lock, G. (2011). *Renewing rural and regional teacher education curriculum* [online resource]. Retrieved from www.rrrtec.net.au

Wood, D., & Zundans-Fraser, L. (2013). Reaching out: Overcoming distance and supporting rural gifted students through educational opportunities. *Australasian Journal of Gifted Education, 22*(1), 42–50.

Young, D. J., & Fisher, D. L. (1996). *School effectiveness research in rural schools*. Retrieved from www.waier.org.au/forums/1996/young.html

12

PARENTS AND GIFTED AND TALENTED CHILDREN

Jennifer L. Jolly

Guiding Questions

- What role do parents and carers play in developing a child's advanced academic potential?
- How does parents' understanding of giftedness impact their ability to support their children's affective and academic needs?
- How does the relationship between schools and parents facilitate the potential of gifted and talented students?

Key Ideas

- Parents often advocate for their child at school; parent-teacher relationships can range from positive to contentious depending on the parental approach and the school's response and understanding of student need.
- Parenting styles influence gifted children's motivation toward learning.
- Understandings of giftedness impact parents' response to their children's academic and affective needs.
- Parents are integral to supporting a child's giftedness and talent development.

Introduction

> "To what extent is any issue simply what all families must confront, and to what extent is this issue unique because of the presence of a gifted child?"
>
> (Colangelo, 1997, p. 359)

194 Jennifer L. Jolly

The role of parents and caregivers in the development of a child's academic, talent, and affective development cannot be understated and is explored by the research literature (Jolly & Matthews, 2012; Garn, Matthews, & Jolly, 2012; Olszewski, Kulieke, & Buescher, 1987). The literature also reflects parents' contributions to the development of youth in sport and musical talent (Bloom, 1985; Gould, Lauer, Rolo, Jannes, & Pennisi, 2006; McPherson, 2009). However, the role of parents and carers in the development of high academic potential is not as well examined or understood — despite a century of research on gifted children, a definitive understanding remains to be achieved. Since the early studies conducted by Terman, parents of gifted and talented children have been part of research into giftedness, but not to the extent that parents' contributions have been reflected in research on typical educational environments, sports, and music. A growing body of empirical literature and a large body of anecdotal evidence exists in regards to the varying levels of support parents provide children; based on parents' reports, these levels of interaction range from damaging, to a laissez fair attitude, to optimal support with purposeful planning. This body of evidence can help to inform parents, schools, teachers, and other stakeholders who work with gifted students and their families.

This chapter discusses what is known about parents of gifted children. It focusses on questions regarding approaches to parenting that are effective in promoting the success of gifted children and how the home environment can help inform teachers' approaches to identification, differentiation, programming models, and counseling options. This chapter will also offer suggestions for future research streams to better help understand this population.

Early understandings of parental influence on gifted children

The first studies of eminence focussed on understanding familial influences on development. Francis Galton's *Hereditary Genius: An Inquiry Into Its Laws and Consequences* (1869) attempted to determine the frequency with which eminence occurred in the population. Galton suggested that the top 1 in 4,000 persons could achieve eminence, which was largely due to hereditary genetics rather than environmental influences. Galton's study did acknowledge the deep influence environmental factors could have on a child's development. Based on Galton and Freud's work, Runco and Albert (2005) argue that

> the role of family variables in an individual's attainment of eminence . . . have long been viewed as essential. The family appears to influence early cognitive development through genes and its emphases (e.g., values, educational opportunities, aspirations, and in some cases, disturbances and conflicts). All else being equal, family variables can make the difference between a fulfilled promise and dismal failure.
>
> *(p. 355)*

Approximately half a century would pass before familial influence would again be seriously considered in reference to gifted children. This renewed interest was subsumed within the renaissance occurring under the umbrella of psychological science during the early part of the 20th century (Jolly, 2005). Lewis Terman's foundational longitudinal study of over 1,500 high-IQ children yielded a sample of children derived from across the state of California, developing into the first comprehensive study of gifted family demographics (Terman, 1925). Additional studies of eminent individuals and familial influence include Goertzel and Goertzel's study of 400 eminent persons in the 1960s, Bloom's seminal work on talent development in the 1980s, and Csikszentmihalyi and colleagues' investigation of talented teenagers in the 1990s (Bloom, 1985; Csikszentmihalyi, Rathunde, & Whalen, 1996; Goertzel & Goertzel, 1962). However, the literature has remained sporadic and uneven in its attempts to unravel these important relationships.

The field of gifted education has since been rather lax in pursuing additional understandings addressing parents of gifted children. The majority of literature has been produced in the United States, with Australia and New Zealand providing limited contributions to these understandings.

Understanding giftedness

For parents and carers to be able to address their child's academic and affective needs, they must construct their own understanding of giftedness as this impacts how they respond to and advocate on behalf of their child (Jolly & Matthews, 2012; Mudrak, 2011). In Australia, where Gagné's Differentiated Model of Giftedness and Talent has been adopted by most states and territories (see Chapter 2 for more detailed explanation), giftedness is defined as a natural ability in the top 10% of individuals, while talent is defined as the development of that natural ability into skills and knowledge in a particular field where a person is performing in the top 10% (Gagné, 1991). In Gagné's model, parents are identified as central figures in the catalytic factor focussing on environment, which may have positive, negative, and neutral impacts dependent on the level and type of intervention (Gagné, 2009). New Zealand's definition of giftedness is far more culture dependent and is envisioned as a special set of abilities and skills to be used as a means to help others (Bevan-Brown, 2009).

As children are identified and labeled gifted, parents begin to develop their own understandings or misunderstandings of what this means for their children in terms of their educational and affective needs. Whether parents' understanding of giftedness aligns with the definition used by the state or individual schools has not been explored by the literature in depth, particularly in the Australian and New Zealand context. However, as the definition of giftedness in New Zealand is drawn from more culturally appropriate practices, the definition may align more closely with parental beliefs.

Parenting styles impact parents' understanding of giftedness. How parents support and foster their children's advanced abilities can enhance growth and achievement or, conversely, lead to underachievement or maladaptive behaviours (Garn et al., 2012; Garn & Jolly, 2014). Parenting styles include permissive, authoritative, or authoritarian (Baumrind, 1966). Permissive parenting suggests little is expected or necessitated from the child, even though parents are responsive to the child. Authoritarian parenting intimates rigid expectations and rules without explanation, whereas authoritative parenting provides clear guidelines and rules set by parents with reasonable contributions from the child. The literature has most consistently considered parenting styles and their impact on gifted children, particularly authoritarian and authoritative styles (Garn, Matthews, & Jolly, 2010).

Authoritarian parenting has been linked to unfavourable outcomes for families of gifted children. The unquestioned authority of parents and a family power structure where parents hold the control provides little autonomy or independence for children (Dwairy, 2004). Authoritarian parents may set goals for their children that are unrealistic or incongruous with children's goals. For example, parents may push children towards career paths such as law or medicine with little regard for a child's own interests or life goals (Morawska & Sanders, 2010). Some parents only use authoritarian parenting styles in particular situations in order to elicit certain behaviours from their children, such as the completion of homework or finishing a task within a specified time period (Garn et al., 2010). In their study of mothers of gifted children, Garn and colleagues found that the "controlling nature of the authoritarian style of parenting creates a social environment that can impede autonomy and relatedness" (Garn et al., 2012, p. 661). These types of controlling environments can lead gifted and talented students to respond by acting out or becoming disengaged (Garn et al., 2012). The use of external motivators such as rewards or punishment provides short-term solutions that can often eventuate in longer-term problems such as underachievement (Garn et al., 2010).

Pilarinos and Solomon (2017) examined parenting styles and the psychosocial difficulties of gifted children. This Canadian study surveyed the parents of 48 primary school-aged children. The overwhelming majority of these mothers and fathers described their parenting style as authoritative regardless of whether or not children were experiencing social difficulties. Mothers reported being more authoritative than fathers, but authoritarian styles among mothers were linked to fewer social difficulties in children, which led the authors to question what this finding means in terms of raising gifted children and the impact of parenting on subsequent psychosocial difficulties.

Parents who interpret their child's above-average abilities as fixed and constant entities often set unrealistic expectations for immediate superior outcomes, rather than focussing on outcomes that result from longer-term growth and nurturance (Mudrak, 2011). Authoritarian parenting styles coupled with unrealistic performance expectations may be transferred to children's own understanding about their abilities, leading them to believe that their giftedness is fixed. Mudrak's study of parental constructs also found "the manifestation of giftedness was in some cases a condition of parental acceptance and when children did not comply, parents responded with dissatisfaction or even anger" (2011, p. 213). The fixed view of a child's abilities, coupled with a tendency to emphasise the differences between children can interfere with gifted children establishing suitable peer groups. Parents of gifted children have reported that they themselves found it problematic to establish appropriate peer groups (Jolly, Matthews, & Nestor, 2013).

Dweck (2012) similarly cautions parents against viewing giftedness as a fixed entity. Unintentionally, parents (and teachers) often reinforce this fixed view of intelligence by saying to their children "you're so great at maths", "you're so clever", or "what a good job you did", without recognizing the process of sustained, targeted effort that is required to take them to the next level of expertise. This is tangentially related to the external pressure often created by parents, which children may internalize as they find it difficult to continually live up to parental expectations of the 'gifted' label (Garn, 2013). The motivation to achieve academically is then derived from these outside pressures and parental expectations, rather than from an internal drive to learn, study, and achieve.

Parental issues and support

The type and quality of the difficulties and challenges faced by parents raising gifted children is largely unknown. An Australian study conducted by Alsop (1997) highlighted the complications parents face in the larger community due to misunderstandings and stereotyping regarding their children's academic needs. Overall, research studies investigating parenting issues are minimal, but several have been undertaken that do suggest the possible need for parenting courses to address the specific needs and issues experienced by many parents of gifted and talented children.

In addition to parenting styles, research has focussed on how parents manage the behaviour of their gifted and talented children. Morawska and Sanders' (2008) survey of over 200 parents of gifted and talented children determined the styles of discipline used and level of confidence in managing their children's behaviours. Parents were also asked to describe their children's social and emotional challenges and factors that would impact these events. Data were also collected from gifted and talented children. These parents reported employing somewhat altered parenting strategies in relation to gifted children when compared to typically developing children. Disciplinary issues tended to revolve around the area of negotiation, which parents considered to be a valued skill until they encountered issues that they did not want to negotiate. Parents did report lower levels of confidence in managing some difficult behaviours, but overall felt effectual in disciplining their children and achieving satisfactory relationships. Morawska and Sanders (2009) suggest parenting programs such as the Gifted and Talented Triple P, which is an adapted version of the Triple P – Positive Parenting Program. The program uses observation, discussion, practice, and feedback in six group sessions to target specific issues in raising gifted and talented children. These issues relate to setting clear expectations, supporting persistence and perseverance, setting effective rules and boundaries, supporting healthy sibling and peer relationships, managing problematic emotions and behaviours, and developing home and school collaboration.

Gifted programming and services

The majority of parents of gifted children seek and approve of gifted programming and services on the whole; they would rather accept limited or flawed services than no services at all. Many parents also feel that gifted services could be expanded (Garvis, 2014), and they tend to be vocal when they perceive that programs and services do not adequately address the academic and affective needs of their child. Parental criticisms of gifted programs tend to coalesce around four specific areas. These include (a) a lack of confidence in a school's ability to meet their child's unique academic and/or affective needs; (b) a perceived inability of teachers to provide challenging content and pedagogy; (c) the probability that a child will be harassed by other students for leaving class to receive gifted services; and (d) lack of communication between the school and families about the nature of gifted programming (Matthews, Ritchotte, & Jolly, 2014). With the lack of a national mandate in Australia, and widely varied state and local gifted education policies across three different school sectors, gifted education programming and services can operate quite differently even within a limited geographic area.

Garvis (2014) investigated parents' perceptions and levels of satisfaction with enrichment programs in Queensland. Despite The Framework for Gifted Education in Queensland requiring gifted provisions within Queensland schools, 62% of the 102 parents surveyed cited that their child's school did not offer gifted programming or services. Those schools that did provide services typically outsourced services and then offered them only during lunch breaks or after school. This also meant that enrichment activities rarely aligned to the regular school curriculum. Finally, parents voiced a lack of transparency in the identification procedures for gifted programs, and the majority felt that more could be done to address their child's needs at school.

Due to schooling situations like the one illustrated by Garvis (2014) and through other studies, parents are often left to assume the role of advocate for their gifted children. Parents of gifted children can garner the reputation of being aggressive or pushy in their journey to seek appropriate services for their child. A study of American parents found that parents of gifted children were twice as likely to contact the teacher when compared to parents of children in regular education (Campbell & Verna, 2007). This is compounded by a perception that teachers are more likely to pursue parental contact for fundraising, volunteering, or to alert parents to a behavioural issue the teacher believes needs to be addressed, rather than to suggest or discuss educational interventions aimed at talent development or developing giftedness. These perceived or real difficulties teachers experience in dealing with parents of gifted children can sometimes encumber the relationship between home and school and the construction of a shared understanding of how to address the student's needs at school (Matthews & Jolly, 2018).

Children spend the majority of their time at home, and the influence of home typically supersedes that of the school. Campbell and Verna (2007) studied high-achieving families from 10 countries (including the U.S., Taiwan, Korea,

Germany, Finland, and China) and found that when home and school climates were more similar, students achieved at higher rates. Effective parents fostered high expectations, a productive work ethic, communication, homework completion, and academic commitment in their children. They cultivated a healthy respect for authority (in particular for one's teacher) and encouraged children to accept responsibility for their own behaviour. Parental expectations were high, but this did not always translate to high levels of parental pressure. Effective parents nurtured a strong work ethic toward school work, by emphasising the role of effort over ability in school achievement and monitoring a child's time to ensure an appropriate distribution between leisure and study. Communication was used effectively to establish a good working relationship between home and school, and to provide avenues for discussing a child's progress or achievement-related issues. Homework offered another opportunity for parents to support their child in the home. Effective parents monitored homework assignments and completion while providing an appropriate space in the home for the work to be done. Although related closely to expectations and work ethic, commitment involved supporting a child's internal motivation to achieve and reinforcing a child's positive self-concept (Campbell & Verna, 2007).

Parental involvement

Parental involvement (PI) is defined as "parents' behaviour at home and in school settings meant to support their children's educational progress" (Karbach, Gottschling, Spengler, Hegewald, & Spinath, 2013, p. 44). Wilder established a positive association between parental involvement and academic outcomes (Wilder, 2014). Largely based on anecdotal reports, it appears that the involvement of parents of gifted children often moves beyond typical volunteer activities and extends to the role of educational advocate. Research on parents as advocates for their gifted children is limited, characterised by qualitative studies with small sample sizes, and largely undertaken in the North American context. This is an avenue for further research in Australia and New Zealand.

A small critical mass of work has explored the advocacy efforts of parents of twice-exceptional children, who have been diagnosed with a specific learning difficulty or other disability in addition to being identified as gifted. Teachers often do not recognise that students can be both gifted and have a learning disability, so "parental advocacy efforts are often undermined by these stereotypes regarding the nature of giftedness" (Krausz, 2017, p. 10). Due to the lack of professional development opportunities in this area, parents may also know more about the academic needs and the cognitive, social, and behavioural profiles of twice-exceptional students than do many teachers (Neumeister, Yssel, & Burney, 2013). In some cases, this perceived power differential on the part of the teacher may undermine parental advocacy efforts. Research by Neumeister et al. (2013) also found that responsibility for monitoring the academic growth of twice-exceptional students fell exclusively to the 10 sets of parents in their study.

In Rubenstein, Schelling, Wilczynski, and Hooks' (2015) phenomenological study of parents of gifted students with autism spectrum disorder (ASD), 13 parents were interviewed to understand the challenges of trying to secure appropriate educational placements. Parents applied different approaches to advocate for their child. These ranged from offering teachers literature or paying conference registration for teachers to relevant events, to advocating strongly for services when teachers were resistant to these more educative efforts. Depending on the collaborative nature of the home-school relationship, outcomes of parents' advocacy efforts ranged from positive to non-existent. In cases where schools did not provide appropriate curriculum, parents found themselves supplementing school education with enrichment activities at home. More often than not, families in Rubenstein et al.'s sample ended up leaving their original schools due to a perceived lack of responsiveness. They either sought other schools or decided to educate their children at home.

Besnoy et al. (2015) also examined the advocacy experiences of parents of twice-exceptional children. Because twice-exceptional children can often have a myriad of learning needs, parents must direct their advocacy skills towards the provision of services to address both learning challenges and strengths. This study included eight parents whose children were identified as gifted with a range of disability diagnoses including Asperger's syndrome, obsessive-compulsive disorder, learning disabilities, and high-functioning autism. The researchers found that "parents in this study were simultaneously advocating for their child's disability and protecting their child's giftedness" (Besnoy et al., 2015, p. 119), again due to teachers' lack of acceptance of the existence of giftedness and disability in the same child. At the outset of their advocacy journeys, parents did not feel confident or knowledgeable about either exceptionality. However, as time progressed, they became conversant in both special and gifted education interventions and best practices, and they became effective and confident activists for their child's educational needs. This parental knowledge was not often viewed positively by schools, who often found "the vigilant nature of parental efforts as obstacles to collaborative partnership" (p. 119).

Margrain's (2010) New Zealand study of gifted early readers highlighted the important role parents can play in seeking out the most appropriate cognitive challenges for their children. The parents in Margrain's study indicated that one of their most effective advocacy strategies centred on scaffolding relationships with their child's teacher. This included volunteering in the classroom and going on class excursions in hopes of building currency for future conversations regarding advanced learning opportunities. Margrain's parents also underscored the importance of being "guided by their children's strengths and interests. . . . Parents strongly rejected that they had explicitly taught the children, possibly wanting to discount notions of formal teaching, hothousing, or being 'pushy' parents" (Margrain, 2010, p. 43).

For students who are most underrepresented in gifted programs, parental advocacy is especially important. A study featuring parents of gifted African American students in a large urban public school system in the U.S. sought to understand

Parents and gifted and talented children **201**

their experience and perceptions (Huff, Houskamp, Watkins, Stanton, & Tavegia, 2005). African American students are 66% less likely to be identified for gifted programs, while Hispanic students are 47% less likely to be selected, when compared to their White peers (Wong, 2016). Comparable data about the proportional representation of minority groups in gifted education are not available in the Australian and New Zealand contexts, but international studies and models may have implications for some populations in this context. Many of the parents in this U.S. study had backgrounds in education, which they drew upon in order to find supplementary materials and work with teachers. The authors noted that

> the parents interviewed had worked to establish such a collaborative relationship; however, they clearly believed that this relationship was based on their similar background and familiarity with the education system and not upon an educational system that was sensitive in reach out to the African American community.
>
> *(2005, p. 219)*

Parents involved in the study worried about families who worked long hours and were unfamiliar with the education system. They felt these families would not be able to negotiate the complexities of the school system and advocate effectively due to the demands on their time and unfamiliarity with the context. For example, one participant explained her interaction with an administrator who was attempting to deny her child access to an Advanced Placement class that she had clearly qualified for, suggesting that "There are lots of Black children who have fallen through the cracks simply because the schools are not receptive. It's like a guarded secret" (Huff et al., 2005, p. 219).

Grantham, Frasier, Roberts, and Bridges (2005) introduced an advocacy model for culturally diverse gifted students, Gifted Program Advocacy Model (G-PAM), in response to underrepresentation of culturally diverse students in gifted programs in the U.S., which "requires parents to coadvocate for equity and excellence" (p. 140). The G-PAM includes four phases: (a) needs assessment, (b) development of advocacy plan, (c) implementation, and (d) follow-up and evaluation. This model was developed to assist parents as they begin their advocacy work on behalf of their gifted children. As parents become better educated about gifted education principles and the barriers that culturally diverse students face to accessing appropriate educational opportunities, the more effective they will be in gaining appropriate programming and services for their children.

Collectively, these studies support previous research on parental involvement and teachers' unpreparedness for certain home-school interactions (Walker & Hoover-Dempsey, 2008). These studies also feature the continuing need to foster home-school relationships. Rather than adversarial relationships with competing needs, parents and schools are stakeholders who can work together focussing on shared interests.

Support in the home environment

Research is clear in establishing the connection between familial support and the development of social abilities in children, and home environments can exert a range of influences on gifted students. Systems developed in the home provide the emotional support and autonomy necessary for successful relationships with friends and other peers outside of the home (Cohen, Patterson, & Christopoulos, 1991). Olszewski-Kubilius, Lee, and Thomson (2014) extended this line of inquiry by examining the relationship between familial influence and social competence for gifted students. They defined social competence as "the social, emotional, and cognitive skills and behaviours that individual needs to successfully engage socially with peers and others to develop rewarding friendships and relationships" (Olszewski-Kubilius et al., 2014, p. 199). Overall, this sample of approximately 1,500 students and their families reported positive family environments with propensities toward open communication, cohesiveness, and positivity. Students from socially competent homes that were less successful described greater instances of chaos, disconnection, and poor communication. Although the families did report levels of rigidity, they were interpreted as positive given that the scaffolds required to support talent development often include structure to accommodate highly scheduled activities.

Wellisch, Brown, and Knight (2012) emphasized the importance of a healthy home environment with a focus on the mental health of mothers. In their Australian study of mothers and gifted children, the authors reported on 11 mothers' personal psychosocial difficulties, including maternal depression and social difficulties, and how these might contribute to their children's social-emotional well-being (however, it was emphasised that the mothers' difficulties were not the only factors contributing to a child's challenges). Mothers' initial misunderstandings of their gifted child's behaviour were rectified in most cases, and adjustments were made to provide more supportive home environments. In addition, the mothers' experiences of depression sometimes confounded problematic social-emotional situations for their children. Rectifying these situations required support for the mothers' mental health.

The influence of home environment and parental support can perhaps be characterised as most intense when homeschooling is implemented for gifted children. This avenue is usually pursued when all other options have been exhausted and parents have become frustrated with the types of support, programming, and services provided at the school or schools their child has attended (Jolly et al., 2013). The number of families choosing to homeschool in Australia due to dissatisfaction with schools' responses to students with advanced learning needs is on the rise (English, 2016). The appeal of homeschooling for parents of gifted learners stems from the potential it offers to shape an education to meet a child's unique educational needs. Parents navigate the options of accelerating content, studying topics in-depth, connecting children with mentors, and finding like-minded peers for their child to work with. Homeschooling provides parents curricular flexibility to respond almost immediately to their child's educational needs, which is often not possible in schools (Jolly & Matthews, 2017). However, research to support the academic efficacy of homeschooling for gifted students (or homeschooling in general, for that matter) has yet to be established.

Final thoughts

The importance of parents' engagement in the development of their child's gifts and talents cannot be understated. Fostering and supporting home-school partnerships and relationships can contribute considerably to the development of children's gifts and potential. Although there is not professional development for parents in the same way that there is for teachers, parents' understandings of parenting styles, supports for motivating their children, and providing an encouraging and appropriate home environment all impact the development of gifted children across the lifespan. Due to the limited research regarding all facets of parenting gifted children, there is still much work left to be done. Specific areas for future research include exploring parents' understanding of giftedness and talent; the challenges in raising gifted children; the role of home-school relationships; parents' experiences of advocacy; and the efficacy of homeschooling.

Discussion Questions

- What elements can foster supportive home-school partnerships to support the education of gifted children?
- How do home environments hinder or reinforce talent development?
- How do parenting styles impact the motivation of gifted and talented children? Do parenting styles vary between mother and fathers?

References

Alsop, G. (1997). Coping or counseling: Families of intellectually gifted students. *Roeper Review, 20*, 28–34.

Baumrind, D. (1966). Effects of authoritative parental control on child behaviour. *Child Development, 37*, 887–907.

Besnoy, K. D., Swoszowski, N. C., Newman, J. L., Floyd, A., Jones, P., & Byrne, C. (2015). The advocacy experiences of parents of elementary age, twice-exceptional children. *Gifted Child Quarterly, 59*, 108–123.

Bevan-Brown, J. (2009). Identifying and providing for gifted and talented Maori students. *APEX, 15*(1).

Bloom, B. (1985). *Developing talent in young people*. New York, NY: Ballantine.

Campbell, J. R., & Verna, M. A. (2007) Effective parental influence: Academic home climate linked to children's achievement. *Educational Research and Evaluation, 13*, 501–519.

Cohn, D. A., Patterson, C. J., & Christopoulos, C. (1991). The family and children's peer relations. *Journal of Social and Personal Relationships, 8*, 315–346.

Colangelo, N. (1997). Counseling gifted students: Issues and practices. In N. Colangelo & G. Davis (Eds.), *Handbook of gifted education* (pp. 353–365). Needham Heights, MA: Allyn & Bacon.

Csikszentmihalyi, C., Rathunde, K., & Whalen, S. (1996). *Talented teenagers*. New York, NY: Cambridge University Press.

Dwairy, M. (2004). Parenting styles and mental health of Arab gifted adolescents. *Gifted Child Quarterly, 48*, 275–286.

Dweck, C. S. (2012). Mindsets and malleable minds: Implications for giftedness and talent. In R. F. Subotnik, A. Robinson, C. M. Callahan, & E. J. Gubbins (Eds.), *Malleable minds: Translating insights from psychology and neuroscience to gifted education* (pp. 7–18). Storrs, CT: The National Research Center on the Gifted and Talented.

English, R. (2016, June). Too cool for school? Why home schooling numbers are increasing in Australia. *Independent Education, 46*(2), 17. Retrieved from http://search.informit.com.au/fullText;dn=473704472522815;res=IELHSS

Gagné, F. (1991). Toward a differentiated model of giftedness and talent. In N. Colangelo & G. A. Davis (Eds.), *Handbook of gifted education* (pp. 65–80). Boston, MA: Allyn & Bacon.

Gagné, F. (2009). Building gifts into talents: Detailed overview of the DMGT 2.0. In B. MacFarlane & T. Stambaugh (Eds.), *Leading change in gifted education: The festschrift of Dr. Joyce VanTassel-Baska* (pp. 61–80). Waco, TX: Prufrock Press.

Galton, F. (1869/1892). *Hereditary genius: An inquiry into its laws and consequences* (2nd ed.). London: Macmillan & Co. Retrieved from http://galton.org/books/hereditary-genius/text/pdf/galton-1869-genius-v3.pdf

Garn, A. C. (2013, June). Parental strategies that support academic motivation. *Parenting for High Potential*, 4–8.

Garn, A. C., & Jolly, J. L. (2014). High ability students' voice on learning motivation. *Journal of Advanced Academics, 25*, 7–24.

Garn, A. C., Matthews, M. S., & Jolly, J. L. (2010). Parental influences on the academic motivation of gifted students: A self-determination theory perspective. *Gifted Child Quarterly, 54,* 263–272.

Garn, A. C., Matthews, M. S., & Jolly, J. L. (2012). Parents' role in the academic motivations of students with gifts and talents. *Psychology in the Schools, 49*, 656–667.

Garvis, S. (2014). Parents' perceptions of gifted and enrichment programs in Queensland, Australia. *TalentEd, 28*, 65–70.

Goertzel, V., & Goertzel, M. (1962). *Cradles of eminence*. New York, NY: Little, Brown & Co.

Gould, D., Lauer, L., Role, C., Jannes, C., & Pennisi, N. (2006). Understanding the role parents play in tennis success: A national survey of tennis coaches. *British Journal of Sports Medicine, 40*, 632–636.

Grantham, T. C., Fraiser, M. M., Roberts, A. C., & Bridges, E. M. (2005). Parent advocacy for culturally diverse gifted students. *Theory Into Practice, 44*, 138–147.

Huff, R. E., Houskamp, B. M., Watkins, A. V., Stanton, M., & Tavegia, B. (2005). The experiences of parents of gifted African American children: A phenomenological study. *Roeper Review, 27*, 215–221.

Jolly, J. L. (2005). The foundations of the field of gifted education. *Gifted Child Today, 28*(2), 14–18, 65.

Jolly, J. L., & Matthews, M. S. (2012). A critique of the literature on the parenting of gifted learners. *Journal for the Education of the Gifted, 35*, 259–290.

Jolly, J. L., & Matthews, M. S. (2017). Why we blog: Home schooling mothers of gifted children. *Roeper Review, 39*, 112–120.

Jolly, J. L., Matthews, M. S., & Nestor, J. (2013). Home schooling the gifted: A parent's perspective. *Gifted Child Quarterly, 57*, 121–134.

Karbach, J., Gottschling, J., Spengler, M., Hegewald, K., & Spinath, F. M. (2013). Parent involvement and general cognitive ability as predictors of domain-specific academic achievement in early adolescence. *Learning and Instruction, 23*, 43–51.

Krausz, L. (2017). Understanding the learning and advocacy needs of a twice-exceptional student through a strengths-based lens: Review of the literature. *Scholarship and Engagement in Education, 1*. Retrieved from http://scholar.dominican.edu/seed/vol1/iss1/10

Margrain, V. G. (2010). Parent-teacher partnership for gifted early readers in New Zealand. *International Journal About Parents in Education, 4,* 39–48.

Matthews, M. S., & Jolly, J. L. (2018). Parents and the development of gifted students. In C. M. Callahan & H. Hertberg-Davis (Eds.), *Fundamentals of gifted education* (pp. 447–456). New York, NY: Routledge.

Matthews, M. S., Ritchotte, J. A., & Jolly, J. L. (2014). What's wrong with giftedness? Parents' perceptions of the gifted label. *International Studies in Sociology Education, 24*, 372–393.

McPherson, G. E. (2009). The role of parents in children's musical development. *Psychology of Music, 37*, 91–110.

Morawska, A., & Sanders, M. R. (2008). Parenting gifted and talented children: What are the key child behaviour and parenting issues? *Australian and New Zealand Journal of Psychiatry, 42*, 819–827.

Morawska, A., & Sanders, M. R. (2009). Parenting gifted and talented children: Conceptual and empirical foundations. *Gifted Child Quarterly, 53*, 163–173.

Morawska, A., & Sanders, M. R. (2010). An evaluation of a behavioural parenting intervention for parents of gifted children. *Behavioural Research and Therapy, 47*, 463–470.

Mudrak, J. (2011). "He was born that way": Parent constructions of giftedness. *High Ability Studies, 22*, 199–217.

Neumeister, K. S., Yssel, N., & Burney, V. H. (2013). The influence of primary caregivers in fostering success in twice-exceptional children. *Gifted Child Quarterly, 57*, 263–274.

Olszewski, P., Kulieke, M., & Buescher, T. (1987). The influence of the family environment on the develop of talent: A literature review. *Journal for the Education of the Gifted, 11*, 6–28.

Olszewski-Kubilius, P., Lee, S-Y., & Thomson, D. (2014). Family environment and social development in gifted students. *Gifted Child Quarterly, 58*, 199–216.

Pilarinos, V., & Solomon, C. R. (2017). Parenting styles and adjustment in gifted children. *Gifted Child Quarterly, 61*, 87–98.

Rubenstein, L. D., Schelling, N., Wilczynski, S. M., & Hooks, E. N. (2015). Lived experiences of parents of gifted students with autism spectrum disorder: The struggle to find appropriate educational experience. *Gifted Child Quarterly, 59*, 283–298.

Runco, M. A., & Albert, R. S. (2005). Parents' personality and the creative potential of exceptionally gifted boys. *Creativity Research Journal, 17*, 355–367.

Terman, L. M. (1925). *Mental and physical traits of a thousand gifted children* [Genetics Studies of Genius, Volume 1]. Stanford, CA: Stanford University Press.

Walker, J. M. T., & Hoover-Dempsey, K. V. (2008). Parent involvement. In T. Good (Ed.), *21st century education: A reference handbook* (pp. 382–392). Thousand Oaks, CA: Sage.

Wellisch, M., Brown, J., & Knight, R. (2012). Gifted and misunderstood: Mothers' narratives of their children's socio-emotional adjustment and educational challenge. *Australasian Journal of Gifted Education, 21*(2), 5–18.

Wilder, S. (2014). Effects of parental involvement on academic achievement: A meta-synthesis. *Educational Review, 66*, 377–397.

Wong, A. (2016, January). Why are there so few Black children in gifted programs? *The Atlantic.* Retrieved from www.theatlantic.com/education/archive/2016/01/why-are-there-so-few-black-children-in-gifted-and-talented-programs/424707/

13

GIFTED EDUCATION IN AUSTRALIA AND NEW ZEALAND

Reflections and future directions

Jane M. Jarvis, Jennifer L. Jolly, and Roger Moltzen

In this chapter, we reflect on key ideas from the text and identify priorities for future research and scholarship in gifted education, with a focus on Australia and New Zealand. *Exploring Gifted Education: Australian and New Zealand Perspectives* represents the first dedicated attempt to bring together scholars from both countries to review the research base on a series of relevant topics in contemporary gifted education. This collaboration comes at a time when an increasing number of authors from New Zealand are submitting work to the (traditionally Australia-dominated) *Australasian Journal of Gifted Education*, and soon after the World Council for Gifted and Talented Children held their biennial conference in Sydney, which included many contributions from Australian and New Zealand scholars and practitioners. Reflection on the state of the field in both countries, and consideration of possible next steps, is timely.

The history and practice of gifted education is not consistent across Australian states and territories, much less between Australia and New Zealand. A central commonality across both nations though is an ingrained cultural concern with egalitarianism, which presents both possibilities and challenges for gifted education. Gifted education scholars in this part of the world have regularly lamented the culturally pervasive 'tall poppy syndrome' that sees high achievers 'cut down' so as not to diminish the status of others (e.g., Gross, 1999). The more recent enhanced focus on accountability for students' literacy and numeracy performance against minimum benchmarks is an additional systemic factor which, based on experience from other parts of the world, has the potential to further undermine attention to advanced learners (e.g., Jolly, 2015). Beliefs among teachers and school leaders that gifted students are already advantaged and do not require specialised attention, or that practices such as academic acceleration are socially and emotionally harmful (e.g., Plunkett & Kronborg, 2011), have also worked against gifted education efforts, as have persistent low academic expectations for students from Indigenous or low socio-economic backgrounds and those living in rural and remote areas. These and similar issues have been discussed throughout this text.

Peters and Engerrand (2016) discuss the challenge of achieving an ideal balance between equity and excellence in programs for gifted learners. They argue that if the pendulum swings too far towards identifying and providing opportunities for learners who currently display excellent performance, it is likely that students from White, socio-economically advantaged families will be disproportionately represented, due in part to inequitable prior educational opportunities. Conversely, an inordinate focus on equity (including proportional representation) might result in programs that fail to achieve the central purpose of nurturing excellence through advanced educational opportunities for those students who are ready to benefit. In Australia and New Zealand, where egalitarianism is a defining cultural principle, the perceived tension between issues of equity and excellence in the education of gifted learners is similarly pertinent and extends beyond questions of identification and representation. Indeed, negotiating that balance is paramount to the identity and survival of gifted education as a field in both countries.

There is no question that the principles of equity and excellence – defined in Australia's 2008 Melbourne Declaration on Educational Goals for Young Australians (MCEETYA, 2008) and New Zealand's *National Education Goals* (Ministry of Education, 2015) – are complementary aspirations for contemporary education. Educators and policy makers would be quick to endorse a schooling system that cultivates outstanding achievement and prepares students for the highest possible levels of contribution to society, at the same time as it systematically ensures access to high-quality learning experiences for all young people, regardless of background or personal circumstances (Jarvis, 2017). Yet, walking the tightrope between these dual goals is clearly no easy feat, and nowhere is this balancing act more precarious than in the education of gifted learners. Any sustainable, integrated, widely supported framework for gifted education must address very real issues of equity and must embody a rationale that is culturally relevant and firmly embedded in a broader educational vision. Authors in this volume have emphasised the need to ensure that gifted students from all parts of the community are represented in research, policy, and practice, and this includes gifted students living with disability, gifted students from various Indigenous cultures, those living in poverty, and very young gifted students and their families. Attention to equity issues in the design of identification, curriculum, and programming practices have also been underscored by chapter authors.

While principles of equity are perpetually discussed in education, including in relation to gifted education, complementary principles of excellence receive far less attention. Looking ahead, this is a discussion that gifted education scholars are well-placed to contribute to and shape. Despite continual documentation (including in the context of multiple government inquiries and reports) of systemic and cultural factors that undermine gifted education efforts, there is little evidence of evolution in the rationale presented for gifted education. Arguments based solely on individual student need are unlikely to be effective in a system characterised by limited

208 Jarvis et al.

(and often discretionary) resources for various groups of students with special needs and pressure to ensure minimum performance standards. And railing against anti-intellectualism, however well-intentioned, has resulted in little progress to date. What opportunities are there to reframe the rationale for advanced educational opportunities in the current educational climate? To offer one suggestion, attempts to define and support the pursuit of excellence might be logically tied to national priorities in science, technology, engineering, and maths (STEM) domains (as discussed by Watters in this volume). Similarly, as one of the few fields of education research concerned with understanding and fostering creativity across disciplines (see Merrotsy, this volume), gifted education is well-placed to advance the national discourse around innovation. And while the education of Indigenous students in both Australia and New Zealand is perpetually discussed in terms of achievement gaps and underperformance, gifted education can offer perspectives on fostering excellence in students from Indigenous populations. Discussions about implementing national curriculum frameworks for the full range of learners, defining and evaluating teachers' performance against national professional teaching standards, and reflecting on students' growth as measured by numeracy and literacy tests and through international comparisons are likely to provide further opportunities for promoting the education of highly able students. In order to remain relevant, gifted education must maintain a place at the table and a strong voice in broader discussions of education in local, national, and international forums.

Linking gifted education concerns to broader educational and national priorities may engender greater support (including financial) for high-quality research. In New Zealand, for example, the Ministry of Education outlines a set of priorities that are clearly reflected in funding for professional learning. Conducting research that both links to government priority areas and is integrated into professional learning initiatives is more likely to attract support than research that seems marginal or relevant to only a small number of students. An example is the commitment of the government and Ministry of Education to the educational success of Māori students. Given the underrepresentation of Māori students in provisions for the gifted and talented, there may be a natural opportunity for gifted education researchers to collaborate with those working in the broader area of responsive pedagogies. Similarly, there may be scope for gifted education researchers to collaborate in larger research teams investigating the outcomes of recent structural changes involving the clustering of schools and early childhood services into Communities of Learning or Kāhui Ako. A Community of Learning is a group of education and training providers (early learning, schools, kura, and post-secondary) working together to help students achieve their full potential. There are important questions about this model that can be addressed through research, and key areas of focus for gifted education researchers might include the implications for academically advanced students as they transition from one level of education to the next, a process that has often presented significant challenges in terms of educational continuity.

As the broader discourse of education continues to become more inclusive, it is critical that scholars from Australia and New Zealand articulate the purpose and place of gifted education in a way that coheres with an inclusive agenda. Arguably, gifted education advocates have not strongly emphasised synergies between gifted and general education or used the language of inclusion to advocate for the place of gifted students in a broader, highly flexible, and responsive system as often as they might, although there are certainly exceptions (for example, see Vialle & Rogers, 2012, and Moltzen, 2006, for discussions of the links between inclusion and gifted education). This is not to say that specialised educational opportunities for gifted learners are unwarranted or should not be advocated; indeed, there is considerable evidence that in the absence of explicit identification and programming for gifted students, teachers are unlikely to provide appropriately challenging learning experiences in the regular classroom (Plucker & Callahan, 2014). Rather, it should be acknowledged that decisions about the education of gifted learners occur within an interdependent system and have palpable implications for all students and for multiple aspects of practice (Jarvis & Henderson, 2014). Effective advocacy (and programming) for gifted education is likely to be most effective when based on a clear rationale for how specialised learning opportunities for gifted students build upon, contribute to, and where necessary diverge from more mainstream teaching and learning practices. Contemporary models in special education, behaviour support, and mental health promotion all reflect a cohesive continuum of intervention ranging from universal strategies for all students through to targeted strategies for some students and then more intensive and individualised interventions for a smaller number of students with more specialised needs; comparable models do exist in the gifted education literature, but they have not become mainstream practice in the Australian or New Zealand contexts, and this leaves gifted education isolated from other major fields of practice in education (Jarvis, 2017). A continuum of provisions for gifted students is discussed in the chapters on curriculum and programming in this volume. The current international focus on talent development approaches to gifted education (Subotnik, Olszewski-Kubilius, & Worrell, 2011) may provide an opportunity for rethinking gifted education in this part of the world in a way that conceptually aligns with aspects of Gagné's (2009) DMGT, with talent development efforts in fields such as sport that enjoy greater cultural acceptance, and with other areas of research and practice concerned with students with special needs.

Regardless of how the argument in favour of gifted education is framed, the future success of the field will certainly depend on the strength of its research base. It will likely always be challenging to convince educational leaders, teachers, and policy makers to allocate resources to the education of students with perceived high potential or already performing at higher-than-expected levels. In the absence of a solid base of evidence about what works in the education of diverse gifted students in relevant local contexts, and the specific benefits of gifted education practices, it may be close to impossible. There is no doubt that the lack of a coordinated local research base represents a significant challenge for the field of gifted education in Australia and New Zealand. Teacher attitudes towards giftedness and gifted education, efforts to educate teachers and school leaders about the nature and needs of gifted students, and students' (predominantly positive) experiences of academic acceleration have been strong local research themes, but there remain significant gaps in the overall research base. Most studies have been small in scale, and a significant proportion of the research base consists of doctoral and master's theses.

In New Zealand, there have been some efforts to conduct coordinated national research, including through a large-scale questionnaire about current practices in schools (Riley, Bevan-Brown, Bicknell, Carroll-Lind, & Kearney, 2004) that is soon to be replicated. There is no comparable, coordinated research in Australia, and both nations would benefit from research documenting the effectiveness of gifted education in multi-faceted ways. Achieving this goal will require a combination of gradually scaling up from quality local research and incorporating gifted education perspectives into broader studies. For example, the Teacher-Led Innovation Fund in New Zealand supports teams of qualified teachers from early learning services, *ngā kōhanga reo*, schools, and *kura* to collaboratively develop innovative practices that improve learning outcomes; this model lends itself to collaboration between teachers and academics developing and researching the effectiveness of specific educational practices, including those relevant for highly able students. It could provide an avenue for documenting the effectiveness of specific gifted education practices across diverse local settings, with a view to subsequently combining these data to offer a more comprehensive evidence base.

Authors in this volume have recommended a range of priorities for future research, reflecting the diversity of topics and approaches that may contribute to an overall evidence base. A common thread across chapters is the principle that gifted students are diverse and that local context matters. This principle is supported by calls for attention to special populations of gifted students in research studies, including those in rural and remote settings, in early education contexts, those considered twice exceptional, and those from Indigenous backgrounds. A second common thread concerns a need for research systematically examining the effects of local, contextual practices, including specific outcomes for student learning. Traditionally, studies of programs and practices (including teacher education programs) relevant to gifted learners have been relatively small-scale and have included descriptions of practice or informal measures of satisfaction or perceived value, but have not included measures of impact on student learning. This is not unique to Australia or New Zealand and represents a core concern for gifted education researchers internationally (Plucker & Callahan, 2014). However, with smaller populations, fewer researchers, and a lack of mandated provision for gifted students, these concerns may be exacerbated for local researchers.

The goal of a coherent evidence base to support advocacy and funding efforts is unlikely to be achieved in this context without coordinated efforts across organisational bodies, academic institutions, and states/territories. Efforts to link gifted education research to broader national and local priority areas, to explore opportunities to use existing large data sources, to develop inter-disciplinary, cross-institutional, and multi-site studies, to incorporate a focus on diverse populations of gifted learners, to document the measured impact of gifted education on student learning, and to examine the applicability of evidence-based international practices in an Australian context should all be priorities for the next phase of gifted education scholarship in Australia and New Zealand, as it seeks to move from the fringes of education research and practice to the mainstream.

References

Gagné, F. (2009). Building gifts into talents: Detailed overview of the DMGT 2.0. In B. MacFarlane & T. Stambaugh (Eds.), *Leading change in gifted education: The festschrift of Dr. Joyce Van Tassel-Baska* (pp. 61–80). Waco, TX: Prufrock Press.

Gross, M. U. M. (1999). Inequity in equity: The paradox of gifted education in Australia. *Australian Journal of Education, 43*(1), 87–93.

Jarvis, J. M. (2017). Supporting diverse gifted students. In M. Hyde, L. Carpenter, & S. Dole (Eds.), *Diversity, inclusion and engagement* (3rd ed.). Port Melbourne, VIC: Oxford University Press.

Jarvis, J. M., & Henderson, L. (2014). Defining a coordinated approach to gifted education. *Australasian Journal of Gifted Education, 23*(1), 5–14.

Jolly, J. L. (2015). The cost of high-stakes testing for high-ability students. *Australasian Journal of Gifted Education, 24*(1), 30–36.

Ministerial Council on Education, Employment, Training and Youth Affairs (MCEETYA). (2008). *Melbourne declaration on educational goals for young Australians.* Retrieved from www.mceetya.edu.au/mceecdya/melbourne_declaration,25979.html

Ministry of Education. (2015). *The national education goals.* Retrieved from https://education.govt.nz/ministry-of-education/legislation/negs

Moltzen, R. (2006). Can 'inclusion' work for the gifted and talented? In C. M. Smith (Ed.), *Including the gifted and talented: Making inclusion work for more gifted and able learners* (pp. 41–55). Oxon: Routledge.

Peters, S. J., & Engerrand, K. G. (2016). Equity and excellence: Proactive efforts in the identification of underrepresented students for gifted and talented services. *Gifted Child Quarterly, 60*, 159–171.

Plucker, J. A., & Callahan, C. M. (2014). Research on giftedness and gifted education: Status of the field and considerations for the future. *Exceptional Children, 80*, 390–406.

Plunkett, M., & Kronborg, L. (2011). Learning to be a teacher of the gifted: The importance of examining opinions and challenging misconceptions. *Gifted and Talented International, 26*(1–2), 31–46.

Riley, T., Bevan-Brown, J., Bicknell, B., Carroll-Lind, J., & Kearney, A. (2004). *The extent, nature and effectiveness of planned approaches in New Zealand schools for identifying and providing for gifted and talented students.* Wellington, NZ: Ministry of Education.

Subotnik, R. F., Olszewski-Kubilius, P., & Worrell, F. C. (2011). Rethinking giftedness and gifted education: A proposed direction forward based on psychological science. *Psychological Science in the Public Interest, 12*, 3–54.

Vialle, W., & Rogers, K. (2012). Gifted, talented, or educationally disadvantaged? The case for including 'giftedness' in teacher education programs. In C. Forlin (Eds.), *Future directions for inclusive teacher education: An international perspective* (pp. 114–122). London: Routledge.

INDEX

2e Students 50–62; Attention-Deficit Hyperactivity Disorder (ADHD) 21; Autism Spectrum Disorder (ASD) 21, 25, 52, 53, 59, 64, 200, 205; Dyslexia 53; Educational Supports 54; Interventions 2, 14, 19, 22, 24, 46, 52, 56, 56, 77, 78, 84, 103, 109, 111, 117, 131, 156, 160, 166, 170, 198, 200, 209; Physical Disability 52; *Savant Skill Curriculum* 59; Specific Learning Disorder (SLD) 21–22, 53, 56–57; Visual or Auditory Processing Disorder 53

abbreviated IQ Tests 25
Aboriginal students 106, 107, 109, 181, 182, 189; Merrotsy 32–49
above-level testing 16, 30
academically gifted 28, 29, 92, 95, 100, 103
acceleration 6, 14, 20, 48, 58, 59, 67, 76–80, 89, 96, 106, 109, 111, 112, 116–118, 128, 129, 133, 134, 139, 149, 150, 160, 181, 189, 206, 210
Achievement Integrated Model 43, 46
affective needs 67, 68, 72, 73, 76, 77, 113, 121, 195, 198; *Ode to Those Bright and Bullied* 73; perfectionism 26, 69, 76, 79, 80, 168; resilience 60, 74, 69–70, 78–79; underachievement 12, 42, 70–71, 76, 79, 80, 145, 187, 190, 196
asynchronous development 66, 71, 76, 77
Attention Deficit Hyperactivity Disorder (ADHD) 21; behaviour checklists 18, 22
Australasian Journal of Gifted Education 80, 150, 167, 206, 211

Australian Association for the Education of the Gifted and Talented (AAEGT) 6, 179; *Australasian Journal of Gifted Education* 80, 150, 167, 206, 211
Australian Curriculum Assessment and Reporting Authority (ACARA) 41, 46, 48, 88, 91, 98, 99, 107, 114, 128
Australian Professional Standards for Teachers 87, 129
Australian Science and Mathematics School 135
Autism Diagnostic Observation Schedule (ADOS) 23
Autism Diagnostic Review – Revised (ADI-R) 23
Autism Spectrum Disorder (ASD) 21, 25, 52, 53, 59, 64, 200, 205

Beghetto, Ronald 32, 37, 45, 46, 47; Autism Diagnostic Observation Schedule (ADOS) 23; Autism Diagnostic Review – Revised (ADI-R) 23; Behavioral Assessment System for Children (BASC-2) 23; Developmental Neuropsychological Assessment (NEPSY-II) 23; Four C Model of Creativity 37, 45; Social Skills Rating System (SSRS) 23; Vineland Adaptive Behavior Scales (Vineland-II) 23; Wechsler Intelligence Scale for Children (WISC-IV) 14, 23, 30; Woodcock-Johnson (WJ-III) Achievement Battery 23
Behavioral Assessment System for Children (BASC-2) 23

214 Index

Bevan-Brown, Jill 8, 10, 17, 25, 61, 66, 74, 78, 89, 91, 114, 120–121, 128, 155–156, 167, 175, 181, 189, 191, 195, 203, 210, 211
Big-C creativity 37, 38
Bloom's Taxonomy 32, 34, 42, 43, 46, 176

Centre for Gifted Education 159, 186
ChallenGE Project 126
Checklist of Creative Positives 38–39
Children of High Intelligence: A New Zealand Study 11
Children or Students with Special Abilities (C/SWSA) 7
Clark, Trevor 50–65
CLEAR 24, 34, 37, 39, 61, 87, 98, 104, 105, 116, 120, 124, 167, 146, 187, 206, 197, 201, 202, 197, 208, 209; Depth and Complexity 99, 104, 109; Differentiated Instruction 99, 105, 130; Schoolwide Enrichment Model 101, 110, 119, 139, 150
Cognitive Assessment System (CAS) 15
Cohen, David 24, 36, 40, 37, 202; *How Creative Are You?* 40
Collaborative Australian Secondary Science Program (CASSP) 141
compensatory rule 20–21
conjunctive rule 20–21
continuum of approach 117, 118, 122
creative positives 38, 39, 48
Creative Problem Solving (CPS) 47, 142; *Middle C* 45
Creativity Characteristics Scale 38; Hartman, Robert K. 38, 48; Renzulli, Joseph 35, 38, 41, 42, 48, 55, 63, 68, 70, 80, 89, 94, 97, 99, 101, 104, 110, 111, 119, 120, 130, 139, 150
curriculum-based assessments 18; Provision-Evaluation-Provision (PEP) 18
curriculum compacting 118

Depth and Complexity 99, 104, 109; Kaplan, Sandra 97, 99, 100, 104, 109, 111
Design and Technologies Curriculum 137
Developmental Neuropsychological Assessment (NEPSY-II) 23
developmental theorists 7; Erikson, Erik 7, 10; Kohlberg, Lawrence 7–10; Piaget, Jean 7, 11
Differential Ability Scales (DAS) 15
differentiated instruction 99, 105, 130; Tomlinson, Carol Ann 98–100, 104, 110, 111

Differentiated Model of Giftedness and Talent (DMGT) 8, 35, 88; Gagne 8–10, 13, 17, 24–25, 35, 45, 47, 48, 88, 89, 92, 114, 128, 153, 158, 167, 195, 204, 209, 211
Disability Discrimination Act 1992 (DDA) 55
Disability Standards for Education 55
Discovering Intellectual Strengths and Capabilities while Observing Varied Ethnic Responses (DISCOVER) 42, 146, 167
disjunctive rule 20, 21, 34
divergent thinking 32, 33, 39; Guilford, J.P. 33, 39, 47
dynamic assessment 19, 26, 182

Early Childhood and Gifted 152–170; *Early Years Learning Framework* 160, 164, 167; The Reggio Emilia 164
Early Years Learning Framework 160, 164, 167
egalitarianism 7, 216, 207
ELEVATE Program 126, 129
enrichment programs 117, 129, 198, 204
Enrichment Triad 48, 99, 110, 119
equity 1, 10, 16, 55, 64, 94, 187, 190, 191, 201, 207, 210
Erikson, Erik 7, 10

Four C Model of creativity 37, 45; Beghetto, Ronald 32, 37, 45, 46, 47; Kaufman, James C. 15, 27, 32, 37, 45, 46, 47, 92
funding 2, 6, 9, 10, 96, 114, 116, 123, 180, 185, 208, 210
Future Problem Solving 42, 134, 144

Gagne 8–10, 13, 17, 24–25, 35, 45, 47, 48, 88, 89, 92, 114, 128, 153, 158, 167, 195, 204, 209, 211; Differentiated Model of Giftedness and Talent (DMGT) 8, 35, 88
Gardner, Howard 42, 47, 89, 92; Multiple Intelligences 32, 89
Gifted and Talented Students: Meeting Their Needs in New Zealand Schools 48, 93, 169, 182
Gifted Education Research, Resources, and Information Centre (GERRIC) 134
Giftedness from an Indigenous Perspective 78, 182, 190, 192
Grant, Anne 20, 27, 152, 154, 156, 158–170, 201, 204, 212
Gross, Miraca 6, 7, 10, 16, 28, 67, 68, 72, 78, 85, 92, 109, 115, 118, 128, 139, 149, 154,

156, 157, 168, 206, 211; acceleration 6, 14, 20, 48, 58, 59, 67, 76–80, 89, 96, 106, 109, 111, 112, 116–118, 128, 129, 133, 134, 139, 149, 150, 160, 181, 189, 206, 210; grouping strategies 76, 140
Guilford, J. P. 33, 39, 47; divergent thinking 32, 33, 39

Hartman, Robert K. 38, 48; Creativity Characteristics Scale 38
Hay, Peta 12–31
Henderson, Lesley 112–133
higher order thinking 131
Hockett, Jessica 99, 108
Hodge, Kerry 105, 111, 152–170, 212
How Creative Are You? 40; Cohen, David 24, 26, 40, 47, 202

Indigenous students 51, 61, 62, 136, 170, 181, 182, 208; *Giftedness from an Indigenous Perspective* 78, 182, 190, 192; Maori 74, 78, 80, 203; Pasifika 35, 61, 173, 181, 182, 186, 189, 190; Torres Strait Islander 9, 61
inquiry approach 141, 164
Integrated Curriculum Model (ICM) 104, 108; VanTassel-Baska, Joyce 14, 18, 17, 28, 29, 30, 84, 88, 91, 92, 94, 98, 102, 103, 104, 106, 108, 109, 111, 120, 122, 131, 133, 141, 150, 184, 191, 192, 204, 211
IQ 5, 7–9, 14–17, 20–22, 26, 27, 29, 30, 37, 39–40, 43, 47, 51–53, 57, 63, 66–68, 100, 109, 120, 126, 130, 140, 145, 153–156, 185, 193, 195, 198, 202, 204, 210; abbreviated IQ tests 15; Cognitive Assessment System (CAS) 15; Differential Ability Scales (DAS) 15; Naglieri Nonverbal Test of Ability 16; Non-Verbal Ability Tests 16, 19; Spatial Test Battery 16, 30; Stanford-Binet Intelligence Scales 14; Universal Nonverbal Intelligence Test 15; Wechsler Intelligence Scale for Children 14, 23, 30

Jarvis, Jane 1–11, 95–111, 206–211
Jellen, K.K. 40, 49; Test for Creative Thinking – Drawing Production (TCT-DP) 40
John Hopkins Center for Talented Youth 136
Jolly, Jennifer 1–11, 193–211
Jung, Jae Yup 5, 18–20, 22–24, 26, 28, 30, 32, 34, 36, 219

Kaplan, Sandra 103, 105, 106, 110, 115, 117; Depth and Complexity 99, 104, 109
Kauffman, James C. 15, 27, 32, 37, 45, 46, 47, 92; Four C Model 37, 45
Kettler, Todd 96, 99, 110, 172, 178, 190
Kohlberg, Lawrence 7–10
Kronborg, Leonie 82–94

learning difficulties 13, 54, 137
learning disabilities 26, 28, 29, 31, 53, 54, 56–58, 60, 63–65, 201, 214
legislation and policy 55, 64, 109, 211; *Disability Standards for Education* 55; *Discrimination Act 1992 (DDA)* 55
little-c creativity 37

Maori 74, 78, 203; Awhinatanga 74; Beavan-Brown, Jill 8, 10, 17, 25, 61, 66, 74, 78, 89, 91, 114, 120–121, 128, 155–156, 167, 175, 181, 189, 191, 195, 203, 210, 211; Gakal 75; Kotahitanga 74; Whakahihi 74
Marland Report 8, 34
mentoring 48, 74, 76, 77, 108
Merrotsy, Peter 32–49
Middle C 45
Ministry of Education: National Administrative Guidelines (NAG 1(c) iii) 56
Moltzen, Roger 5–11, 206, 211
Multiple Intelligences 32, 89; Gardner, Howard 42, 47, 89, 92
Multiple Menu 99, 110

National Administrative Guidelines (NAG 1(c) iii) 56
National Curriculum Board 41, 48
New Zealand Association for Gifted Children 167
New Zealand Ministry of Education 9, 41, 56, 74, 86, 87, 89, 115–118, 130
New Zealand's National Administration Guidelines 114
nominations 17, 20, 25, 30
non-performance methods 14, 20, 24, 25
non-verbal ability tests 16, 19

Parallel Curriculum Model (PCM) 99; Tomlinson, Carol Ann 98–100, 104, 110, 111
parents 187–199
Parkyn, George 5, 11
perfectionism 26, 69, 76, 79, 80, 168
performance methods 14, 20, 24, 25

Piaget, Jean 7, 11
Plunkett, Margaret 171–192
professional development 28, 82, 84, 85, 87, 90, 93, 100, 104, 113, 115, 122, 123, 125, 129, 133, 144, 149, 164, 165, 166, 184, 188, 203
professional learning 82–91, 93, 109, 116, 122, 123, 129, 172, 208, 212
program evaluation 113, 116, 124, 125, 127, 128
Provision-Evaluation-Provision (PEP) 18

The Reggio Emilia approach164
Reis, Sally 29, 36, 58, 59, 62, 65, 66, 71, 74, 76, 85, 86, 107, 110, 116, 122, 125, 136, 145, 156
Renzulli, Joseph 35, 38, 41, 42, 48, 55, 63, 68, 70, 80, 89, 94, 97, 99, 101, 104, 110, 111, 119, 120, 130, 139, 150; Creativity Characteristics Scale 38; Enrichment Triad 48, 99, 110, 119; Scales for Rating the Behavioral Characteristics of Superior Students (SRBCSS) 38; Schoolwide Enrichment Model 101, 110, 119, 139, 150
resilience 60, 64, 69–70, 78–79
Response to Intervention (RTI) 22, 28
Riley, Tracy 112–131
rurality 177–192

Savant Skill Curriculum 59
Scales for Rating the Behavioral Characteristics of Superior Students (SRBCSS) 38
Schlichter, Carol 56; Talents Unlimited 56, 65
Schoolwide Enrichment Model 101, 110, 119, 139, 150; Renzulli, Joseph 35, 38, 41, 42, 48, 55, 63, 68, 70, 80, 89, 94, 97, 99, 101, 104, 110, 111, 119, 120, 130, 139, 150
scope, gifted programs 20, 98, 104, 113, 115, 116, 122, 127, 129, 142, 143, 208
Section 504 Title II 55
Senate Inquiry into the Education of Gifted Children 86
Social Skills Rating System (SSRS) 23
Spatial Test Battery 16, 30
Specific Learning Disability (SLD) 15–22, 53, 56–57
Stanford-Binet Intelligence Scales 14
Stein, Morris I. 19, 30, 36, 48, 71, 80, 133, 137, 145, 148, 149, 200, 205
STEM (Science, Technology, Engineering, and Mathematics): Australian Science and Mathematics School 135, 150;

The Big Science Competition 134; Gifted Education Research, Resources, and Information Centre (GERRIC) 134; John Hopkins Center for Talented Youth 136; John Monash Science School (Victoria) 135; North Carolina School of Science and Mathematics 136
Sternberg, Robert J. 36, 37, 47, 48, 94, 128, 130
sustainability, gifted programs 113, 123, 125, 127

talent development 2, 10, 12, 47, 52, 70, 79, 81, 83, 84, 86, 88, 89, 91, 92, 102, 108–110, 130, 190, 191, 193, 195, 198, 202, 203
talent search 16, 25, 30, 134; above-level testing 16, 30
Talents Unlimited 56, 65; Schlichter, Carol 56
Tannenbaum, Abe 9, 11, 30, 88, 89, 94, 97, 130, 169; Sea Star Theory of Giftedness 88
teaching strategies 64, 91, 93, 106, 141, 146, 168; Collaborative Australian Secondary Science Program (CASSP) 141
Test for Creative Thinking – Drawing Production (TCT-DP) 40; Jellen, Hans G. 40, 49; Urban, K. K. 29, 40, 49, 75, 159, 172, 184, 175, 177, 178, 180, 188, 191, 106, 200
Tomlinson, Carol Ann 98–100, 104, 110, 111; differentiated instruction 99, 105, 130; Parallel Curriculum Model (PCM) 99
Torrance, E. Paul 38–40, 48, 150
Tournament of the Minds 42, 146
twice-exceptional students see 2e Students

underachievement 12, 42, 70–71, 76, 79, 80, 145, 187, 190, 196
Universal Nonverbal Intelligence Test 15
Urban, K. K. 29, 40, 49, 75, 159, 172, 184, 175, 177, 178, 180, 188, 191, 106, 200; Test for Creative Thinking – Drawing Production (TCT-DP) 40
U.S. Study of Mathematically Precocious Youth (SMPY) 103

Van Tassel-Baska, Joyce 14, 18, 17, 28, 29, 30, 84, 88, 91, 92, 94, 98, 102, 103, 104, 106, 108, 109, 111, 120, 122, 131, 133, 141, 150, 184, 191, 192, 204, 211; Integrated Curriculum Model (ICM) 104, 108
vertical curriculum 138, 139

Vineland Adaptive Behavior Scales
(Vineland-II) 23
Visual-Spatial Abilities 15; Cognitive
Assessment System (CAS) 15;
Differential Ability Scales (DAS) 15;
Universal Nonverbal Intelligence Test 15

Wardman, Janna 66–81
Watters, James 132–151

Wechsler Intelligence Scale for Children 14,
23, 30; Autism Spectrum Disorder (ASD)
21, 25, 52, 53, 59, 64, 200, 205
Wheel Work 42–44, 47; Bloom's Taxonomy
32, 34, 42, 43, 46, 166
Woodcock-Johnson (WJ-III) Achievement
Battery 23; Autism Spectrum Disorder
(ASD) 21, 25, 52, 53, 59, 64, 200, 205
Wormald, Catherine 50–65

PGMO 04/11/2018